The Virtues
Or the Examined Life

AMATECA
Handbooks of Catholic Theology

AMATECA is an international series of Handbooks of Catholic Theology, initiated by Eugenio Correcco and Christoph Schönborn. To date, it comprises 22 volumes in 10 languages. As representatives of university theology and members of the Church, the authors strive to maintain a proper balance in the treatment of controversial subjects in light of the belief of the Church and its magisterium. The foundations of the series, guaranteeing the theological identity of the individual volumes, are to be found in the theologies of Hans Urs von Balthasar and Henri de Lubac.

THE VIRTUES
Or the Examined Life

Romanus Cessario, O. P.

Continuum

London New York

First published in North America and the United Kingdom 2002 by

The Continuum International Publishing Group Inc
370 Lexington Avenue, New York, NY 10017

The Continuum International Publishing Group Ltd
The Tower Building, 11 York Road, London SE1 7NX

First published in Continental Europe 2002 by
LIT VERLAG Münster – Hamburg – Berlin – London
Grevener Str. 179   D-48159 Münster

Printed in Germany

© 2002 by LIT VERLAG

Library of Congress Cataloging-in-Publication Data

Cessario, Romanus.
   The virtues, or, The examined life / Romanus Cessario
     p. cm.
   Includes bibliographical references and index.
   ISBN: 0-8264-1388-9 (hardcover)-- ISBN 0-8264-1389-7 (pbk.)
   1. Theological virtues. 2. Cardinal virtues. I. Title: Virtues II.
   Title: Examined life. III. Title.
   BV4635.C29   2002
   241'.4–dc21   2002003456

ACKNOWLEDGEMENTS

"Per recompensationem beneficiorum
amicitia conservatur"
Summa theologiae IIa-IIae q. 106, a. 2

Friendship, observes Aquinas, is preserved by the acknowledgment of a favor received. First of all, I would like to express my appreciation to the governing board of L'Associazione Manuali di Teologia Cattolica (AMATECA) for the kind invitation to participate in this important theological project. Special gratitude goes to Mr John Janaro and Mrs Lisa Lickona for providing helpful observations about the manuscript, and to Mrs Susan Needham for her gracious assistance in preparing the English edition. For introducing this study of the virtues with his intelligently lithe prose, I am happy to acknowledge my indebtedness to Jesuit Father John McIntyre. And by dedicating this book to Father Thomas Dominic Rover, I want above all to recognize with profound gratitude the Dominican brother who first instructed me about truth and friendship.

CONTENTS

INTRODUCTION

In "The Principle and Foundation" at the beginning of his Spiritual Exercises, St Ignatius teaches that all creatures exist in order to lead all human beings to arrive at our supernatural life of glory. This perception not only grounds a characteristically Ignatian optimism, but it also indicates the basis for a certain Jesuit intransigence. That is, in the concrete or existential order, creatures either do help, or they do not. In other words, Ignatian realism admits of no medial position between helping and hindering, except perhaps in the classroom.

Speaking then of "all other things on the face of the earth," Ignatius makes his sobering illation: "Hence, man is to make use of them in as far as they help him in the attainment of his end, and he must rid himself of them in as far as they prove a hinderance to him." Indeed, the compound sentence embodies the double task that Ignatius assigns to all human acts: personal salvation and the greater glory of God.

Moreover, during the progress of the Spiritual Exercises, the director is able to concretize three motives more and more concisely. As the exercitant deepens within himself the virtues of faith, hope, and charity, what von Balthasar calls, "the form of God in the world" today, he conforms himself ever more consciously to the divine will. Next, he finds in the example of Christ a complete witness to the action of God in human affairs. Finally, in contemplating the love of the Most Blessed Trinity, he unites himself with the radical source of all goodness. Depending, therefore, on the level of one's development, the Exercises disclose three principal motives underlying authentic Christian behavior: personal salvation, the example of Christ, and the love of God. This divine pedagogy enables the disciple to recognize himself, however obliquely, as the language of God.

During the first week of the Exercises, the motives for action may strike one as really minimalist: do good, commit virtue, avoid sin. However, unless we recognize these as commandments and not as counsels, we are in danger of losing our souls and our very selves as well (Mt 16:25, Lk 21:19). That is, the exercitant must let God be God and appropriate the will of God through what St Paul calls "the obedience of faith" (Rom 1:5, 16:26). If it takes all of our energies and attention just to obey the commandments of God, then Ignatius advises "the first method of prayer," which reflects systematically on the ten commandments, the seven capital sins, the three powers of the soul, and the five senses. Motivated largely by an eschatological imperative, this first stage puts the exercitant under judgement. Only when he can acknowledge his own radical sinfulness – in thought, word, act, and omission – can the retreatant recognize the divine mercy and the need for personal freedom.

In several places, Ignatius notes that interior mortification is considerably more difficult than external penances, and more fruitful. Still, he is willing to recognize that human acts, motivated by faith and animated by a reverential fear, produce very elementary results that ensure a measure of personal holiness. Indeed, for many people not all of them "anonymous Christians" this represents their personal best before God and the world. Their frail efforts, however, never quite bridge the gap between faith and world. Caught up in their own pursuits and narrowed by the concerns of "flesh and blood" (Mt 16:17), they never perceive the living God as the heart of this world.

If freedom from personal sin presents an adequate rationale for human behavior, it certainly does not satisfy Ignatius and his companions. Instead, they look to the imitation of Christ: "to know him more intimately, to love him more ardently, to follow him more closely." As the design of God, Christ the King discloses God's gracious plan for us (DS 3004) and reveals himself as the embodiment of all creation (Eph 1:10). Because the following of Christ translates the wisdom of God in space and time, in history and culture, it assures us of those kerygmatic sources associated with Christian dignity, reminding us that we are indeed "a chosen race, a royal priesthood, a holy nation, a people set apart." Moreover, an awareness of the whole Christ leads to both *ecclesia* and *communio*, making us really Emmanuel (Mt 1:23). In short, it is precisely in the Church that we appropriate the form of Christ.

Ever since *Gaudium et spes* (7 December 1965), the Church has described the Christian vocation as one of transforming the *sæculum*. The laity especially are charged with the responsibility "to permeate and perfect the order of temporal affairs with the spirit of the gospel: (c.225, 2). Pope John Paul II has reiterated this challenge in his Apostolic Exhortation *Christifideles laici* (30 January 1989). So the Christian strategy seeks to impose a christological form on otherwise neutral or intractable elements in order to "redeem the time" (Eph 5:16). This means that individual Christians must be so united to the Lord as to continue the radical involvement that we discern in the meditation on the incarnation. The Christian too, as an *instrumentum conjunctum*, works immanently to relate the world and its structures to the energy of the resurrection. Inevitably, a sinful world resists this kind of orientation, which means that the faithful follower not only confronts the cross daily (Lk 9:23) but also lives with "the mark of the nails" (Jn 20:25). This engagement with the world, then, encounters the same kind of opposition that beset the Lord. But despite the interminable wrestle with principalities and powers, the disciple already has the assurance of victory (1 Jn 5:14), for he remains united to the source, the norm and measure of all human behavior. By cooperating with the risen Lord, the individual believer becomes the hands and the heart, the feet and the eyes of the Lord. Accordingly, each in his or her own way extends the kingdom, making the *sæculum* worthy of the Lord himself. For all believers, then, the Christ becomes the appropriate *figura* that contains and shapes christic action.

Yet, we can perceive still another, a more profound level in Ignatius's spirituality to motivate human action. In the "Contemplation for Obtaining Divine Love," Ignatius presents us with an image of the Most Blessed Trinity. Here, we see God conducting himself "as one who labors." Ignatius clearly sees the Godhead as constantly working, tirelessly sustaining, and always striving to realize the original plan of creation. Consequently, Ignatius would have us collaborate with the energies of the triune God. So the form of God, which commences with baptism, concludes with the vision of God. At the very least, it comprises a global view. Perhaps we can locate here the origin of the Ignatian *magis* (cf Jn 5:17). Father Pedro Arrupe, for example, was fond of quoting Ignatius's insight, "the more universal the good, the more divine it is." Fervently animated by the love of God, the true follower enters into the world's structures and plants therein the seed that we recognize as the word of God (Mk 4:14). Indeed, the new evangelization recommended by Pope John Paul II seems to presuppose and require this kind of cosmic perspective. This appreciation in turn prompts a reflection on "the divine milieu."

If the encounter with the world and its structures appears impossibly vast and complex, the encounter with God remains supremely personal. As von Balthasar points out, to the extent that we are chosen, we become persons. The Ignatian maieutic persuades us that Almighty God calls each one of us by name. This means that he not only chooses us, but he personalizes us as well. This perception remains consonant with the teaching of Vatican II which declares the human person as "the only creature on earth which God wills for itself" (*GS* 24). The more personal our relations with the Blessed Trinity become, the more central the divine milieu in our lives. Speaking of that center, Teilhard de Chardin observes that it manifests "the absolute and final power to unite." Herein, I submit, we find a contemporary focus for our current energies. What makes it worthy of our attention may well derive from an awareness that it belongs equally to God.

These reflections on the radicals of Christian behavior will seem perfectly apparent to those familiar with the *Spiritual Exercises*. Although they begin with a concern for personal salvation, the rhythm moves next to a personal encounter with Christ. Sometime during the Fourth Week, one which celebrates the mystery of the risen Lord, the *Exercises* disclose the trinitarian cadence that unifies and explains this faith-event. In many ways, these three radicals correspond to the three levels which Father Bernard Lonergan has distinguished: common sense, theory, and interiority. For the director, however, the challenge lies in effecting a shift from the essential understanding to the existential deed.

St Ignatius learned very well from his Dominican masters at the University of Paris. At the rue S. Jacques, not too far from his *collège* Sainte-Barbe, he studied with Mathieu Ory, Jehan Benoît, and Thomas Laurent "for priesthood and not for grades." Following the tradition of the convent, his teachers took him systematically through St Thomas's *Summa theologiae* and not the more traditional Commentary on the *Sentences*. This discipline enabled Ignatius to understand the fruits of his own prayer life and experience. Neither an intellectual not an academician himself, Ignatius nevertheless respected the discipline of the classroom to the extent that in his *Constitutions* [464] he prescribes St Thomas and the *Summa* as one of the principal texts to be expounded in theology. In presenting this tract on the virtues, Father Romanus Cessario exemplifies that fidelity to the Dominican charism which the conciliar fathers praised and encouraged. To paraphrase Father Lonergan, his method illustrates the *via analytica*; the more impatient (or prompt) Ignatius prefers the *via synthetica*. At any rate, I am very privileged to share in this complementary discourse, for it reveals the current *catholica* in action. Perhaps Ignatius says it best when he gives us his "first rule" for getting things done: "so to trust in God as if the complete success of the undertaking depended on yourself and not at all on God, but so to arrange the matter as if everything depended on God and not at all on yourself." For all of its wit, the paradox attempts to coalesce the selflessness of man within the selflessness of God. For the sake of the kingdom.

Ad Majorem Dei Gloriam!

Feast of St Thomas Aquinas
28 January 1993

Rev. John P McIntyre, SJ
Faculty of Canon Law
Saint Paul University
Ottawa, Ontario, Canada

Part I

The Theological Virtues

CHAPTER 1
FAITH AND THE LIFE OF CHRISTIAN VIRTUE

1. WHAT THE ANGELS SEE: NATURE AND GRACE

Although human and angelic intelligences perform differently, the classical distinction between what the angels see in the morning and what they see in the evening suggests an important truth about the knowledge available to everyone who lives by faith in Jesus Christ. The notion that the angels possess two kinds of vision first appears in St Augustine's commentary on the biblical account of creation, the *De Genesi ad litteram*, Book IV, chapters 22–31, where the Doctor of Grace speaks about a "morning" and an "evening" knowledge of the angels. The subsequent theological tradition enlarged on the distinction, for, as Hugh of St Victor remarks, "there are many questions about this angelic nature, from which the curiosity of the human mind cannot manage to find rest."[1] So in his *Summa theologiae*, it comes as no surprise to discover that St Thomas Aquinas explains Augustine's intuition on angelic knowledge.

> Augustine invented the expressions "morning" and "evening" knowledge as part of his interpretation of the six days of creation recorded in Genesis... [He] called "morning knowledge" the angels' knowledge of things in their primordial beginning, namely as they exist in the Word; and "evening knowledge" their knowledge of created reality as existing in its own nature.[2]

Because the "darkness of night" more properly characterizes the knowledge of the bad angels who fixate on created reality, Aquinas rejects the view that we can speak about an angelic "nocturnal" knowledge. He goes on to explain that since morning and evening both connote daylight, "both types of knowledge expressed by these terms belong to the angels who are enlightened."[3]

No Christian theologian would contest that what the angels see in the morning, namely, everything as it exists in the divine Word of creation, forms the only basis for genuine theological reflection. St Paul himself testifies to the centrality of this type of knowledge when he reminds the Colossians that Christ "is the image of the invisible God, the firstborn of all creation; for in him all things were created, in heaven and on earth, visible and invisible" (Col

---

[1] *De Sacramentis* Bk 1, chap. 5, no. 19 (*PL* 176:254).
[2] *Summa theologiae* Ia q. 58, a. 6.
[3] Ibid.

1:15,16). While we frequently associate theology with the reality of God and his works, with mysteries such as the Trinity, the resurrection of Christ, and the immaculate conception of the blessed Virgin Mary, theological reflection also and properly extends to what men and women do. In other words, Christian faith determines ethical issues. And so the virtues of the Christian life are among those visible realities that find their fullness in Christ. Indeed, the second-century Christian author Origen affirms this truth when he writes: "Do not be surprised that we speak of the virtues loving Christ, since in other cases we are wont to regard Christ himself as the substance of those very virtues." [4]

Because Christ remains the source of all moral goodness for the person who accepts the message of the Gospel, the Church asserts that Christian moral teaching possesses a distinctive specificity. In a variety of ways, contemporary theologians emphasize the important link between right Christian conduct and authentic Christian belief. Hans Urs von Balthasar, for example, identifies Christ as the "concrete and personal norm" of the moral life. [5] This means *inter alia* that without an effective union with Christ, no human person can in practice achieve the perfection of the moral life that conduces to beatific fellowship with the Trinity, and to the company of the saints and angels. Moreover, "it is Christ, the last Adam, who fully discloses humankind to itself and unfolds its noble calling by revealing the mystery of the Father and the Father's love." [6] In other terms, only the person who embraces a life of Christian virtue lives fully according to the norm of moral truth that Christ, the "image of the invisible God," communicates to the world, and so in Christ achieves the perfection of his or her human nature.

Because of their superior intelligence, the angels know the divine mysteries in the Word with great clarity. We on the other hand know faith-truths darkly, that is, only by believing the Word of God, First Truth-Speaking. [7] In any case, St Augustine's distinction refers to what the angels know after their irreversible choice to love God. And because of the moral darkness that characterizes the sin of the world, faith-truths about human conduct sometimes seem especially obscure to the person who still must learn to appreciate the spiritual measure that Christ establishes for human life. Certainly, a more profound contemplative pondering of revealed truth – an effort, in faith, to see more clearly what

---

[4] Origen, *Commentary on the Song of Songs*, Bk 1, in Origen, *The Song of Songs: Commentary*, trans. R.P. Lawson (Ancient Christian Writers, vol. 26; Westminster, MD and London, 1957), p. 89.

[5] Hans Urs von Balthasar, "Nine Theses in Christian Ethics," in *International Theological Commission: Texts and Documents 1969–1985*, ed, Michael Sharkey (San Francisco, 1989), p. 108.

[6] *Gaudium et spes*, no. 22.

[7] Aquinas even speculates whether the angels possessed this clarity about faith-truths even before their confirmation in glory (See *Summa theologiae* IIa-IIae q. 5, a. 1).

the good angels see in the "morning" when everything appears in the "perfect image" – forms a basic feature of the dynamism of Christian living. Does this mean, however, that faith knowledge alone can supply moral instruction for the Christian believer? Traditionally, the Church gives a negative reply to that question. Human reason with its inherent capacity and proper object is not abrogated by the gift of faith. The human being enlightened by faith in Christ continues to engage the world with his or her rational faculty of intelligence. And in order to grasp the full splendor of the Christian life, it is important to know the reasons why authentic human knowledge helps Christian belief, especially in matters that concern the proper conduct of human life.

The fact that reason preserves its full vigor within the context of Christian life indicates a genuine role for philosophy within a Christian understanding of the world and of the human person. In his Gifford Lectures (1931 – 32), Étienne Gilson raised the issue of a Christian philosophy: "I call Christian, every philosophy which, although keeping the two orders formally distinct, nevertheless considers the Christian revelation as an indispensable auxiliary to reason." [8] Whether or not we accept this specific proposal, Gilson at least gives an account as to how the believing Christian can consider the "esse rerum," the being of things, from a standpoint formally distinct from that of divine faith. And if this personal quest for wisdom develops into an organized intellectual inquiry, we can rightly call the person who practices it a Christian philosopher. Philosophical knowledge seeks after "esse rerum quod in propria natura habent"; that is, it seeks to disclose the proper natures that things have in themselves. Though philosophy can achieve only a limited grasp of the nature of things, philosophical learning still represents a discursive effort on the part of the human person to attain what the angels see in the evening, a "knowledge of created reality as existing in its own nature." The Church, moreover, encourages this effort, and she does so on the authority of St Paul: "Ever since the creation of the world his eternal power and divine nature, invisible though they are, have been understood and seen through the things God has made" (Rom 1: 20).

The Christian knows that there are limits to the "principles and causes" that philosophers seek. Aristotle's "first philosophy," it is true, invites us to contemplate the existence of the highest Truth, but even the few who successfully achieve this goal attain only an oblique, inferential knowledge of this ultimate principle; that is, a knowledge of the dependence of created beings on a unique source that all people call God. [9] Because he fully grasped the difference between the God of the philosophers and the God of Abraham, Isaac, and

---

[8]   *The Spirit of Medieval Philosophy* (New York, 1940), p. 37.
[9]   See *In De Trinitate* Bk 5, chap. 4.

Jacob, Aquinas offers an uncharacteristically melancholic remark about those persons who rely on human reason alone to discover the truth about human existence.

> Because Aristotle saw that there is no other human knowing in this life except through the speculative sciences, he held that man cannot reach a complete, but only a relative happiness. Thus it is clear what great anguish the noble genius of philosophers has experienced over the course of time. [10]

But while the Christian believer escapes this sad lot, he or she still needs to experience some of the anguish of the philosophers. For as one theologian points out, "if man does not make definite contact with God at one point that is not grace (in the theological sense of the word), then the God who reveals himself cannot address man meaningfully. Hence the solemn declaration by the Church that the existence of God can in principle be naturally known (DS 3004, 3026) and that the human soul is immortal (DS 1440)." [11] When the Church champions the dignity of the human calling and restores hope to those despairing of any higher destiny, she recognizes that her message meets the deepest desires of the human heart. At the same time, because of the supernatural sense of faith, the People of God receive a truth that exceeds the capacity of human knowledge, the truth that sets them free (see Jn 8: 32).

Let us return to the distinction that both St Augustine and St Thomas Aquinas make between the morning and evening knowledge of the angels – their cognitio "matutina" and "vespertina" – in order to see what application it might have for theological ethics. Aquinas explains the basis for distinguishing the two types of angelic knowledge in the following way: "For the being of things flows out from the Word as from a first [or primordial] principle, and this effusion terminates in the being of things which they possess in their proper nature." Aquinas talks about a "flow of being" that spreads from the creative source of all things in God and terminates in the variety of created natures that exist in the world. [12] The outpouring of divine truth resembles this flow of being. In Aquinas's view, one finds the unexpectable completion of metaphysics in Christian revelation. Through divine revelation, God communicates a knowledge of all reality as it exists in his Son, even though believers still enjoy the capacity to acquire a genuine knowledge of real beings as they exist in themselves. One American philosopher even goes so far as to assert that "re-

---

[10] Contra gentiles Bk III, c. 48.

[11] Edward Schillebeeckx, Revelation and Theology, vol. 1 (New York, 1967), pp. 154, 155.

[12] Because he firmly grasps the full implications of the Christian doctrine of creation ex nihilo, Aquinas recognizes that all created natures possess but never exhaust their proper act of being. The very contingency of created beings derives from the tenuous grip that they have on existence, whereas the divine omnipotence and infinitude rest on the identity of essence and existence that belongs uniquely to God. In other words, Aquinas's explanation of the "flow of being" remains free of emanationism or other pantheistic connotations.

vealed theology promises a vision of the principles which the metaphysician seeks, even desires." [13]

2. NATURAL AND GOSPEL LAW

The Pastoral Constitution on the Church in the Modern World, *Gaudium et spes*, acknowledges the legitimacy of a twofold source for moral truth. For example, in one place, the Church affirms "that underlying all changes there are many things that do not change, and which have their ultimate foundation in Christ who is the same yesterday, today, and forever," whereas in another place the Council itself "seeks to recall before all else the unchanging force of the natural law of peoples and of its universal principles." [14] *Gaudium et spes*, then, gives us reason to suppose that the Christian believer can respect two complementary sources for moral truth, namely: (1) the explicit revelation of Christ, and (2) the created structures of human reality that the Christian tradition calls natural law. Each one, of course, possesses its distinctive methodology, certitude, and object. With the eyes of faith, the believer learns the marvelous things that lie hidden in Christ, whereas a metaphysics of morals instructs about "the being of things which they possess in their proper nature." This twofold approach to moral truth explains why the Second Vatican Council described the supreme norm for all human conduct as a law that is both "natural and gospel (*lex naturalis et evangelica*)." [15]

Within the realm of human conduct, the Christian thinker can legitimately ponder the "esse rerum," the "being of things" from two standpoints. From the first standpoint, the believer peers into the actual economy of salvation and beholds what even the angels long to see. As a communication of the truth about God and the secret purpose of his will (see Eph 1:9), revelation concerns divine and supernatural realities. But this knowledge comes only through faith in Christ, for "in fact, it is only in the mystery of the Word incarnate that light is shed on the mystery of humankind." [16] From the second of these standpoints, the believer gains a universal perspective from "the unchanging force of the

---

[13] Mark D. Jordan, *Ordering Wisdom: The Hierarchy of Philosophical Discourses in Aquinas* (Notre Dame, IN, 1986), p. 178. Jordan further explains this connection: "If there is a methodological difference between metaphysics and theology, there is no material segregation of them in the texts [of Aquinas]. The discourse of metaphysics is not closed at some point below theology in the hierarchy of sciences. The reader passes imperceptibly from one discourse to another. Indeed, it is not as if one were passing outside of metaphysics, even though one knows that metaphysics itself cannot prove the necessity of a higher realm. It is rather that one finds the unexpectable completion of metaphysics in revelation" (p. 177).

[14] *Gaudium et spes*, nos. 10 & 79.

[15] *Gaudium et spes*, no. 79.

[16] *Gaudium et spes*, no. 22.

natural law of peoples and of its universal principles." This results in a knowledge of natural law and virtue that holds true for all humankind. Just as the
angels gaze on the same truth in the morning and in the evening, so faith and
reason bring the human person face to face with the single truth that remains
rooted in the divine Being and is made known "from seeing the light of the
gospel of glory of Christ who is the image of God" (2 Cor 4:4).

The truths of faith, however, surpass the scope of the human intellect; they
cannot be measured by the human intellect's inherent criteria for evidence. In
believing, therefore, the intellect, under the impulse of the will's command,
effected by grace, assents to what exceeds its natural requirements and capacities, namely, the truthfulness of God revealing. According to the truth of the
Catholic faith, Christ himself stands at the center of the entire revelatory process. Faith then comes from God, both as a free gift of grace that causes faith's
required assent, and as a lavish outpouring or effusion of doctrine about those
things that pertain to our salvation.

The New Testament clearly affirms that the human person discovers God
in knowledge and love, and that the perfection of Christian existence achieves
a consummation of this intentional union. In the Gospel of John, Jesus himself
instructs us: "It is written in the prophets, 'And they shall all be taught by
God.' Everyone who has heard and learned from the Father comes to me" (Jn
6:45). This means that Christian theology effectively includes "all knowledge
taught us by God's grace." [17] So in its certitude, intrinsic worth, and ultimate
purpose, Christian theology ranks above all other human sciences. And the
Christian tradition accordingly reserves the attribution of "truly wise" for the
person who seriously learns about God: "That person who considers maturely
and without qualification the first and final cause of the entire universe, namely
God, is to be called supremely wise; hence wisdom," says Aquinas, "appears
in St Augustine as knowledge of divine things." [18] Whereas some knowable
things, such as developments in medical science, do not fall immediately under
the purview of divine faith, the Church understands the divine wisdom that
she mediates as inclusive of truths about human life. "When," therefore, "the
Magisterium proposes 'in a definitive way' truths concerning faith and morals,
which, even if not divinely revealed, are nevertheless strictly and intimately
connected with Revelation, these must be firmly accepted and held." [19]

God graciously extends his saving instruction to matters of human conduct in order to promote the welfare of the human race; indeed, as St Gregory
of Nyssa expresses it, only the believer grasps that the goal of a virtuous life

---

[17] *In primam partem*, q. 1.
[18] *Summa theologiae* Ia, q. 1, a. 6.
[19] Congregation for the Doctrine of the Faith, *Instruction on the Ecclesial Vocation of the Theologian*, no. 23.

is that we become like God himself. [20] When Aquinas talks about human actions as ordered to beatific union with God, he carefully points out how God's holy instruction *sacra doctrina* both treats divine realities and regulates human conduct.

> The *sacra doctrina* is more theoretical than practical, since it is mainly concerned with the divine things that are, rather than with things men do; it deals with human acts only in so far as they prepare men for that achieved knowledge of God on which their eternal bliss reposes. [21]

Christian theology falls within the larger communication of divine truth that constitutes God's holy instruction to his people. Moral theology thus differs from philosophical ethics, even though the history of religious ethics verifies the tendency to consider practical sciences separately from dogmatics, and eventually as purely secular studies. Thus the 18th-century English philosopher David Hume in his *Natural History of Religion* (1757) mistakenly anticipated that "religion will be driven out by stronger secular convictions derived from natural regularities." But nothing exhibits more natural regularity than "the supreme rule of life that is the divine law itself." The Church identifies this supreme rule of life with "the eternal, objective and universal law by which God out of his wisdom and love arranges, directs and governs the whole world and the paths of the human community." [22] And so the Second Vatican Council does not hesitate to repeat the celebrated phrase from the *Confessions* of St Augustine, "It is for yourself that you have made us, Lord, and our hearts are restless, until they repose in you." [23]

3. THE VIRTUOUS LIFE

When Aquinas describes the unique characteristic of gospel life, he writes: "Now it is the grace of the Holy Spirit, given through faith in Christ, that is predominant in the law of the New Covenant, and that in which its whole power consists." [24] Because as St Ambrose reminds us, "the Holy Spirit does not proceed by slow, laborious efforts," the Christian Church must always remain attentive to the active interplay of human nature and divine grace that

---

[20] St Gregory of Nyssa, *Orationes de beatitudinibus*, Sermon 1, in St Gregory of Nyssa, *the Lord's Prayer* and *The Beatitudes*, trans. Hilda Graef (Ancient Christian Writers, vol. 18; Westminster, MD and London, 1954), pp. 85–96.

[21] *Summa theologiae* Ia q. 1, a. 4. Because moral truths can fall under the same "formal light" or reason, *viz*, God as First Truth Speaking, moral theology forms a true part of the *sacra doctrina*.

[22] The Decree of the Second Vatican Council on Religious Freedom, *Dignitatis humanae* no. 3.

[23] St Augustine, *Confessions*, Bk 1, chap. 1 (*PL* 32: 661), as cited in *Gaudium et spes*, no. 21.

[24] *Summa theologiae* Ia-IIae q. 106, a. 1.

expresses the heart of the New Law. [25] *Gaudium et spes* affirms that the Holy Spirit "leads the Church into all truth (see Jn 16:13), and he makes it one in fellowship and ministry, instructing and directing it through a diversity of gifts both hierarchical and charismatic, and he adorns it with his fruits (see Eph 4:11 – 12; 1 Cor 12:4; Gal 5:22)." [26] The moral theologian must recognize the supreme importance that the grace of the Holy Spirit holds in the life of the member of Christ's Body. [27] For the Christian believer, the theological life amounts to the exercise of both the three theological virtues, faith, hope, and charity, and the moral virtues, prudence, justice, fortitude, and temperance. However, because this virtuous life reflects the fullness of Christ's messianic grace, the theological tradition further holds that each believer enjoys the special divine assistance of the gifts of the Holy Spirit, who "intercedes for the saints according to the will of God" (Rom 8:27).

The inspired Word of God supplies an instruction, a Torah, that is quite detailed, and that in the interpretation given it by Jesus and his New Testament followers enjoys universal validity. While the Ten Commandments summarize the Old Testament Torah, the virtues of love, faith, and hope, the cardinal virtues and their facilitating gifts of the Spirit, as well as the differing gifts of ministry given to the members of the Body of Christ express the moral teaching of the sacred Scripture in its Christian fullness. For the precepts of Scripture do not of themselves constitute a complete ethics apart from the virtues of character which they form and express. As Christ himself teaches, "A good tree brings forth good fruit" (Mt 7:17).

The moral theologian can make fruitful use of the notion of *habitus* as a way to explain the virtues of character. *Habitus* provides a way for the theologian to explain that grace really transforms the principal psychological capacities of human nature, and at the same time allows the person to use these capacities in ways that are creative and easily adapted to new situations. As real *habitus* of the supernatural order, the theological and infused moral virtues enable a person to sustain an interpersonal communion with God. *Habitus* do not establish routine. Indeed, instead of inhibiting the exercise of human autonomy, *habitus* provide the indispensable condition for the realization of au-

---

[25] St Ambrose, *Commentary on Luke*, Bk 2, chap. 19, no. 22 (*CCL* 14:39).

[26] *Gaudium et spes*, no. 4.

[27] The German philosopher Martin Heidegger has exercised considerable influence on 20th-century European philosophy, and consequently on a great deal of theological thought and writing. In a recent study, a French author has remarked that his influence has sometimes led Christian thinkers to confuse the "destiny of Being" with the "design or plan, to use a Pauline term of grace." See Daniel Bourgeois, *L'un et l'autre sacerdoce* (Paris, 1991), p. 84. For some further considerations, see Otto Herman Pesch, "Christian Existence According to Thomas Aquinas," *The Etienne Gilson Series* 11 (Toronto, 1989).

thentically free and responsible Christian behavior.[28] Sometimes, it is true, we refer to sanctifying grace as an "entitative" *habitus* of the soul, but this way of speaking represents an extended use of the concept.[29] Rather, as real *habitus* of the supernatural life, infused virtues shape the capacities or powers of the human soul (*potentiae animae*) that form the basis for knowledge and love – namely, the intellect for faith and prudence, and the rational appetite, or will, for the virtues of charity, hope, and justice. Only sanctifying grace can simultaneously elevate and perfect these powers, so that a person can "do everything in the name of the Lord Jesus, giving thanks to God the Father through him" (Col 3:17). To consider theological faith, for example, as a *habitus* proper to the Christian reflects a longstanding theological intuition about how God bestows the gift of faith. In his treatise entitled *The Divine Names*, the 5th-century Christian author known as Dionysius the Areopagite writes:

> Faith is the permanent Ground of the faithful, which builds them in the Truth and builds the Truth in them by an unwavering firmness, through which they possess a simple knowledge of the Truth of those things which they believe.[30]

By a judicious and creative use of the Aristotelian category of *habitus*, the moral theologian affirms that for those "justified by faith in Christ" (Gal 2:17), this "unwavering firmness" forms a personal quality or trait of their whole moral lives.

In the Old Testament we find emphasis on such key virtuous *habitus* as righteousness (*sedeq*), mercy (*hesed*), and fidelity ('*emet*), but it is clear from Christ's own teaching on the Great Commandment and from St Paul's discourse in First Corinthians 13 that charity (the equivalent to *hesed*) constitutes the supreme Christian virtue and that it extends to both God and neighbor. Additionally, St Paul makes it clear that both faith and hope remain directly related to charity. In the history of moral theology, these three virtues, traditionally called the theological virtues, have always been regarded as providing the whole shape of Christian ethics and with full biblical warrant.

The four cardinal virtues (temperance, fortitude, justice, and prudence), derived from Plato, reinterpreted by Aristotle, and transmitted by the Stoics, are referred to once in the Book of Wisdom: Wisdom "teaches temperance and prudence, justice, and fortitude, and nothing in life is more useful for men

---

[28] Aquinas stresses that the radical source or principle of human action, and consequently freedom, remains the human potencies/capacities, *viz*, in *Summa theologiae* IaIIae q. 49, a. 4: "But it is obvious that the nature and notion of a capacity is to be a source of action. And so every *habitus* whose possessor is a capacity is connected primarily with action."

[29] See *Summa theologiae* IaIIae q. 50, a. 2.

[30] Dionysius the Areopagite, *The Divine Names and The Mystical Theology*, trans. C. E. Rolt (London: SPCK, 1979), chap. 7, no. 4 (p. 153).

than these" (Wis 8:7). [31] While this one quotation, in a work marked moreover by Greek influence, hardly suffices to give the cardinal virtues their capital importance, their traditional use as organizing principles for ethics still can be explained by the following considerations. Prudence signifies the equivalent of the "wisdom" constantly portrayed in the Old Testament as a gift of God without which a righteous life is impossible. The New Testament repeatedly speaks about this wisdom as given even to the little ones in the messianic age and encourages the Church to maintain a prudent watchfulness "for the sake of prayer" (1 Pt 4:7). Justice of course constitutes a central theme of both the Old and the New Testament; it is necessarily included in the very notion of "love of neighbor." Thus the sacred Scriptures constantly exhort and guide us to respect the rights of others and to do so with a practical wisdom or prudence that exceeds mere legalism, and this out of piety for the heavenly Father (see Col 4:1). The mystery of the Cross gives a central place in Christian virtue to martyrdom and the patient endurance of suffering for the sake of Christ, that is, to fortitude and with it to nonviolence rather than the aggressiveness which predominated in the Greek notion of virtue. "In the world you face persecution. But take courage; I have conquered the world" (Jn 16:33)! Finally, the celibacy of Jesus, his teaching on divorce, and St Paul's pastoral instructions make clear that temperance in the form of chastity, whether married, celibate, or virginal, has a special Christian emphasis. "For the grace of God has appeared, bringing salvation to all, training us to renounce impiety and worldly passions, and in the present age to live lives that are self-controlled, upright, and godly, while we wait for the blessed hope, and the manifestation of the glory of our great God and Savior, Jesus Christ" (Tit 2:11 – 13).

The traditional view originating in St Augustine that the theological and cardinal virtues are completed by the gifts of the Holy Spirit, the beatitudes, and the fruits of the Spirit (Gal. 5:22 – 23) helpfully organizes a considerable amount of Christian revelation. According to patristic exegesis, the "fruits" are acts of the virtues, whereas the beatitudes are perfect fruits that proceed from the virtues operating under the influence of the gifts. The gifts, which are to be distinguished from the special gifts of ministry mentioned by Paul in First Corinthians 12, are recounted as given to the Messiah in Isaiah 11:23 (see Rev 5:6). According to the official teaching, these gifts are given to all Christians in baptism to facilitate the working of the other virtues by rendering the Christian docile to the guidance of the Holy Spirit, so that he or she shares in a divine, rather than a merely human, mode of judging and acting. This theory of the gifts is of utmost importance in the history of spiritual theology,

---

[31]   For a complete Biblical introduction to moral theology, see Benedict M. Ashley, O.P., *Living the Truth in Love* (New York: Alba House, 1996).

and to neglect it would be to reinforce the disastrous separation of moral from ascetic and mystical theology which took place in the post-Tridentine period. An example of this separation of the virtues and gifts from moral theology is to be found in the *Directorium Asceticum* or, *Guide to the Spiritual Life*, first published in 1752 by the Jesuit spiritual author Giovanni Battista Scaramelli. [32] At the same period, then, that Hume announced the divorce of revelation from human reason, the *Directorium Asceticum* disengaged both the moral virtues, which it describes as the "immediate dispositions for Christian perfection," from the theological virtues, especially charity, which it recognizes as "the essence of Christian perfection," from the canons of moral theology. It was possible to conceive of such a divorce during a period when moral theology was exclusively governed by the juridically-inspired principles of the casuists' manuals.

But Christian revelation offers no grounds for such an awkward separation. If we ponder the pneumatology that runs throughout the New Testament, there can be no doubt that in promising the Paraclete Jesus in fact promised that the outpouring of the Holy Spirit that was to herald the messianic Age (see Acts 2:14 – 36) was about to begin. True Christian freedom, which leads to the pursuit of a good life, comes only from the Holy Spirit; "the Lord is the Spirit, and where the Spirit of the Lord is, there is freedom" (2 Cor 3:17). And the early Church experienced the distinction between the observance of the commandments in the human mode of dutiful obedience and the Spirit-inspired and facilitated fulfillment of these same precepts with profound insight and joy. With this end in view, St Paul constantly urges his converts to grow to Christian maturity and docility to the Spirit. The numbering and classification of the gifts is less significant than the fact they are given in the plenitude symbolized by the number seven. Actual reference to the various qualities of action and insight assigned to the traditional seven names of the gifts, Wisdom, Understanding, Counsel, Fortitude, Knowledge, Piety, and Fear of the Lord can be found scattered through both Testaments. But the important truth remains what St Paul teaches the Romans about the meaning of adoptive childhood: "For all who are led by the Spirit of God are children of God . . . and if children, then heirs, heirs of God and joint heirs with Christ if, in fact, we suffer with him so that we may also be glorified with him" (Rom 8:14,17).

4. THE GIFTS OF THE HOLY SPIRIT

The received tradition of the Middle Ages provided Thomas Aquinas with the resources required for constructing a theology based on the gifts of the Holy

---

[32]   Giovanni Battista Scaramelli (1687 – 1752), *Direttorio ascetico* (1752); English translation, 4 vols. (London, 1924).

Spirit. [33] Although published in 1911, the latter work still remains a principal source for the period up to Aquinas. Over the course of roughly two decades (1252 – 1272), Aquinas applied his extraordinary talent for consolidation and synthesis to the biblical glosses and patristic texts that furnished sundry interpretations of the well-known text of Isaiah 11:2 – 3. [34] Aquinas's teaching about the gifts integrates his doctrines on the intra-Trinitarian life of relations and processions, on the temporal missions of the Son and Spirit, and on the indwelling of the Paraclete in the souls of the just with his practical theology of the Christian life. Indeed, as a comparative study of his writings indicates, Aquinas's views concerning the nature and function of these gifts continued to evolve even while he was drafting the *Summa theologiae* [35] The final redaction of his gift-theology falls within the treatise on the individual virtues in the *secunda pars*. [36]

In the *secunda-secundae*, Aquinas makes a key methodological decision that shapes his theology of the gifts. He accepts the established pairing of the seven gifts with the seven cardinal moral and theological virtues. This tradition of the *Spiritus septiformis*, the sevenfold Spirit, dates from the Latin Church of the fourth century. [37] Although theologians had previously suggested other means of inserting the gifts into the structures of Christian theology, Aquinas settles for the paradigm that associates the gifts with the virtues, the Beatitudes, and the fruits of the Holy Spirit.

A simple reading of the New Testament itself urges the theologian to ponder the gifts of the Holy Spirit. For example, in taking leave of his disciples, Jesus told them, "It is good for you that I go away; for if I do not go away, the Paraclete will not come to you; but if I go, I will send him to you" (Jn 16:7). In

---

[33]   For a general history of the theology of the gifts, see G. Bardy, F. Vandenbroucke, A. Bayez, M. Labourdette, C. Bernard, "Dons du Saint-Esprit" in *Dictionnaire de Spiritualité* 3, cols. 1641- 1957. For the development of the doctrine in the patristic tradition, consult Albert Mitterer, "Die sieben Gaben des Hl. Geistes nach der Väterlehre," *Zeitschrift f?r katholische Theologie* 49 (1925), pp. 529 – 566 and Ambroise Gardeil, "Dons du Saint-Esprit II. Partie documentaire et historique," in *Dictionnaire de théologie catholique* IV, cols. 1748 – 1781.

[34]   2 "And the Spirit of the Lord shall rest upon him, the spirit of wisdom and understanding, the spirit of counsel and might, the spirit of knowledge and the fear of the Lord. 3 And his delight shall be in the fear of the Lord." The traditional list of seven Gifts results from the fact that the Septuagint version used "piety" instead of "fear of the Lord" in verse 2.

[35]   Edward D. O'Connor, C.S.C., provides one of the best studies of Thomist theology of the gifts in *The Gifts of the Spirit*, vol. 24 of the Blackfriars translation of the *Summa theologiae* (London/New York, 1974). For a detailed examination of the evolution of St Thomas's thought on the gifts, see especially Appendix 4, pp. 110 – 130.

[36]   The only text in the *tertia pars* that says anything significant about the gifts occurs in IIIa q. 7, a. 5, where Aquinas inquires concerning the grace of Christ.

[37]   In 385, Pope Siricius, for instance, speaks of "the invocation of the sevenfold Spirit with imposition of hands by the bishop." See his *Letter to Himerius* (DS 183).

brief, theological reflection concerning the status, function, and purpose of the gifts of the Holy Spirit articulates the precise nature of this promised divine aid. According to the formulation of Aquinas, for example, these gifts shape the personal psychology of a believer in such a way that the person can respond positively to those *instinctus* that we customarily ascribe to the Holy Spirit. [38] In other terms, the gifts round out the exercise of the moral and theological virtues in the commonplace experiences of the Christian life, to the extent that they remain indispensable for Christian perfection.

Aquinas presents some basic elements of his teaching on the gifts in question 68 of the *prima secundae*. [39] Following a schema established by St Albert the Great [40], St Thomas relates that his predecessors supplied a variety of arguments to explain how one can distinguish the gifts from the virtues. The rudimentary scholastic thesis that one ought to differentiate the virtues from the gifts apparently originates with Philip the Chancellor. [41] Aquinas, however, argues that these earlier attempts to provide a suitable reason for the distinction missed the mark. Thereupon, he ventures another approach. Taking his cue from Scripture's own way of speaking, St Thomas observes that Holy Writ uses the term "spirit" for what the theologians call a gift. By underscoring the inherent connection between *spiritus* and *motus*, Aquinas then defines the gifts as habitual dispositions in the believer to receive special divine inspirations or promptings that surpass the basically human mode of acting established by virtue. [42]

---

[38] Fr Servais Pinckaers continually emphasizes the importance of the gifts for those issues that nettle contemporary theology, for example, see his *Les sources de la morale chrétienne. Sa méthode, son contenu, son histoire*, 2e édition revue et augmentée (Fribourg, 1990), pp. 164–167.

[39] Although the eight articles of this question assume a conception of the gifts that Aquinas will later modify, a brief resumé of certain pertinent points nonetheless provides important basic information. In the plan of the *prima secundae*, qq 68–70 treat the Gifts of the Holy Spirit, the Beatitudes, and the Fruits of the Holy Spirit respectively.

[40] See his *In III Sententias*, ed. Borgnet (Paris, 1894), d. 34, A, a. 1 [614–620]: "An dona sunt virtutes?"

[41] See Philip the Chancellor, *Summa de bono*, edited by Nicolai Wicki, *Corpus Philosophorum Medii Aevii. Opera Philosophica Mediae Aetatis Selecta*, Vol. II (Berne, 1985), Pars Posterior, *De bono gratie in homine* II, D, "De septem donis Spiritus Sancti," Q. I "Utrum dona sint virtutes" [1106–1113]. In addition, see O. Lottin, *Psychologie et morale aux XIIe et XIIIe siècles*, vol. III (Louvain, 1929, 1930), p. 363.

[42] This definition represents a change from Aquinas's earlier opinion in *Scriptum super Libros Sententiarum* ed., M. A. Moos (Paris, 1929–1947) III, d. 34, q. 1, a. 1 [1110–1115], where he describes a gift simply as perfective of a superhuman mode of action in the individual: "dona a virtutibus distinguuntur in hoc quod virtutes perficiunt ad actus modo humano, sed dona ultra humanum modum . . . "

According to the seventeenth-century Dominican theologian John of St Thomas, this new mode of gift-activity produces some startling outcomes.[43] For example, he argues that once a virtuous act comes under the influence of the gifts, the action acquires an entirely new moral character or species. For the Thomist tradition of moral theology, this means that one deals with an entirely new sort of action. The reason, of course, for this strong affirmation lies in the unique regulatory principle that governs the working of the gifts. In order to illustrate how diverse modes of activity can work on the same material action, the Iberian commentator uses the simple image of a boat moved both by the rowing of oarsmen and by the force of the wind:

> This interior illumination, this experiential taste of divine things and of other mysteries of the faith, excites our affections so that they tend to the object of virtue by a higher mode than these very same ordinary virtues do themselves. This happens to the extent that our affections obey a rule and measure dependent upon higher realities, *viz*, that interior prompting (*instinctus*) of the Holy Spirit according to the rule of faith and his illumination. As a result, the gifts effect a different kind of moral action, that is, they establish a distinctive moral specification; indeed we are led to a divine and supernatural end by a mode which differs from the rule formed by our own efforts and labors (even in the case of infused virtue), that is, one formed and founded upon the rule of the Holy Spirit. In a similar way, the work of oarsmen moves a ship differently than the wind does, even though the waves waft it toward the same port.[44]

John of St Thomas employs the example of two categorical causes, *viz*, oarsmen and wind, to explain two *modes* of a single divine activity in the person: a human mode, when the infused and theological virtues remain under the direction of our own ingenuity and resources, and a supra-human mode, when the same virtues come under the influence of the gifts.

Common experience supports this distinction. As the evident contrasts in fervor among the members of the Church make clear, each justified believer retains the capacity to direct the progress of his or her supernatural life. In simpler terms, human reason remains the directive rule or measure for the virtues, even for the infused moral and theological virtues. But the Holy Spirit, like a prompter on a theatrical set, can inspire a virtuous action in accord with a measure that surpasses that of human reason. The First Letter of John refers to

---

[43] See John of St Thomas, "De donis Spiritus Sancti," in *Cursus theologicus. In Summam Theologicam D. Thomae* I-II, Disputatio XVIII in the Vivès edition, vol. VI (Paris, 1885). Written in 1644, this commentary is among the classical *loci* for a theological understanding of the gifts; thus, the 17th-century Carmelite theologians at Salamanca said: "De hac materia tam docte, tam profunde et luculenter agit, ut palmam aliis, immo et sibi ipsi alia scribenti, praeripere videatur" (*Cursus theologicus, De spe*, Disp. 4, dub. 4, n. 43). For further information, see Javier Sese, "Juan de S.T. y su tratado de los dones del Espiritu Santo," *Angelicum* 66 (1989), pp. 161–184.

[44] Disp. XVIII, a. 2, n. 29.

this action: "... but the anointing which you received from him abides in you, and you have no need that any one should teach you; as his anointing teaches you about everything ... " (1 Jn 2: 27). [45]

The believer requires these special gifts so that a virtuous Christian life may achieve its full flourishing. [46] In order fully to appreciate the import of this thesis, we must recall that no adequate proportion exists between human nature and the goal of beatific fellowship with God. As we learn from everyday experience, even Christians engage in the pursuit of those created goods that remain proportionate to them more easily than they aspire to the divine Good, which constitutes subjective Beatitude. "And so the moving of reason is not sufficient," affirms St Thomas, "to direct us to our ultimate and supernatural end without the prompting and moving of the Holy Spirit from above." [47] In other terms, the life of faith and grace in itself does not ensure that the Christian will use these divine gifts in a godly way.

As Advocate and Comforter, the Holy Spirit, on the other hand, pushes the believer beyond the restrictions of human inclination and judgment in matters that pertain to eternal life. As we have seen, St. Paul corroborates this basic theological truth when he speaks about those who are led by the Spirit of God as "heirs" to the Kingdom (see Rom 8:14–17). But the process unfolds step-by-step, and so Aquinas compares the Holy Spirit to a teacher who gradually leads an apprentice to a sure grasp of a particular discipline by providing moments of insight that elucidate both its methods and content.

Although the topic has no parallel in his other writings and, for that matter, no precedent in any other theologian's work, Aquinas next inquires whether or not the gifts themselves form distinctive *habitus* The biblical term *spiritus* of course suggests something transient, even charismatic, in character. But as the gifts render an individual continually and actively receptive to divine promptings indispensable for Christian perfection, so they form a permanent part of the believer's moral character. Wherefore, Aquinas contends, the Gospel of John recounts that Jesus reassures his disciples with the promise that the Counselor "dwells with you, and abides with you" (Jn 14:17). In explaining this fusion between the spontaneity of an inspiration and the permanence of a settled disposition, John of St Thomas frequently points to the Scriptural witnesses that authorize this scholastic thesis. [48]

---

[45] Cajetan uses this text in his commentary *In primam secundae* q. 68, a. 1, *in loco.*

[46] For a brief, but comprehensive, treatment of how Aquinas understands the importance of the Holy Spirit in the Christian life, see Luc Somme, "La rôle du Saint-Esprit dans la vie chrétienne, selon saint Thomas d'Aquin," *Sedes Sapientiae* 26 (1988), pp. 11–29.

[47] *Summa theologiae* Ia-IIae q. 68, a. 2.

[48] See for example, Disp. XVIII, a. 2, n. 8: "Ratio et fundamentum est, quia in primis in ipsa Scriptura significantur ista dona dari per modum permanentiae, dum dicitur Isai. XI:

As formed *habitus* in the believer, the gifts shape the moral character of the Christian in determined ways. For instance, they perfect us in the *sequela Christi* in the same way that the virtues of personal discipline, i.e., fortitude and temperance, are said to perfect the irascible and concupiscible appetites. The virtue of temperance, in the Aristotelian view, so moderates the concupiscible powers of the soul that the truly temperate person performs actions according to the measure of right reason, but without the strain, interior struggle, and determined effort that accompanies the exertion of those who do not possess the virtuous *habitus* The gifts establish this kind of conformity in the Christian, so that we need not struggle after the promptings of the Holy Spirit. And as the witness of the saints unmistakably indicates, the gifts do this without inducing a colorless uniformity into Christian living.

It is worthwhile to observe that, like any philosophical concept put to use in theology, the notion of *habitus* takes on a certain analogical elasticity. An infused *habitus* supplies certain personal dispositions in the believer which render the creative living of a Christian life prompt, joyful, and easy. [49] In the case of the gifts, for instance, although Aquinas does not seem to envisage that one can reject a divine prompting, he would still insist that the *habitus* does not destroy human freedom. Rather, the gifts infallibly produce in the believer a sort of ordered spiritual liberty that characterizes New Testament existence. [50] St John of the Cross seeks to capture the paradoxical status of the gift- *habitus* when he writes: "From the time I sought nothing because of what I myself wanted," he wrote, "everything was given to me by God, even though I did not ask for it." [51]

'Requiescet super eum Spiritus Domini, spiritus sapientiae, et scientiae, etc.' ... ergo ista dona habent statum permanentiae."

[49]   For a neglected but still useful study on the notion of *habitus* in the Christian life, see Placide de Roton, O.S.B., *Les Habitus. Leur Caractère spirituel* (Paris, 1934), pp. 149 – 163.

[50]   In more technical terms, theology understands the Gifts as instances of a *gratia operans*, i.e., graces in which the divine initiative accounts for the direction of the human will. In the case of a *gratia operans*, the action of the will does not proceed because of a prior discursive process of the mind as regulated by the virtue of prudence. A movement of divine grace supplies for this ordinary working of our self-determination. Still, the will must consent to its own act. Hence, once the divine initiative is freely, though passively, received, the individual becomes the active cause of his or her own subsequent activity. The divine causality prolonging itself into this action forms a *gratia cooperans*.

[51]   For example, see his teaching in *Subida al Monte Carmelo* Lib. III, c. 20, n. 4: "Hay otro provecho muy grande y principal en desasir el gozo de las criaturas, que es dejar el corazón libre para Dios, que es principio dispositivo para todos las mercedes que Dios le ha de hacer, sin la cual disposición no las hace."

5. FAITH AND THE GIFTS OF UNDERSTANDING AND KNOWLEDGE

Two gifts of the Holy Spirit particularly aid the faith in Christ that the New Testament says remain indispensable so that the power of the Holy Spirit might be set loose in the world. [52] And for this reason, the theological tradition situates and interprets the gifts of Understanding and Knowledge within the framework of theological faith. Because theological faith sanctifies human intelligence, it constitutes a special theological virtue. Through faith, says Aquinas, the mind is wed to God. God's own Truth and Word achieves this union in the human person such that the one who believes the preaching of the Gospel gives full credence to what is set forth as divinely revealed. The Second Vatican Council has this important word to say about the relationship of theological faith to the growth of the Church. "Tradition and scripture together form a single deposit of the word of God, entrusted to the church." Through a personal assent to the credal propositions that embody divine revelation, the Christian believer is progressively shaped into a full member of Christ's body. "Holding fast to this [deposit], the entire holy people, united with its pastors, perseveres always faithful to the apostles' teaching and shared life, to the breaking of bread and prayer." [53] Christian belief changes every aspect of human life and makes out of the human race a holy people ready to confess the "treasure of revelation." [54]

The gifts that facilitate theological faith particularly sustain the act of belief by which the Christian lays hold of and appropriates the articles of faith that represent the mysteries of the Christian religion. The fifth-century abbot Faustus of Riez takes up the theme of the union that faith accomplishes between God and humankind: "What wedding can this be," he inquires concerning the Marriage Feast of Cana, "but the joyful marriage of man's salvation, a marriage celebrated by confessing the Trinity and by faith in the resurrection." [55] Aquinas's teaching on the articles of faith emphasizes their instrumentality in the effusion of divine instruction that comes from God to the Church, and so he treats them as truth-bearing propositions over which the Magisterium enjoys particular prerogatives. [56] Moreover, this view represents the common under-

---

[52] For a fuller treatment of the gifts that aid the theological virtue of faith, see my *Christian Faith and the Theological Life* (Washington, D.C.: The Catholic University of America Press, 1996).

[53] *Dei verbum*, no. 10.

[54] *Dei verbum*, no. 26.

[55] Faustus of Riez, *Sermo 5, de Epiphania* 2 (*PLS* 3: 560–562).

[56] Aquinas in fact considers the *articuli* as directly related to the structure of the Church. For example, the distinction which he draws between "implicite credere" and "explicite credere" reveals the instrumental nature of the *articuli fidei*. In coordination with this distinction, Aquinas further establishes a hierarchization of the articles themselves and a certain hierar-

standing of the Church: "The task of authentically interpreting the word of God, whether in its written form or in that of tradition, has been entrusted only to those charged with the Church's ongoing teaching function, whose authority is exercised in the name of Jesus Christ." [57] The Magisterium fosters theological faith, and everything that it proposes for belief, as being divinely revealed, is drawn from the one deposit of faith. In exercising its magisterial authority, the Church fulfills Christ's promise to his disciples that they would never be left spiritual orphans.

As the "spouse of the incarnate Word," the Church enjoys the continued help of the Holy Spirit. Although rationalist interpretations of Christian belief, such as those provoked by the seventeenth-century Cartesian spirit of clear and distinct ideas, eclipse this important qualification, it remains true that human cognition, even in the act of faith, experiences its limitations more than its prowess in the face of divine truth. [58] Because of this in-built cognitive limitation, the gifts of Understanding and Knowledge although perfective of the act of faith must draw their effective power from the virtue of charity. Unlike the virtues of faith and hope that do not accompany the Christian to heaven, charity even now abides in the Church here below as the identical reality that flourishes in the company of the saints above. This given of the theological life explains why Aquinas associates the gift of Wisdom, which is the most eminent gift of the Holy Spirit, with charity, which is the theological virtue that most perfectly embodies the divine reality.

5.1. THE GIFT OF UNDERSTANDING

As its two components, viz, "intus" and "legere" indicate, the Latin etymology for understanding ("intellectus") suggests a sort of intuitive reading between the lines. In the Aristotelian account of human knowledge, the intellectual habitus called "understanding" triggers the intellect to scrutinize the indemonstrable first principles of the speculative intellect. Precisely as indemonstrable, we can fittingly compare these first principles with the articles of faith, for the supernatural mysteries of Christian faith rest on nothing other than the divine Truthfulness. Hence, Aquinas posits the analogy between natural understand-

---

chy among believers (see *Summa theologiae* IIa-IIae q. 2, a. 6; q. 2, a. 5; q. 2, a. 7; q. 2, a. 8; q. 5, a. 3 & ad 2).

[57] *Dei verbum*, no. 10.

[58] For an original essay about the cognitive and the affective dimensions of Christian belief, see Richard Schaeffler, "Spiritus sapientiae et intellectus–spiritus scientiae et pietatis–Religionsphilosophische Uberlegungen Verhaltnis von Weisheit, Wissenschaft und Frömmigkeit und ihrer Zuordnung zum Geiste" in *Weisheit Gottes–Weisheit der Welt. Festschrift für Kardinal Ratzinger zum 60. Gerburtstag* (St Ottilien, n.d.) Band I, pp. 15–35. The author frames his reflections with the gifts of the Holy Spirit.

ing and the gift of the same name.[59] Just as natural understanding enables the human mind to grasp the first principles of speculative and practical reasoning, so the gift of Understanding aids theological faith to penetrate what is contained in the article of faith. In this way, the gift of Understanding fosters theological faith. Even if the believer can neither immediately see nor demonstratively know the object of faith, he or she can still perceive "the light [which] shines in the darkness" (see Jn 1:5). Since the articles serve as notional principles for the development of faith-knowledge, the gift of Understanding enables the infused *habitus* of faith to fathom the truths expressed in these propositions as formulated.

The gift of Understanding does not so illumine the act of belief that faith no longer operates in its characteristic darkness. And since the penetration or seizure of the articles of faith does not result in a discernment that destroys the mystery of faith, the act of belief still remains constituted by its lack of evidence. Hence, the gift of Understanding does not have a special object other than that of theological faith. On the contrary, since the gift allows the believer to perceive more clearly the distance between the hidden *res* or divine reality itself and the *enunciabile* or truth-bearing proposition that manifests it, the gift actually heightens the suspense of faith's inevidence. And Understanding accomplishes this goal, even as it bolsters the believer to adhere with greater precision and clarity to the truth that is believed.[60] "Since it develops out of connaturality for and union with divine things, the gift of Wisdom," explains John of St Thomas, "does not supply a comprehensive knowledge concerning the highest causes; the gift rather deepens our grasp of these causes by way of a quasi-affective, mystical knowledge."[61] The same holds true for the gifts of Understanding and Knowledge.

Only charity, of course, can account for the quasi-instinctive discernment which the gift of understanding brings to the act of belief.[62] Given its own

---

[59] In accord with his revised vision of the gifts in the *Secunda secundae*, Aquinas discusses understanding as part of the treatise on the virtue of faith (see IIa-IIae q. 8). His treatment takes into account four distinct elements: First, the nature of the gift of understanding (aa. 1 - 3); second, the subject in which the gift resides (aa. 4 – 5); third, the relationship of understanding to the other gifts (a. 6); and lastly, the Beatitude and Fruit of the Holy Spirit which the medieval tradition associated with this gift (aa. 7, 8). In general, the treatises on the gifts in the *Summa theologiae* provide a good example of Aquinas's organizational method and of his *via doctrinae*.

[60] To arrive at knowledge by a means other than that of seizing a representation of the thing known accounts for the "quasi-experiential" character of such a knowledge. The mystics speak about a "ray of darkness" which strengthens the intellect in conformity to Truth.

[61] Disp. XVIII, a. 4, n. 8 [636].

[62] The gift of Understanding belongs to everyone who participates in divine charity. The function of a gift always remains "to aid" the act of its respective virtue. Thus, the act of "assent" which constitutes divine faith is complete in itself. According to the teaching of the Church,

proper dynamics, affective knowledge tends to degage from the human mode of conceptual knowledge. Yet, John of St Thomas rightly emphasizes that this penetration denotes a judgment; it is not achieved immediately as a result of simple apprehension. But in order to distinguish Understanding from the judgment of discursive reasoning associated with the other intellectual gifts, John of St Thomas speaks about a simple or discriminative judgment. He describes this as a "certain sympathy with spiritual things [which] arouses understanding to discern spiritual realities from corporeal ones . . . " [63] Consider the article of faith that Mary is immaculately conceived. The gift of Understanding makes possible a sharpened and superior penetration of the terms which express the mystery "immaculate"; "conception"; "mother." The penetration of these terms, moreover, opens up a world of religious experience unique to each of the faithful, grounding the personal depth and affective resonance of the believer's relationship to the immaculate Mother of God. At the same time, the common propositions enshrined in the articles of faith guarantee a unity of faith and practice within the one Body of Christ.

In his discussion of the acquisition of the virtues, Aristotle describes two different ways to learn about a virtuous life, and these methods help to explain how the judgment of Understanding functions in the life of the believer. First, an individual can acquire a specific moral virtue through learning about the virtue; for example, by studying about the principles of good nutrition, a person can develop the techniques for maintaining a healthy diet. But the same person can also learn about temperance in food and so acquire the virtue of abstinence through observing closely how an abstemious person eats. For even if a temperate person knows nothing speculatively about good nutrition, he or she has developed the knack for making right judgments concerning nourishment as a result of having consumed the right amount of food over a long period of time. In other words, the person who connaturally observes moderation in eating, experiences the virtue. If this occurs in ordinary human experience, why

---

it can exist even in one who does not actually love God thus, a "dead" faith, as it is called. The gift of understanding, however, supposes this assent. Charity moves the believer to an "understanding" of divine things which results in concretely appreciating as a personal truth that which faith proposes for assent. See *Summa theologiae* II-II q. 8, a. 4.

[63] Disp. XVIII, a. 3, n. 19 [609]. It remains a constant element of Thomist epistemology that the appetite cannot acquire knowledge. Even divine charity cannot know something except in a metaphorical way. So, in order to explain how the gift of Understanding grows as a result of the union of the believer with God who is the Highest Good, one must have recourse to *knowledge by conformity*. Formed faith observes the measure of faith as a knowing; it represents a human mode of knowing because the mind still must appropriate the *articuli fidei*. Faith illumined by the gifts corresponds to a supra-human mode of knowing. Love penetrates the representation of faith's Object. Nonetheless, the gift does not replace or subordinate the theological virtue. As a distinct gift of grace, Understanding remains a cognitive attainment of First Truth, but as a Truth actually loved.

cannot the believer know of and judge about divine truths as a result of having experienced and loved them?[64] Understanding works in this connatural way. "But the knowledge which moves one toward a right ordering of love, thereby reaching a more profound experience of divine things, belongs to the gift of Understanding." [65]

As a distinctive endowment of the spiritual life, "the gift of Understanding does not sharpen and perfect the mind through study and metaphysical inquiry, but by mystical connaturality and union with divine truths." [66] In the case of the gift, however, divine love itself begets the desire for a right appreciation or estimate or understanding of the loved reality. John of St Thomas portrays this dynamic as follows:

> Knowledge and judgment of spiritual and supernatural truths happens both through study and speculative inquiry... and through connaturality, love, and experience. In his *On the Divine Names*, c. 3, Dionysius wrote concerning Hierotheus that "he had not only attained to divine things, but he had suffered them as well." Anyone suffers divine things when he is stirred to love and is moved by the Holy Spirit above the level measured by human rules. The term suffer is employed since acting under obedience and subjection to the motion of another amounts to a sort of suffering or receiving.[67]

The saints even speak about the "*pondus amoris*" – the weight of love – that draws the believer towards God. This weight of divine love enables the saints to penetrate the hidden mysteries of divine truth. It is through the gift of Understanding that the Fathers of the Church gain a depth of insight into the implications of the biblical witnesses. For instance, St Ambrose recognizes in the biblical account of the Visitation a significance for the spiritual well-being of the whole Church: "Mary's son, who is beyond our understanding," the saint assures us, "is active in his mother in a way that is beyond our understanding." [68] Since it comes about "through the intimate understanding of spiritual things which they experience," the theological exegesis practiced by the Fathers surpasses in value for the Church that which is developed exclusively on the basis of scientific expertise in higher criticism.

The gift of Understanding grasps the Christian mysteries, especially those that disclose the economy of salvation, as actual happenings. Those saints who see into the events of Christ's life, for example, the Annunciation, the Nativity, the Passion, the Resurrection, and so forth, best personify the gift of Understanding. For those who possess this gift love to meditate on the Scriptures and

---

[64]   Disp. XVIII, a. 3, n. 48 [620].

[65]   Disp. XVIII, a. 3, n. 46 [619].

[66]   Disp. XVIII, a. 1, n. 46 [619].

[67]   Disp. XVIII, a. 3, n. 45 [619].

[68]   St Ambrose, *Homily on Luke*, Bk 2, chap. 19, 22 – 23 (*CCL* 14, 39 – 42).

to "ponder with assent," according to the apt phrase of St Augustine, the incarnate truths of salvation. [69] Aquinas, moreover, links this pondering with the moral life: "Only the one who makes no mistake about the final end of human life possesses a correct appreciation of it, and firmly cleaves to this end as the greatest good." [70] In the Christian view, the moral life instrumentally obtains the *doctrina* which gives ultimate meaning to the human vocation the beatific vision, so that all the mysteries of the economy pertain equally to the moral teaching of the Church. [71] There exists then an organic link between the practice of the Christian faith and the articles of doctrines of the faith. To ponder the truth of faith facilitates the practice of Christian virtue, and from a different perspective, a virtuous life opens our hearts and minds to the illumination that the Christian mysteries offer to those who accept them. [72]

5.2. THE GIFT OF KNOWLEDGE

As the Aristotelian notion of "science" suggests, the gift of Knowledge (*scientia*) aids theological faith by means of a different sort of graced-activity. [73] John of St Thomas again explains:

> [Knowledge] grounds a movement of the Holy Spirit which moves the mind not by a direct light, as if one were to shine a light into a dark room, but through an internal experience an affective connaturality with the truth by which it can supernaturally seize the realities about which it judges." [74]

In addition, he describes the gift's proper activity as resolutive or analytical judgment-making; so, like Wisdom, the gift of Knowledge scrutinizes the causal explanations underlying the *sacra doctrina*. [75] The gift of Knowledge itself principally concerns the ascending relationships between effects and their causes and, only in an oblique way, the descending relationships between the sovereign causes and their effects. Since the theological tradition associates the highest explication of divine truth with the gift of Wisdom, the gift of Knowl-

---

[69] See *On the Predestination of the Saints*, c. 2; Aquinas interprets this definition in *Summa theologiae* IIa-IIae q. 2, a. 1.

[70] *Summa theologiae* IIa-IIae q. 8, a. 5.

[71] John of St Thomas even considers that the gift of Understanding segues into the *lumen gloriae*. See Disp. XVIII, a. 3, n. 66 [627]: "Ergo donum intellectus in patria non est aliquid distinctum a virtute attingente Deum in se, qui est habitus luminis gloriae." In the following number (n. 67), the commentator qualifies this position.

[72] See *The Catechism of the Catholic Church*, no. 89.

[73] Aquinas treats the gift of Knowledge in the four articles of *Summa theologiae* IIa-IIae q. 9 as follows: the nature and object of the gift (aa. 1,2); its speculative character (a. 3); and the associated Beatitude (a. 4).

[74] Disp. XVIII, a. 4, n. 56 [653].

[75] Disp. XVIII, a. 4, n. 1 [634].

edge remains fixed on the created effects of the divine agency in the world.[76] And though indissociably linked with Christ's instrumentality and energized by divine charity, the gift's proper activity in the believer compares favorably with the "evening knowledge" of the angels, that is, when the angels learn from God's perspective about the innate structure of reality in itself.[77]

The cognitive links between the mind and its object remain an underlying basis of the process of knowledge-judgment which does not, however, imply a falsifying distance or separation between subject and object. In other terms, the beginning and the end of this process lies in the object as really existing. According to the canons of realist epistemology, the judgment of knowledge preserves the mind from being confined to the closed world of its own creations, by leading it back to the open world of things as they actually exist. The gift of Knowledge aids the believer to escape from the vicious circle of subjectivity which confuses human concepts for the truth about the living God. The gift "resolves" because it brings together disparate truths acquired by faith into a single vision about God's action in the world. Aquinas, therefore, explains that "only those enjoy the gift of Knowledge who possess a sure judgment on matters of faith and practice from the outpouring of grace, so that they never stray from the straight path of righteousness."[78] The long tradition of the Church affirms that the mind cannot be satisfied by anything less than this, for theology remains a continuation of faith's quest for something which surpasses the confines of human imagination.

Although in a mode different from that of discursive theology, knowledge scrutinizes the composition of a given article as well as its possible relationship to other doctrines of faith. "Although knowledge proceeds from created causes," explains John of St Thomas, "it can still move from them to the divine, just as we can grasp something of the invisible God by knowledge of

---

[76] John of St Thomas briefly recapitulates this distinction: "Haec [scientia] autem est habitus judicativus evidenter veritatum scibilium per causas vel effectus (ut comprehendamus scientiam propter quid et quia, a priori et posteriori) ita tamen quod quando fit hoc judicium per causas inferiores et creatas, est scientia; quando per supremas, est summa scientia, quae sapientia dicitur, juxta quod etiam Augustinus dicit XIII de Trinitate, cap. XIX: 'Sapientia divinis et aeternis, scientia humanis et temporalibus attributa est rebus' " (Disp. XVIII, a. 4, n. 50 [650]). The commentator immediately remarks, however, that one must interpret this augustinian distinction between divine and human things as referring to two formally distinct ways of thinking about reality.

[77] Aquinas explains St Augustine's distinction between the "morning" and "evening" knowledge of the angels in *Summa theologiae* Ia q. 58, aa. 6,7. In the French edition (Paris, 1984), p. 556, n.6, J.-H. Nicolas explains that the two "knowledges" do not entail diverse objects, but two different ways of knowing; he translates the definition in article 6 as follows: "connaissance du soir [est] la connaissance de l'être créé comme existant dans sa nature propre" (p. 554).

[78] *Summa theologiae* IIa-IIae q. 9, a. 3 ad 3.

those things which he has produced." [79] The commentator further remarks that, inversely, the gift of Wisdom extends to created things, with the result that together the gifts of Knowledge and Wisdom equip the believer to interpret reality from God's standpoint. This capability of Knowledge suggests theology's explicative function, for Knowledge analyzes a truth-statement or faith-proposition. As a "science of the saints," Knowledge leads us to appreciate aspects of a divine mystery that purely rational argumentation in itself can not disclose. All in all, the gift of Knowledge strengthens the believer's hold on the aggregate of the articles of faith as expressed in the Creed.

To continue with the example of the immaculate conception, the gift of Knowledge facilitates our judging the implications of this doctrine for other mysteries of the faith. These include both those that are articulated in propositions and those that are not. For example, one can consider Mary's unique privilege as a starting point for additional inquiries concerning such questions as whether it was possible for her to commit sin, whether during her lifetime our blessed Lady possessed full knowledge of Christ's person and his mission, whether the example of her virtues succors Christian living, and still other questions that can develop this faith-proposition. Knowledge also illumines the relationship of this article of faith to other Marian doctrines, such as the Assumption, as well as to all the other doctrines of faith, especially those that touch the reality of sanctifying grace. The one who lovingly contemplates the immaculate conception does not confront simply a "dogma" about the Mother of God, but the whole drama of salvation as the blessed Virgin personally represents it. "Her Son," St Ambrose reminds us, "is active in his mother in a way beyond our understanding," so that from Mary we learn about the true joy of life.

The Church Fathers traditionally coupled the beatitude "Blessed are those who mourn" with the gift of Knowledge. John of St Thomas explains this connection in light of the judgment which knowledge enables the believer to make concerning created realities.

> To have a perfect union with God and experience his immense goodness, requires stripping oneself of creaturely things and possessing a *knowledge* of their poverty, humiliation, and bitterness; such considerations, furthermore, lead us to cling more closely to God, whom we come to know better as we distance ourselves from creatures. [80]

The gift of Knowledge, he continues, helps the believer to make accurate and precise judgments about created goods in the context of a Christian value system. [81] And since knowledge provides a correct estimate about created realities

---

[79] Disp. XVIII, a. 4, n. 60 [654].

[80] Disp. XVIII, a 4, n. 57 [653].

[81] Ibid.

in themselves, it also allows the believer to recognize the privative results of misusing created goods. This does not mean, however, that the gift of Knowledge leads to a dour moralism, as if a gift of the Holy Spirit would develop a rigid spirit. Indeed, the gifts bring "sweet refreshment from above." Nonetheless, because knowledge critically regards the entire body of revealed truth – and, the immaculate conception serves as a good example in this context – this gift also moves the believer to make the right judgment about human failures and their providential purpose in the Christian life.

Because there exists an intrinsic relation between knowledge as the right estimation about created realities in themselves and knowledge as analysis of the propositions of faith, only those moved by the Holy Spirit enjoy the gift of right judgment in matters of faith and morals. Why is this so? We discover the answer in what the Holy Spirit teaches the Church about the truth of God's yearning: "Love, then, consists in this: not that we have loved God but that God has loved us and has sent his Son as an offering for our sins" (1 Jn 4, 10). Indeed, only the saint both knows and understands that God loves us, not because we are good, but because he is. By faith therefore, the saint already possesses God's mercy, his life, and his love. This vocation, moreover, remains open to all those who hear the saving doctrine which the ministers of Christ's church preach. Thus, in his *Book on the Holy Spirit*, St Basil writes: "As we contemplate the blessings of faith even now, like a reflection in a mirror, it is as though we already possessed the good things our faith tells us that we shall one day enjoy." [82]

6. THE GIFT OF WISDOM

In the commentary that accompanies the following verse from the *Spiritual Canticle*, St John of the Cross observes five specific characteristics of divine wisdom:

The breathing of the air,
The song of the sweet nightingale,
The grove and its living light
In the serene light,
With a flame that is consuming and painless. [83]

First, the Carmelite mystical author explains that the verse speaks about the giving of the Holy Spirit from God to the person and from the person to God. Secondly, John of the Cross tells us that we read here about the rejoicing that comes from the fruition of God's work. Next, the verse speaks, he says, about

---

[82]   See *On the Holy Spirit*, chap. 15, nos. 35 – 36 (*Sources Chrétiennes*, vol. 17 bis, pp. 364 – 370).

[83]   John of the Cross, *The Spiritual Canticle*, 39.

the possessing of knowledge of creatures and of their orderly arrangement. Then, it tells about contemplating God in himself. Lastly, the text points to the person's total transformation in charity. On this fifth point, St John of the Cross offers a description of the transformative powers of divine Wisdom.

> This transformation is not like the one the soul possesses in this life, for although the flame in this life is very perfect and consummating in love, it is still also somewhat consuming and destructive, acting as fire does on coal; although coal is conformed with and transformed into the fire, and does not fume as it did before the transformation, still the flame which consummated the coal in fire consumed and reduced it to ashes. [84]

This remark from the Carmelite tradition introduces the gift of Wisdom that accompanies divine charity. Because the gift of Wisdom crowns the whole of the Christian life, we can suitably consider this gift by way of introduction to the virtues that develop human character in the image of Christ.

Aquinas clearly gives the gift of Wisdom central place in his moral theology. We know that Aquinas takes up the Augustinian theme that identifies beatific fellowship as the goal or end to which all human life tends by reason of the very nature that God's wise providence and design bestows on it. As a complement to this important intuition about the meaning of human life, Aquinas develops a full moral teaching. He analyzes the human act, its object, end, and circumstance; the form of the moral good, the passions, *habitus*, and virtues, sin and law, and the peculiar features of the new dispensation of grace. These matters all precede the discussion of the theological life that is contained in *Summa theologiae* IIa-IIae qq. 1 – 44. Significantly, Aquinas places his treatise on the gift of the Holy Spirit that represents the perfection of the Christian life, the gift of Wisdom, before the long discussion of the moral virtues (qq. 47 – 170) and of the states of life (qq. 171 – 189) that are established in the Church. And though Aquinas gives no other example of vices that thwart the gifts of the Holy Spirit, he does devote a short question to the contrary of wisdom, folly. By these literary devices, Aquinas reminds us that all the moral virtues and the states of life represent so many different ways in which the Christian believer embodies divine wisdom in the world. For through a life of virtue, the Christian exhibits a "measure of judgment in contemplating divine things or in directing human affairs according to divine standards." [85]

From all of this we can conclude that the gift of Wisdom differs considerably from the other gifts that the tradition associates with the theological and cardinal moral virtues. Aquinas never relented on his original intuition that because of the perfection that charity possesses, the highest virtue does not require a special gift to assist its implementation. In this completeness, char-

---

[84]   Ibid., 14.
[85]   *Summa theologiae* IIa-IIae q. 45, a. 5.

ity remains substantially different from both faith and hope. But Aquinas still held to the established pattern of assigning the gift of Wisdom to the theological virtue of charity, so that his small treatise on Wisdom more describes the entire life of Christian virtue, than a special help for a particular virtue. [86]

Aristotle's *Metaphysics* supplies Aquinas with a definition of Wisdom that serves to open up this reflection on Christian life: it belongs to the wise person to consider the highest cause of things. [87] Commenting on this definition, Aquinas remarks that one can consider the highest cause in one of two ways, either simply, as when one considers the highest cause in a particular area of inquiry, or universally, as when one looks at everything that is from a total and universal perspective. For Aquinas, only the person capable of measuring and ordering things in accord with divine norms, *viz*, how God knows the world to be, participates in this universal or supremely objective viewpoint.

At first glance, the approach of Aquinas might seem to differ from that of St Augustine, who describes wisdom as a conformity to the highest love instead of a quality of intellect. Aquinas of course recognizes the intrinsic ordination of knowledge to love that directs the Christian life, but he also affirms that this direction leads to a fuller and more comprehensive grasp of the "object" as both known and loved. Thus he concludes, "the gift of Wisdom differs from the acquired intellectual virtue of wisdom. The latter comes through human effort, the former 'comes from above' (Jas 3: 15)." [88]

Within the total plan of the *Summa theologiae*, the gift of Wisdom appears as the full and existential deployment of the *sacra doctrina* For this gift enables the believer "to judge aright through a certain connaturality with divine things." [89] While the root of this connaturality with divine things remains theological charity, which alone makes us true friends of God, the gift of Wisdom nonetheless remains an intellectual endowment. Why? The proper act of wisdom is to judge, and judgment necessarily involves an act of the intellect. John of St Thomas has this to say about the difference between Wisdom and the gift of Counsel that assists the act of prudential judgment.

> Finally, the gift of Wisdom differs from the gift of counsel. It is true that Wisdom is directive of actions in as much as they are regulated through eternal laws

---

[86] See Kieran Conley, O.S.B., *A Theology of Wisdom* (Dubuque, Iowa 1963), especially pp. 1 – 104.

[87] *Metaphysics* Bk 1, chap. 2 (982a8)

[88] See *Summa theologiae* IIa-IIae q. 45, a. 1, ad 2.

[89] See the crucial text in *Summa theologiae* IIa-IIae q. 45, a. 2: "A correct judgment made through rational investigation belongs to the wisdom which is an intellectual virtue. But to judge aright through a certain fellowship with them belongs to that wisdom which is the gift of the Holy Spirit... Now this sympathy (*compassio*), or connaturality with divine things, results from charity which unites us to God: he who is joined to the Lord is one spirit with him (1 Cor 6: 17)."

contemplated in wisdom. Nevertheless, over and above this there is need for the
gift of Counsel corresponding to prudence, which directs the moral virtues. The
virtue of prudence is distinguished from the virtue of wisdom in this, that prudence regulates according to human rules acts done here and now. On the other
hand, wisdom is not immediately regulative of action. It is contemplative and
knows the Supreme Cause, upon which depends the essential knowledge of the
rules of the actions. Furthermore, it establishes and defends the universal principles upon which such rules depend.

The relation of the gift of Counsel and the gift of Wisdom is as follows: The
gift of Counsel directs immediately the actions of the soul moved by the Holy
Spirit to choose correctly and well and to find the mean even in things which
are very doubtful. It is noted in the Book of Machabees: "Good counsel came
into their minds (1 Mach 4: 45)." The gift of Wisdom, on the other hand, is not
immediately regulative of activity. It contemplates divine things, both as they are
in themselves, and secondarily, as they are the higher rule of action. Activity is
still immediately directed by human rules. [90]

This interpretation of Wisdom does not enhance the intellectual part of the
human person to the detriment of the whole person; indeed, the Christian must
always be ready to account for the reasons of the heart that the mind knows
not. At the same time, the authentic Thomist understanding of Wisdom does
not require us to make the will a knowing capacity. The New Testament texts
that insist on the primacy of love in the Christian life encourages us to respect
the importance of thinking about the truth in love. From this, one can easily
discern that the gift of Wisdom also shapes the way in which the Christian
tradition conceives of the contemplative life.

7. OUR LADY AND THE RECOLLECTED LIFE

In his biblical commentary on the Sermon on the Mount, St Augustine associates the gift of Wisdom with the seventh beatitude, "Blessed are the peace-
makers for they shall be called children of God" (Mt 5: 9). According to patristic exegesis, a peaceful spirit above all characterizes the person who remains
united with Christ. For according to the testimony of the angels at the nativity
of the Lord, peace belongs by preference to "those whom God favors" (Lk 2:
14). St Paul further develops the notion of God's favor in explicitly Christological terms: "For those whom he foreknew he also predestined to be conformed
to the image of his Son, in order that he might be the first-born among many
brethren" (Rom 8: 29). As an icon of the divine tranquillity, the peacemaker
embodies the order of divine wisdom and love in the world.

---

[90] John of St Thomas, *The Gifts of the Holy Spirit*, trans. W. D. Hughes (New York, 1950),
      chap. 4, no. 28.

An ancient spiritual adage reminds us that the supremely peaceful God settles his peace on everything. "Tranquillus Deus tranquillat omnia." Thus Aquinas assures us, a peacemaker is one who brings about peace in himself or in others. The spiritual authors customarily recommend a recollected life as the surest path to both attaining personal peace and establishing peace within the human community. The recollected spirit, nourished by a life of vocal prayer and meditation, especially manifests itself through the correct judgments that the person of interior peace makes concerning divine things and the world. In sum, peace flows from a recollection, and recollection from the knowledge that we are God's children. "Now we are called children of God," says Aquinas, "in so far as we participate in the likeness of his only begotten and natural Son, according to Romans, 'They are the ones he chose especially long ago to become true images of his Son,' who is Wisdom Begotten." [91]

As the fruit of charity and the gift of Wisdom, peace points to a number of Christological themes pertinent to the fullness of the theological life: First, God's wise, though hidden, plan for establishing and renewing the order of creation; secondly, the requirement that sinful men and women attain the renewal of their godly images, so that they might become more and more conformed to the image of the Eternal Son, "who is Wisdom Begotten;" and consequently, the reality of the communion of saints, or the Church that embraces all those to whom God effectively addresses the call to sanctity. St Paul hints at the pattern that exists between the Covenant of creation and the New Covenant that is written in the blood of Christ: "For it is the God who said, 'Let light shine out of darkness,' who has shone in our hearts to give the light of the knowledge of the glory of God in the face of Jesus Christ" (2 Cor 4: 6). And as images of this glory, the Christian believer enjoys the benefits of a tranquil life, even amid the anxieties of a changing and hostile world.

St Paul warns, "Let no one deceive himself. If any one among you thinks that he is wise in this age, let him become a fool that he may become wise. For the wisdom of this world is folly with God" (1 Cor 3: 18). As a warning against this sort of perverse foolishness *stultitia*, the Christian tradition urges us to adopt a life of prayer and spiritual discipline in order to acquire divine wisdom. For those who do not accept the wisdom of the Gospel, no matter how much human wisdom they may have, stand condemned to an impoverished, if not outright silly, sort of life. "The unspiritual man does not receive the gifts of the Spirit of God, for they are folly to him, and he is not able to understand them because they are spiritually discerned" (1 Cor 2: 14).

St John of the Cross says that the fire of divine charity is "somewhat consuming and destructive." In order that we might be made worthy partakers of

---

[91] *Summa theologiae* IIa-IIae q. 45, a. 6.

the divine life, what is unspiritual in every believer requires the purification that the Holy Spirit brings. "God has revealed to us through the Spirit. For the Spirit searches everything, even the depths of God. So also no one comprehends the thoughts of God except the Spirit of God" (1 Cor 2: 10,11). This sort of spiritual purification runs so deep in the human soul, that superficial conformity to rules or a mere general intention to do God's will never suffices to bring about what St Paul carefully designates as being "conformed to the image of his Son." In the Church, one discovers this kind of divine wisdom; in fact, spiritual authors speak about the Holy Spirit as the soul of the Church.

In their spiritual treatises, the medieval authors of the Cistercian Order frequently applied a verse from the Book of Wisdom to the Blessed Virgin: "From eternity, in the beginning he created me, and for eternity I shall not cease to exist" (Wis 24: 9). The Church venerates Mary as the Seat of Wisdom because the virgin mother of the Savior, who as St Ambrose reminds us "remains active in his mother in a way that is beyond our understanding," ranks first among all the elect. She also reigns as Queen of Peace. Mary's place in the Church derives principally from her divine maternity. In fact, we hear the Trinitarian echo in the words that announce her special mission in the Church: "And the angel said to her, 'The Holy Spirit will come upon you, the power of the Most High will overshadow you; therefore the child to be born will be called holy, the Son of God' " (Lk 1: 35). Because she is the mother of Christ, Mary also serves as the spiritual mother of all those who are incorporated into Christ. Rightly do the Christian faithful venerate our Lady as the Mother of the Church. Those who look for peace in themselves or human insight, rather than in Mary and the wisdom that God alone provides through the power of the Holy Spirit, will do well to recall the words from the Book of Wisdom that the Church's liturgy allegorically places on Mary's lips: "Come to me, you who desire me, and eat your fill of my produce ... Those who eat me will hunger for more, and those who drink me will thirst for more" (Wis 24: 19, 21).

CHAPTER 2
THEOLOGICAL HOPE AND CHRISTIAN
EXPECTATION

1. THE VIRTUOUSNESS OF THEOLOGICAL HOPE

Catholic theologians generally distinguish between hoping and believing. The 12th-century Cistercian spiritual author William of St.-Thierry nonetheless confesses in his *Meditations*: "I am bold to say that I do not truly know whether I hope for something other than that which I believe. You, Lord are my belief, you are my hope." [1] The Christian believer holds fast to the divine truths that are necessary for salvation. As a specific virtue of the Christian life, theological faith perfects human intelligence; to adapt the words of the Fourth Gospel, faith consecrates the human mind in Truth (Jn 17: 17). Still, even though properly speaking faith remains a virtue of the intellect, the act of faith requires more than the exercise of human intelligence. Christian belief relies on the energies of human appetite. Because the mysteries of faith surpass the inbred capacities of human intelligence, the human will must supply the required momentum for making the act of fiduciary assent. And because belief demands that we rely on the word of another, the virtue of faith necessarily involves commitment to a person, to the loving God who reveals his truth in the world. Faith commitment of this kind occurs only under the influence of divine grace, as each person is drawn to embrace the ultimate goodness that the Church announces through the preaching of the Gospel.

Whereas the intellect finds its perfection in knowing the truth, the human will because of its particular psychological structure reaches its own perfection through embracing the good. For the Christian theologian, "good" always denotes a real, predicamental quality of being that exists as a result of the divine causality. This means that the resemblance to divine goodness that leads us to call something good is inherent in the thing itself, belonging to it as a form and therefore giving identity to it. Because his love is the cause of their goodness, God is said to love created things. "God's love," Aquinas reminds

---

[1]   William of St.-Thierry, *Meditations*, no. 10, trans. Sr Penelope (Spencer, MA, 1971), p. 147.

us, "pours out and creates the goodness in things."[2] And so all true goodness in the world variously and verily participates in the very goodness which belongs identically to the persons of the blessed Trinity. Moreover, Christ instructs us that even the created goodness of his humanity points to God alone: For when a certain ruler asked Jesus, "'Good Teacher, what must I do to inherit eternal life?' Jesus said to him, 'Why do you call me good? No one is good but God alone' " (Lk 18: 18,19). For the Christian believer, theological hope represents a reaching out for the ultimate goodness that is God himself and so initially perfects the passive capacity in the human being to find complete fulfillment only in God, a capacity that God himself has made part of being human.[3]

Before we can examine the virtuousness of theological hope, it is useful to recall some of the anthropological presuppositions that undergird the classical treatment of the theological virtue of hope. Using the language of personal fulfillment, the German philosopher Josef Pieper provides a general description of hoping:

> Hope, like love, is one of the very simple, primordial dispositions of the living person. In hope, man reaches "with restless heart," with confidence and patient expectation toward... the arduous "not yet" of fulfillment, whether natural or supernatural.[4]

As a characteristically human endeavor, then, hoping incarnates a reaching out for anything that is perceived as good, and for the anticipated fulfillment that the possession of something good brings.

Four features of hoping in general merit special attention. First, hope concerns only the movement toward what perfects the human person, toward good objects or ends that enhance the personal dignity of one endowed with spiritual powers. But if a person were to encounter something destructive, the reaction would take on a different shape, for when something evil faces us we experience repugnance or fear. Second, hope looks toward the future, for a person never hopes for what he or she already possesses. Hope seeks a good object that still lies in the future; the person who presently and actually realizes the

---

[2] *Summa theologiae* Ia q. 20, a. 2. For the Christian moral theologian, this notion implies that extramental good shapes the development of human freedom and choice. In this sense, real moral good is to be distinguished from what some British moral philosophers consider moral realism, namely, a form of moral argument which supposes that the grounds for moral truth lie only in some part outside of the moral agent. The British philosopher Roger Scuton, for instance, distinguishes between a strong and a weak naturalism on the basis of how strongly one makes the logical inference between the 'good' and whatever is judged to be good. See his "Attitudes, Beliefs and Reasons" in *Morality and Moral Reasoning*, ed, John Casey (London, 1971), p. 57.

[3] See Servais Pinckaers, O.P., "Le désir naturel de voir Dieu," *Nova et Vetera* 51 (1976), pp. 255–273.

[4] Josef Pieper, *Hope*, trans. Mary Frances McCarthy, S.N.D. (San Francisco, 1986), p. 27.

attainment of something desired reacts with joy. Third, we speak about hoping only when the attainment of the good, future object involves some difficulty or an element of arduousness. Otherwise, when it is a case of someone seeking a good that is easily achieved, the person experiences the simple emotion of desire, which belongs properly in the concupiscible appetite. In fact, the precise note of being difficult to attain establishes the formal object of hope and explains why we find hope among the irascible or contending emotions, instead of the concupiscible or impulse emotions. For if there were nothing difficult to surmount in achieving a particular good, the concupiscible or impulse emotions themselves would suffice to ensure that the human person aspired to such goods. Finally, only something that is attainable elicits hope; a person must judge that the hoped-for reality lies within the realm of possible options. When this is not the case, the individual who is definitively impeded from obtaining any good required for human perfection experiences despair.

The emotion of hope shares in the general dynamics of human longing. As part of the psychological makeup of the human person, hope expresses itself in two ways. First of all, hope exists at the level of the basic sense appetites, *viz*, as one of the five irascible or contending emotions that serve to strengthen the human person against the difficult situations that life presents. As a human emotion, sense hope arises spontaneously whenever a person encounters a good which, though its achievement may entail sizable difficulties, still emerges as a realizable good. This expectation comprises the simple, primordial movement of the human person toward an expected good. St Augustine writes: "You have only to show a leafy branch to a sheep, and it is drawn to it. If you show nuts to a boy, he is drawn to them. He runs to them because he is drawn, drawn by love, drawn without any physical compulsion, drawn by a chain attached to his heart." [5] However, the natural emotion of hope, like the simple disposition of love, lacks the distinctive quality of virtue. For by definition, virtue establishes a person in the stable pursuit of the good, whereas the spontaneity associated with any sheerly emotional response excludes the sort of stability that the definition of virtuousness requires.

On another level, hope designates a moral or human virtue. As is true of all human virtue, the moral virtues that resemble hope, such as magnanimity and munificence, involve a reasoned choice toward the achievement of a good course of action. But in the form of a moral virtue, hope specifically affects human appetite; it even strengthens the irascible or contending appetites. In other words, moral hope begets courage. Since natural hope involves excelling in formidable activities or undertaking lavish projects, these virtues, as I have said, include qualities of soul such as magnanimity and munificence. "Mag-

---

[5]   St Augustine, *Treatise on John*, 26, 4 – 6 (*CCL* 36, 261 – 263).

nanimity," says Aquinas, "coincides with courage in as much as it strengthens the mind for a strenuous task." [6] And from this connection, the moral theologian recognizes the excellence that hoping achieves in other virtues related to cardinal fortitude, such as long-suffering and constancy.

The Christian tradition treats hope as an analogical concept. As an identifiable human trait, hoping signifies both a simple emotion that arises in response to perceiving sense objects, as well as specific actions associated with certain moral virtues. These latter enjoy the common purpose of ensuring that a person remains fixed in the pursuit of a difficult good according to the order of right reason. "Confidence," says Aquinas, "implies some form of hope: for confidence is hope strengthened by a firm supposition." [7] Within this range of analogical understanding, the exact nature of theological hope emerges. For the theological virtue of hope takes up these common themes and incorporates them into a life of specifically Christian dimensions.

The theological virtues relate the believer directly to God; these endowments of grace establish the human person in an active and full relationship with the Persons of the blessed Trinity, a relationship made possible for us by the saving work of Jesus. As a theological virtue, hope's special function is to unite the believer with God as his or her supreme and ultimate Good. Theological hope fixes our attention and our emotional energies onto the "dawn from on high" (Lk 1: 78). And for this reason, St Paul encourages us to "be sober, and put on the breastplate of faith and love, and for a helmet the hope of salvation" (1 Thes 5: 8).

It might seem that any as yet future good, even so great a one as the divine Goodness itself, could not serve as a suitable object for virtue, given that virtue, by definition, makes its possessor good here and now. In fact, some theologians have argued that hope should not be numbered among the theological virtues, for by hoping we do not attain God, rather we establish a certain state of affairs that remains within the human condition, viz, the self's movement toward the possession of God. Aquinas, however, sets forth a unique and important way to justify the virtuous character of hope. He explains that "in all things subject to regulation and measure, their being good is reckoned on the basis of their reaching the rule (or measure) proper to them." [8] Virtue puts right reason into emotion, and like all virtue, hope looks to establish the proper measure for a specific human activity. More specifically, the virtues of hope shape the proper emotional response that a person should demonstrate when faced with some future, difficult, but attainable good. Thus, while hope by definition remains

---

[6]   *Summa theologiae* IIa-IIae q. 129, a. 5.
[7]   *Summa theologiae* IIa-IIae q. 129, a. 6, ad 3.
[8]   *Summa theologiae* IIa-IIae q. 17, a. 1.

unfulfilled with respect to reaching its object, the very act of hoping possesses a suitable perfection in itself and therefore qualifies as a truly virtuous activity. By its very nature, then, hoping is tendential.

Aristotle distinguishes magnanimity from hope precisely on the basis of whether persons are able to attain a difficult good by their own efforts, as happens in the case of magnanimous men and women, or whether they are able to reach a goal only with help from others. It is this distinction which opens up for Aquinas a way to clarify the distinctively virtuous quality of theological hope. He says:

> When it is a case, then, of hoping for something as possible to us precisely through God's help, such hope, *by reason of its very reliance upon God*, reaches God himself. Evidently, then, it is a virtue, since it makes one sphere of human activity to be good and to reach one of the rules it is supposed to reach. [9]

The perfection involved in hoping lies, in other words, in the confident way that the believer turns toward God. This reliance, moreover, constitutes the basis for establishing that proper measure or rule that the definition of virtue requires in order that both doer and action manifest a certain perfection.

In this reliance on the divine help, we can again distinguish theological hope from the simple emotion of desire. While desire implies a certain movement toward a future good, it does not form the basis for a theological virtue. Why not? Aquinas replies: "No virtue is called desire, because desire does not imply any present clinging or spiritual contact with God himself." [10] In another text, Aquinas enlarges on this topic:

> To be sure one who hopes is imperfect with respect to what he or she hopes to obtain and does not yet possess. But such a one is perfected as to this, that he or she already reaches the rule proper to his actions, namely God on whose help he relies. [11]

Hoping belongs to the wayfarer, but it also perfects the Christian on life's journey, for by assuring one's reliance on God, it braces the believer to confront the difficulties and spiritual trials that remain part of Christian living.

2. HOPE AND THE PROMISE OF HAPPINESS

In order to understand clearly the formal object of theological hope, we must consider the important truth that God alone constitutes the supreme Good for the human person. When Aquinas asks whether human happiness ultimately consists in the vision of God's very essence, he concludes that the personal relationship with God which we call beatitude is indeed the supreme happiness

---

[9] Ibid.

[10] *Quaestio disputata de spe*, a. 1, ad 6.

[11] *Summa theologiae* IIa-IIae q. 17, a. 1, ad 3.

for each member of the human species. [12] To speak about humankind's ultimate beatitude as consisting in a "direct vision of the divine essence" implies that the rational soul is capable of an immediate intuition of God's very being, upon which follows a spontaneously elicited joy, the thorough beatification of the whole person. [13] The scholastics traditionally designate the human creature's share in God's blessedness as "formal beatitude," which they distinguish from the supremely blessed life of God in himself or "objective beatitude."

The theological virtue of hope relates the believer to objective beatitude, that is, the very blessedness of God, but with special reference to formal beatitude. In other words, hope draws the Christian toward the blessed vision of God which the company of the saints on high actually enjoys and which fulfills all their desires. The Christian who hopes seeks God *for himself or herself*. In technical language, the formal object of theological hope is God-as-possessed.

In the excesses of 17th-century French spiritual idealism, some actually spoke about *l'amour pur*, a love so disengaged from the self that it could conceivably continue even in the damned. [14] This account obviously has nothing in common with Christian hope. At the same time, when we say in theology that hope seeks God for the hoper, that is, the loving embrace of God's goodness for me, we do not thereby subordinate God to either the human creature or to the whole of creation. The believer does not hope for God as one might instrumentally use something created in order to achieve some personal perfection. Rather the Christian desires God for himself or herself because God alone stands as the true ultimate end or goal of each human being's personal existence. As is clear from the general norms of Christian loving, we can never subordinate another person as a means of self-fulfillment. Since this is true

---

[12]   See *Summa theologiae* Ia-IIae q. 3, a. 8. Aquinas also considers whether a creature can find fulfillment in "seeing" the divine essence in Ia q. 12, aa. 1–11. He further contrasts this kind of vision-knowledge of the divine essence with both the knowledge of God which the human person has in this life through natural reason and through the gift of divine grace. In his commentary on *Summa theologiae* IIa-IIae q. 4, a. 8, Cajetan observes that in this life the knowledge of God through grace is not necessarily a higher mode of knowledge than that through reason, which provides its own sort of evidence. Rather faith's excellence derives from its formal object, namely, First Truth-Speaking. For a discussion of God's own knowledge which he shares with the blessed in heaven as source of faith and the *sacra doctrina*, see *Summa theologiae* Ia q. 1, a. 2 and IIa-IIae q. 2, a. 3.

[13]   Thomists traditionally distinguish the mind's grasp of the divine essence from the will's joyful elation which results from beholding it. Moreover, they insist that this beatific joy relates to the vision of God in the same way that a specific property belongs to an essence. On this question, Scotus held the view that joy itself is the formal constitutive of beatitude. In general, we can assume that such speculations reflect different anthropological positions. For Aquinas, "the ultimate happiness of humankind consists in its highest activity, which is the exercise of one's mind" (*Summa theologiae* Ia q. 12, a. 1).

[14]   For further information, see Ronald Knox, *Enthusiasm* (New York, 1950).

of our love for human persons, it is all the more true of our love for God. As Cardinal Cajetan aptly remarks, in theological hope, "we hope for God for ourselves, but certainly not on account of ourselves – *Speramus Deum nobis, non vero propter nos*." [15]

St Jerome warns against the Pelagians, "Rely not on your wisdom, virtue, or talent, but on God alone; for he it is who directs your footsteps in your pilgrimage to the heavenly home." [16] This fundamental Christian belief points to another aspect specific to theological hope. What motivates a Christian to hope that he or she will eternally possess God? What grounds our expectation that we will receive such great benefits from him? How can one maintain this hope throughout a lifetime of falling many times and in the face of many other signs of our unworthiness? In a short essay on hope, Aquinas provides a direct answer to these questions.

First, Aquinas recapitulates the basic teaching that hope's virtuousness lies precisely in its proper reliance on the divine help.

> Faith is not considered a virtue except in so far as it assents to the testimony of the First Truth . . . likewise hope obtains the status of virtue from the fact that one clings to the help of the divine power while moving towards eternal life. However, were one to seek out human assistance, either one's own or from another, in order to look for this perfect good without the divine help, this would be a serious sin. [17]

Theological usage distinguishes a virtue's formal terminative object from the formal mediating object. The scholastic theologians describe the formal mediating object as the medium whereby the virtuous person reaches the formal object of the virtue. This amounts to explaining what exactly motivates a person to cling to God in theological hope.

> Therefore, as the formal (mediating) object of faith is First Truth (Speaking), whereby as through a certain medium the believer assents to those things which he or she believes the material object of faith so also the formal (mediating) object of hope is the help of the divine power and mercy (*auxilium divinae potestatis et pietatis*), on account of which the movement of hope reaches out for the goods hoped for, *viz*, the material object of hope. [18]

The Christian gospel places the experience of God's mercy at the very heart of the theological life. "Christ is not separated from sinners," says St Augustine, "rather he is judged with them. The thief escapes, and Christ is sentenced. The criminal receives forgiveness; the one who forgives the sins of all believ-

---

[15] *In Secundam secundae* q. 17, a. 5, no. 8.

[16] St Jerome, *Adversus Pelagianos*, Bk 3; see St Jerome, "The Dialogue Against the Pelagians," in *Dogmatic and Polemical Works*, trans. John N. Hritzu (The Fathers of the Church, vol. 53; Washington, DC, 1965), pp. 230–378.

[17] *Quaestio disputata de spe*, art. 1.

[18] Ibid.

ers stands condemned." [19] The saints underscore the experience of the divine mercy and compassion as an indispensable part of the Christian life. Aquinas's distinctions give theological expression to this authoritative teaching on Christian salvation.

Within the larger perspectives of theological discussion, the commentatorial tradition that followed after Aquinas questioned why a Christian would expect to attain the full possession of God. While some commentators agreed that God's merciful omnipotence indeed accounts for the efficient cause of our actually attaining the vision of God, they rejected the view that the divine power can serve as a formal cause of our hoping for it. In other words, there is nothing in the divine omnipotence that gives a specific reason for theological hope as such, and so God's omnipotence does not serve as hope's formal mediating object. Rather, as the 17th-century Jesuit commentator Francisco Suarez argued, the very goodness of God himself suffices to explain why someone would be motivated to hope in God.

But there is something of the incomplete in this explanation. For Suarez's position fails to take account of the fact that the divine power must not only account for the actual achievement of eternal happiness, but also for our intending toward it, for our very spiritual clinging to God in hope amidst the difficulties and obstacles of the present life. And only God's all-powerful mercy adequately expresses the reason that a Christian believer in the present sin-marked economy of salvation can hope to attain beatitude. Hope shapes the Christian believer to seek the vision of God not simply as a good but as it is a possible good. This happens only in virtue of God's merciful aid, the effective expression of his disposition to save us. Thus, divine omnipotence and mercy specify hoping in a motivational way. [20] Aquinas's position supports the view that the pilgrim Church constantly requires succor in its journey to the heavenly homeland or *patria*. Alone, the human creature remains impotent to reach the goal of beatific fellowship with the saints and, moreover, experiences frustration in the effort by the experience of personal and communal sin. The formal mediating object of theological hope reminds us that God's omnipotent mercy, his fatherly care, both can and will overcome these obstacles to our well-being.

Ultimately, since it is through the sacrifice of Christ that God communicates his redeeming mercy, the mystery of the Incarnation forms the foundation for Christian hope. St Paul explicitly points to Christ as the one who guarantees the validity of Christian hope: "But I am not ashamed, for I know whom

---

[19] St Augustine, *Tractatus super Joannem* 31, chap. 7 (*PL* 35: 1642).

[20] I am indebted to William J. Hill, O.P., *Hope* (2a2ae. 17–22), vol. 33 of the Blackfriars translation of the *Summa* (New York 1966), p. 148, note 11 for this summary of the position which John of St Thomas defends in his *Cursus Theologicus* XVII, Disp. IV, art. 1, no. 17.

I have believed, and I am sure that he is able to guard until that Day what has been entrusted to me" (2 Tim 1: 12). Christian hoping, then, is unique to the actual order of salvation history. Nevertheless through the virtue of hope, each believer already participates in the promised eschatological salvation. Aquinas takes full account of St Paul's words to the Romans: "and hope does not disappoint us, because God's love has been poured into our hearts through the Holy Spirit which has been given to us" (Rom 5: 5). In this context it is important to recall that the Jesuit commentator Suarez failed to signal trust in God's mercy as a constitutive part of hope's formal motivating object. But Aquinas's insistence on God's merciful omnipotence reminds us that, because of personal sin, the believer never outgrows the need for a loving confidence in God's mercy. "And because 'we all make many mistakes' (Jas 3: 2)," the Council of Trent warns, "each of us ought to keep before his eyes the severity of judgment as much as the mercy and goodness ... for our whole life must be examined and judged not by our judgment but by that of God." [21]

Theological hope relates the Christian directly to God, so it includes among its material objects all of the good things that the Christian believer lovingly looks forward to receiving: the vision of God, the accompanying bliss, the resurrection of the body and its glorification, and fellowship with the blessed. [22] Theological hope also entitles the Christian to expect the secondary material objects, that is, created instruments of hope that form part of the Christian dispensation for salvation. This means above all the instrumental causality of Christ's humanity, but it also includes spiritual goods such as grace, the infused virtues, the gifts of the Holy Spirit, the maternal mediation of the Blessed Virgin Mary, the intercession of the saints, and the forgiveness of sins, especially mediated through the sacraments of reconciliation and holy anointing. But one can also legitimately hope for temporal goods in so far as these conduce toward beatitude, such as holy friends, good health, psychological equilibrium,

---

[21] Council of Trent, "Decree on Justification," chap. 16 (*DS* 1545–1550).

[22] Christian hoping ceases at death, when the believer hears Christ say, "Come, you that are blessed by my Father, inherit the kingdom prepared for you from the foundation of the world" (Mt 25: 34). The Church, moreover, has officially taught that the beatific vision does not await the general resurrection of the dead (*DS* 1304–1306). Accordingly, we believe that the separated souls of the just do experience the beatitude of heaven. Furthermore, we recognize in faith that these blessed ones together comprise the company of the saints with which the Church on earth enjoys a special form of communion. At the same time, the resurrection of the body also belongs to the body of Christian truths to which we give our profession of faith in the Creed. Although theological reflection on matters which pertain to eschatology necessarily involves a certain degree of speculation, the common teaching of the Church maintains that the resurrected body also participates in the effects of beatitude. Aquinas expresses this belief beautifully when he says that "participation in the glory of Christ's body renders our bodies glorious" (*Summa theologiae* IIIa q. 56, a. 2).

and so forth. Again, Aquinas compares these material objects of hope with the material objects of theological faith, namely, the articles of the Creed:

> Just as those things that are believed as faith's material object are all referred to God even though some of them are created, e.g., the dogma that God created all creatures and that the person of the Word takes up the body of Christ in a hypostatic unity, so also all those things which are hoped for as material objects of hope are ordained to the one hoped-for end which remains the enjoyment of God. Towards this kind of formal beatitude we hope to be helped by God not only spiritually, but also with physical benefits. [23]

This treatment gives us an insight into how Aquinas overcomes the apparent tensions between future and realized eschatology, between the modern dichotomy of material and spiritual. St Augustine expresses the same matter succinctly: "Those blessings alone are the object of the theological virtue of hope that are contained in the Lord's Prayer." [24]

3. HOPE AND THE LOVE OF DESIRE

In its root meaning, to love means to will a good to someone. [25] On this basis, the Christian tradition distinguishes between two kinds of love, namely, the love of benevolence (*amor benevolentiae*) and the love of desire or concupiscence (*amor concupiscentiae*). Benevolence signifies the willing well to another, or disinterested affection, that properly characterizes the love of friendship (*amor amicitiae*). And since the one to whom we benevolently will a good thereby becomes united with us in a true bond of friendship, only other persons ought to comprise the authentic recipients of true benevolence. According to the gracious design of God's mercy, the Christian believer embraces not only the self and other persons such as neighbors and the angels in this kind of loving, but even God himself.

Concupiscence signifies willing a good to oneself, the desire of what is good for the subject; a wanting that is not necessarily disordered, for it is implanted in us by the author of nature and continues under the reign of grace. By loving this way, we seek for ourselves some authentic good, including those things that are predominately useful or delightful goods. Theological hope remains rooted in this kind of love. Of course, it is possible to affirm that a person hopes for God as his or her formal beatitude without implying that the person

---

[23] *Quaestio disputata de spe*, art. 1. See also, *Summa theologiae* IIa-IIae q. 17, a. 2, ad 2.

[24] *Enchiridion de fide, spe et caritate*, chap. 114; see St Augustine, "Faith, Hope and Charity," trans. Bernard M. Peebles, in *Writings of St. Augustine* (The Fathers of the Church, vol. 2; New York, 1947), pp. 369–472.

[25] See *Summa theologiae* Ia q. 20, a. 2: "God therefore wills some good to each existing thing, and since loving is no other than willing good to someone, it is clear that God loves everything."

thereby subordinates God to the person's own self-interest. Aquinas provides us with a good philosophical analysis of the interrelationship between the two kinds of love.

> Love is twofold: one kind is perfect; the other kind is imperfect. Love of something is imperfect when someone loves a thing not that he might wish the good in itself to the "thing," but in order that he might wish its good to himself. This is called by some "concupiscence," as when we love wine, wishing to enjoy its sweetness, or when we love some person for our own purposes or pleasure. The other kind of love is perfect; in this the good of anything is loved in itself, as when loving someone, I wish that he himself have the good, even if out of that fact nothing falls to me. This is said to be the love of friendship, whereby anyone is loved for himself (*secundum seipsum*). This is perfect friendship, as is said in *VIII Ethicorum*. [26]

In other words, to consider the love of desire (*amor concupiscentiae*) as an imperfect expression of love does not imply moral wrongdoing. Rather the love of desire is imperfect in the same way that one can consider motion as imperfect, *viz*, as an act of a being which has not reached its final term.

When the object of the love of desire includes some non-personal thing, the ultimate referent (the end "to which" or *finis cui*) must always be the one who loves: e.g., I love money because I can put food on the table for my family or sexual pleasure because it involves joyful union with my spouse. Otherwise such love would be disordered, as when a miser loves money only for the sake of money or the profligate sexual gratification only for the sake of sexual gratification. But when God is loved with desire, as happens in theological hope, one can still wish the goodness of God for the self without entailing a disordered subordination of God to one's own personal purposes. In this regard, God and even created persons differ from such things as wine, money, or sexual gratification. For while within the proper circumstances and given the right conditions, one can seek good things solely on account of the self, the Christian can never consider God in that way. Indeed, to seek to use any person only as a means for one's own fulfillment forms the heart of selfishness.

Virtuous hoping does not leave the hoper in frozen isolation; there exists a mutual relation between the hope of desire and the love of friendship. Moreover, this inter-connectedness of loves reflects a more basic inter-action that transpires within the human person. Aristotle describes "a sort of circle formed by the acts of the soul: for a thing outside the soul moves the intellect, and the thing known moves the appetite, which tends to reach the things from which

---

[26] *Quaestio disputata de spe*, art. 3, "Utrum spes sit prior caritate." The reference to Aristotle's *Nicomachean Ethics* runs as follows: "Perfect friendship is the friendship of men who are good, and alike in virtue; for these wish well alike to each other *qua* good, and they are good in themselves."

the motion originally starts." [27] Insofar as hope looks for and moves toward the hoped-for good, it springs from a love of desire. But insofar as the one hoping looks out for the help which is needed to attain this good, the hoping disposes him or her toward a love of benevolence or friendship. For the hoper comes to love the one who provides the means for attaining the sought-after good. [28] Hope leads to charity, writes Aquinas, "for when a person hopes to receive something good from God, he or she is led to see that God should be loved for his very self." [29]

Because the theological virtues always point to God as their proper and immediate object, they remain radically different from any ordinary kind of human believing, hoping, or loving. Still, we can discern in the experience of human friendship a model for the way that faith leads to hope and hope to charity. Aquinas offers a good illustration of this in the *Summa contra gentiles*:

> The love that a man has for others arises in man from the love that he has for himself, for a man stands in relation to a friend as he does to himself. But a person loves himself in as much as he wishes the good for himself, just as he loves another person by wishing him good. So, by the fact that one is interested in his own good he is led to develop an interest in another person's good. Hence, because a person hopes for good from some other person, a way develops for him to love that other person in himself, from whom he hopes to attain the good. Indeed, a person is loved in himself when the lover wishes the good for him, even if the lover may receive nothing from him. Now, since by sanctifying grace there is produced in us an act of loving God for himself, the result was that we obtained hope from God by means of grace. However, though it is not for one's own benefit, friendship, whereby one loves another for himself, has of course many resulting benefits, in the sense that one friend helps another as he helps himself. Hence, when one person loves another, and knows that he is loved by that other, he must get hope from him. Now by grace one is so established as a lover of God, through the love of charity, that he is also instructed by faith that

---

[27] See *Quaestiones disputatæ de veritate* q. 1, a. 2 where Aquinas gives this account of Aristotle's teaching in Bk 3, chap. 9 of the *De anima* (433a14ff).

[28] William J. Hill, *Hope*, p. 137, offers this helpful illustration: "In willing food to the hungry, it is apparent that my love goes out to both bread and man, but hardly in comparable ways. There are actually two goods here, one (loved with an *amor concupiscentiae*) enriches my hungry fellow man, the other (loved with an *amor amicitiae*) enriches me. The enriching act is in the former case an 'appropriation;' in the latter it is only a 'communion.' The good which derives to me is precisely the full realization of my humanity, the most perfect deployment of my liberty under the direction of intelligence, the fulfillment of myself in the construction of the human community. In short, one cannot truly love a friend and in supernatural charity it is God who is now the friend without becoming thereby ennobled."

[29] *Quaestio disputata de spe*, a. 3. In its most proper and formal sense, hope concerns only the one who makes the act of hope; and so formally speaking, Christian theologians argue that a person can not hope for another person's eternal beatitude. The tradition, however, does allow that someone can draw other persons into his or her hoping on the condition that there exists a true bond of charity so that such persons are regarded as "other selves."

he is first loved by God: according to the passage found in 1 John 4: 10: "In this is charity: not as though we had loved God, but because he hath first loved us." It follows, then, from the gift of grace that we get hope from God. It is also clear from this that just as hope is a preparation of man for the true love of God, so also man is conversely strengthened in hope by charity. [30]

This text recalls the organic connection that binds together theological faith, hope, and charity; as virtues of the Christian life, each of these infused qualities of soul unites the human person to God in ways that affect the principal human powers.

Hope, nevertheless, forms a distinctive theological virtue. Theologians distinguish hope from charity on the basis of the distinction between the love of desire and the love of friendship. By theological charity, we love God for his own sake, that is, with a love of benevolence or friendship. Both faith and hope share this in common, namely, that by these theological virtues we enjoy a personal, immediate union with God. Faith brings knowledge of the truth; hope brings reliance on God's help to bring us to blessedness. Hope looks to God as a source from which other good things come to us. From this intrinsic ordering of the theological virtues, it is easy to recognize that there exists a connection between the truth that the believer comes to accept from hearing, *ex auditu*, and the hope that this message kindles in his or her heart. Jesus begins his ministry "proclaiming the good news of God, and saying, 'The time is fulfilled, and the kingdom of God has come near, repent, and believe in the good news' " (Mk 1: 14 – 15).

4. THE PROVISIONAL CHARACTER OF HOPE

While every virtue affects the whole person, it is important to know which human capacities a particular virtue shapes. We know that faith constitutes a perfection of the intellect; it makes us knowers of the truth. The virtues of theological love perfect the powers of human appetite, that is, the rational appetite or will of the believer. As the rational appetite forms the subject of theological hope, this virtue deals with the desires of the heart, for, as Aquinas explains, "corresponding to the movement of the inferior appetite where there is emotion, there is a movement of the superior appetite without emotion." [31] It is important to recall that by describing hope as a virtue of the rational appetite, Aquinas departs from the Augustinian tradition that classified hope as a virtue of the memory. While it is true that hope can purify the human memory of the recollection of past sins, it only accomplishes this by helping us confront the

---

[30] *Summa contra gentiles*, Bk 3, c. 153, no. 2, trans. Vernon J. Bourke (Notre Dame, IN: University of Notre Dame Press, 1975).

[31] *Summa theologiae* IIa-IIae q. 18, a. 1.

future with a renewed confidence in God's merciful omnipotence. In this way, whatever in our past might inhibit our here and now confidence in God's mercy no longer intimidates us. "The thief escapes," St Augustine reminds us, "and Christ is sentenced."

Aquinas defines hope as a confident movement toward the future, and therefore catalogs it as a virtue that belongs to the provisional *status viatoris*, to the state of the wayfarer. We know that neither the blessed nor the damned can possess hope. For the blessed already possess the beatitude that hope longs after; in them, hope gives way to the joy that accompanies the beatific vision. But for those in hell, no hope of reform remains. In fact, the very realization that they can never reach beatitude characterizes the anguish that the damned suffer. And so Aquinas argues that "it is no more possible for the damned to consider blessedness as still open to them than for the blessed to conceive of it as not already possessed." [32] But wayfarers find themselves in neither condition, and so theological hope urges them on.

Indeed, a proper understanding of theological hope requires an adequate estimation of the wayfaring condition a proper conception of temporality. Since time marks the movement of change, philosophical forms of idealism, which develop out of the assumption of a split between mind and body, deal with temporality only in oblique ways. And so thinkers influenced by idealistic systems of thought find it easy to close the person off in an abstract world of human conceptions, and to constrain the human person within the tyranny of rationalism. On the other hand, existentialist philosophies, which refuse to place limits on human temporality, deny the provisional status of the wayfarer by imagining a kind of ultimate significance to this passing world. Because the heavenly city is sought on earth, humanists turn hope into a form of expectation for a better life. As much as these trends still affect theological investigation today, the theologian must protect the virtuousness of hope from those ideologies that threaten to detranscendentalize it.

The *status viatoris* implies human creatureliness. In Christian theology, hope aims at overcoming everything that keeps the human spirit from reaching perfection. [33] Indeed the various replacements for Christian hope proposed by different ideologies (and sometimes uncritically adopted by theologians) inevitably presuppose that sin and its effects are permanent features of the human situation. One either refuses to accept that the sinful status of the creature can be overcome or argues that the penalties of sin form part of authentic human existence. Neither option is theologically satisfying. Indeed, moral theologies that compromise moral truth usually fail to appreciate the full scope of

---

[32] *Summa theologiae* IIa-IIae q. 18, a. 3.
[33] See Aquinas's *Quaestio disputata de spe*, aa. 1–4.

the merciful omnipotence of God made available to us in Christ. Rather than "easing the burden" of the moral life, these theologies in effect urge people to live without the comfort in God's love that theological hope both promises and provides. Since theological hope serves the state of the wayfarer, this virtue provides everything that the pilgrim Church requires in order to reach its goal, and with a unique certitude that verifies the very transitoriness of earthly life.

The Catholic Reform of the 16th century steadfastly refused to accept the argument advanced by Protestant theologians that knowledge of one's own salvation ought to be included among the material objects of faith, that is, as something positively revealed by God. Here Luther's attempt to discover fiduciary faith led to a confusion between what the mind can know in faith and what the will can achieve through hoping. We must respect the limitations that belong to both kinds of human activity. *Qui stat, caveat ne cadat*! "Let the one who stands," St Paul exhorts us, "take care not to fall" (1 Cor 10: 12). Moreover, the Council of Trent affirms that every believer should maintain an unshaken hope that God will provide what is required for salvation: "Even though all should place a most firm hope [*firmissimam spem*] in God's help and rest in it, let no one promise himself with absolute certainty any definite outcome." [34]

In order to grasp accurately the full significance of this discussion, the theologian distinguishes certitude into its cognitive form, when the intellect is fixed on a truth, and noncognitive or affective certitude. Affective certitude is a form of practical knowledge that directs any operation to its proper end, *viz*, either as realized or as tending toward an end. According to Aquinas's explanation, this special kind of certitude compares with the sureness that moral virtues exhibit with respect to their objects, a tendency that can be described as connative. "The tendency of hope toward its end is marked by such certitude as this," says Aquinas, "in actual fact a derivation from faith's certitude found in the cognitive power." [35] But since hope's certitude resides in the will, the character of the rational appetite predominates in its operations; and in this sense it differs both in kind and degree from the certitude that only the intellect can achieve.

As a virtue of the wayfarer, hope develops in us a connatural clinging to God, a sure expectation that God will provide whatever we need to reach happiness, even though the thought of our own resources and the feebleness of our own efforts might otherwise incline us to think otherwise. The practical reliability of the moral virtues serves as model for hope's certitude. The moral

---

[34] Council of Trent, "Decree on justification," chap. 13 (*DS* 1540 and 1541): "nemo sibi certi aliquid absoluta certitudine polliceatur, tametsi in Dei *auxilio firmissimam* spem collocare et reponere omnes debet" (emphasis added).

[35] *Summa theologiae* IIa-IIae q. 18, a. 4.

virtues supply the human person with "second natures" which serve as real principles for human action, so that our appetites infallibly will follow the order of right reason. In a similar way, theological hope gives us a "new nature," one that places our desire for God firmly within the ambience of his merciful omnipotence. In summary, the graced Christian believer possesses the cognitive certitude of faith that a mercifully omnipotent God offers the gift of salvation to all men and women and, as long as the person personally appropriates this truth held by faith, the affective certitude of hope enables him or her to live a life of mature confidence in God's power. Among the blessed, the certitude of hope gives way to joyful realization of the divine Goodness, whereas in the wayfarers, the members of the pilgrim Church, this certitude still exists in a tendential state.

As a true theological virtue, hope shapes the Christian to trust in God's merciful omnipotence as the formal means whereby he or she anticipates a full share in the divine goodness. But within the economy of Christian salvation, Christians must appeal as well to the personal agents that the divine goodness has established in the world. So the Christian hoper confidently relies on the merits of Christ, on the maternal mediation of the Blessed Virgin Mary, Mother of the Church, on the intercessory prayer and help of the communion of saints, and on any other means that aid Christian hoping. [36] St Bernard was especially fond of invoking the Blessed Virgin Mary as a source of hope: "You will not lose hope when you call on her; you will not err when you think about her." [37] This praiseworthy practice does not mean that we place our hope in any creature for that which God alone can provide. It does mean, however, that God really uses secondary, instrumental causes in the working out of our salvation. The belief in the communion of saints represents the awareness that each person works out his or her salvation only within the social reality of the Church. As Mother of the Church, the Blessed Virgin Mary forms the center of this reality. Mary is the mother of fair hope: "Ipsam rogans non desperas, ipsam cogitans non erras."

5. DESPAIR AS ANTICIPATION OF NONFULFILLMENT

Because it rests principally on an error in faith-judgment, the roots of despair lie not in sentiment or mood, but in an act of the intellect. For the person tempted to despair supposes that God will not provide what is required to reach

---

[36]   The capital grace of Christ forms the foundation for this theological doctrine about created instruments; within the Church their exists a hierarchy of holy helpers among whom our blessed Lady holds the primary place. Thus, the Church suitably invokes her as "spes nostra," i.e., our hope.

[37]   St Bernard, Homilia 2, super "Missus est," (PL 183: 71).

salvation; and because such a supposition contradicts Christ's explicit promise, this disposition toward God constitutes a sinful posture. The theological tradition describes despair as an example of an offensive turning toward God – a *conversio offensiva*, i.e. an anti-theological vice. In the case of moral vice, the human person turns toward another creature in a disordered way, and thereby turns away from God. The wrongful *conversio ad creaturam* always entails *aversio a Deo*. But by engaging in the anti-theological vices, the Christian actually "turns" toward God in a disordered way, that is, the believer takes up a wrong attitude with respect to God's goodness. Despair especially exemplifies this sort of anti-theological vice. From a theological point of view, despair arises as a result of an error in judgment about the existence and/or nature of God's saving action. But the vice of despair denotes the felt conviction that God will not provide what *my* salvation requires or that he will not forgive *my* sins. While a variety of cultural and psychological factors create an atmosphere conducive to despairing, despair itself is the false notion that results from these factors. And so, despair constitutes an "offensive turning" toward God, *viz*, not as toward a merciful and omnipotent Father, but rather as to a god who is either incapable or unwilling to save me.

Even when expressed in theoretical terms, however, despair does not entail a sin against faith. The person who despairs *affectively* excludes himself or herself from the universal implications of the faith judgment that God wills all to be saved, though such a one may hold fast to the truth on intellectual grounds. And so despair about one's personal salvation can actually coexist with the act of belief that God wills the salvation of all humankind.

Since despair results primarily in an internal contradiction within the human person, those who are sensitive to the requirements of good pastoral ministry recognize the need to explain fully the gospel of hope to despairing persons, even before making an effort to correct one or another moral vice. For the repeated commission of serious sin frequently indicates that the sinner has forgotten or never learned the truth about God's merciful love. "Because the one who forgives the sin of all believers stands condemned," St Augustine reminds us, "the criminal receives forgiveness." [38] Indeed, the person who does not experience the merciful help of the heavenly Father as a real and practical good, finds it difficult to abide in the truth that God is merciful, that Christ has died for the sins of the world, and that the forgiveness of sins really exists within the Church of faith and sacraments. And the person in such a condition needs the power of the Holy Spirit, for the practical dynamics of despair eventually lead to sins against faith, that is, sins that actually reject or abandon the reality of the Christian mysteries themselves.

---

[38]   See note 22.

The two vices that the classical spiritual heritage assigns as the most frequent causes of despair are spiritual sloth – what Kierkegaard calls the "despair
of weakness" – and unchastity. According to the view of Gregory the Great,
cynicism about spiritual goods and compromises in living a chaste life frequently mask a life of practical despair. The confessor, spiritual director or
Christian counsellor should recognize that a reciprocal relationship exists between these moral vices and the anti-theological vice and constantly remind
the person caught in habitual sin of God's merciful love and forgiveness. In
a certain sense, despair amounts to a special sin against the redemption. "If
sin could truly not be forgiven," Aquinas says, "then it would not be a sin to
doubt forgiveness of sin." [39] But the truth of the matter is that sin has been
forgiven and theological hope brings the sinner into contact with a merciful
God. To call people from despair and the blackmail of the devil is one of the
chief pastoral responsibilities in the modern Church; all Christians, but especially priests (whose sacramental character points toward penance and the
Eucharist), need to see this as a constitutive part of proclaiming the gospel of
peace.

The true seriousness of despair lies in its anti-theological character. Once
separated from the goodness of God, the one without theological hope is left
vulnerable to other sorts of sin and, eventually, prone to spiritual death. The
suicide of Judas depicts the biblical model for despair. As I have said, the
spiritual tradition of the Church identifies unchastity and spiritual sloth (e.g.,
neglect of prayer, recollection, the sacrament of penance) as the sins that most
easily persuade one to fall into despair. But the remedy for despair outstrips in
vigor its causes. St Bernard advises that we call to mind the wounds suffered
by Christ as a sure way to bring back hope to the heart that, in the tempest
of pusillanimous and diffident feelings, has drifted from its moorings. "I have
fallen into a grievous sin," says the saint, "my conscience is alarmed, yet shall
it not be troubled; for I will call to mind the wounds of my Lord, who was
bruised for our iniquities. What sin can be so deadly as not to be healed by the
death of Christ?" [40]

6. THE FALSE HOPE OF PRESUMPTION

"There are two things that kill the soul," says St Augustine, "despair and false
hope." [41] Because it acts directly against the formal motivating object of theo-

---

[39] *Quaestiones disputatæ de malo* q. 3, a. 15.

[40] St Bernard, *Sermo in Cantica*, 61; see Bernard of Clairvaux, *On the Song of Songs III*, trans.
      Kilian Walsh and Irene M. Edwards (Cistercian Fathers Series, 31; Kalamazoo, MI, 1979).
      pp. 140–148.

[41] *Sermo 87*, chap. 8 (*PL* 38, 535).

logical hope, despair immediately appears as a sinful disorder. Presumption or false hope, on the other hand, mimics authentic theological hope, even though this anti-theological vice also constitutes an "offensive turning" toward God. St Bernard aptly contrasts this deceptive sin against theological hope with despair. "Fear of God's judgments, apart from hope, casts us down into the pit of despair; while indiscreet hope, unmixed with a reasonable fear, engenders a hurtful security." [42] Those who presume on God's merciful omnipotence want his sovereign goodness and forgiveness outside of the order that is established by the divine wisdom and justice. St Thomas cites the example of a person who "hopes to obtain pardon without repentance or glory without merits." In short then, presumption establishes an "unwarranted reliance upon God." [43] Because this vice urges us erroneously to imagine that God gives pardon to those who persist in their sins or leads those to glory who shirk from an upright life (see Jas 1: 22), presumption constitutes a vicious attitude in the Christian soul.

Certain periods in the history of spirituality supply examples of this offensive posture toward God. During the course of the 16th-century Reform, the Protestant divines laid great emphasis on the place that interior experience holds in the Christian life. In an effort to address the Catholic need for "inner spiritual experiences," the Jesuits and other spiritual directors developed various "methods" for prayer and meditation. These methods, however, provided the unexpected and unwelcome result of centering so much concentration on the self that considerable anxiety arose among those who practiced these methods. The leaders of the Quietist movement, especially the Spanish Miguel de Molinos (1640 – 1697), sought to address this uneasiness among the faithful by counselling that internal states or dispositions counted little in the spiritual life. Quietism accordingly developed into an aberration unwittingly generated by the Catholic Reform in the 16th and 17th centuries. By effectively urging people to think that God rewards us without reference to merits and virtue, the Quietist guidelines and mentality veered toward institutionalizing presumption. The Quietists, moreover, promoted a sort of acquired contemplation that moved a person away from making imperated acts of the will and therefore inhibited the believer from the effective practice of virtue. Quietism may even have promoted forms of moral turpitude. Molinos, the Spanish spiritual master, was in fact charged with innumerable counts of sexual misconduct, and subsequently his theories lost their popular appeal. If the charges against Molinos are accurate however, we can inquire whether the Quietist principles do not adumbrate the distinction, today widely held among certain moral theologians,

---

[42] St Bernard, *Sermo in Cantica*, 6; see Bernard of Clairvaux, *On the Song of Songs I*, trans. Kilian Walsh (Cistercian Fathers Series, 4; Spencer, MA, 1971), pp. 32 – 37.

[43] *Summa theologiae*, IIa-IIae q. 19, a. 1, ad 2.

between the "transcendental level" of human intention and the "categorical level" of human acts. This deceptive cleavage of human conduct from human meaning has led many moral theologians to argue that all forms of bodily human conduct remain as so many neutral appendages of interior spiritual states, which alone can determine an act's moral worth.

Presumption denotes an affective movement of the creature that is motivated by a false judgment about how God's mercy conforms to his justice and wisdom. In the final analysis, the one who presumes does not understand that God's plan for our salvation includes our complete interior transformation. This entails both the work of image-restoration restoring the full character of the human being as *imago Dei* through the forgiveness of sins and image-perfection causing spiritual excellence in the Christian believer through the infused virtues and gifts of the Holy Spirit. The one who despairs forgets that forgiveness of sins is available in the Church; the one who presumes denies that Christian salvation bestows an entirely new capacity for action. It is not true that Christian belief and hope leave people the way they are; divine grace changes and renews those who welcome it. In the Christian life, a person cannot "travel north and south at the same time," i.e., one cannot persist in a sinful turning toward a creature and at the same time imagine that God's mercy ignores the turning away from him implied by the very nature of sin. According to the tradition, presumption springs from vainglory and pride, the most serious of the deadly sins. "This sort of presumption," Aquinas teaches, "appears to spring directly from pride; implying, in effect, that one thinks so much of himself that he imagines God will not punish him nor exclude him from eternal life in spite of his continuing in sin." [44]

7. THE GIFT OF THE FEAR OF THE LORD

Aquinas's treatise on the gift of Fear of the Lord illustrates both his comprehension of the Christian spiritual tradition and his insight into the psychological dimensions of the human person. In his treatise on the theological virtues, the Dominican neo-scholastic theologian Reginald Garrigou-Lagrange remarked: "Quidam dicunt quod S. Thomas non est psychologus, sufficit hic articulus [*Summa theologiae* IIa-IIae q. 19, a. 1] ad probandum contrarium, contra deliramenta protestantium, jansenistarum, et Kantii. S. Thomas optime utitur gladio distinctionis." [45] To be sure, Father Garrigou-Lagrange's exasper-

---

[44] *Summa theologiae* IIa-IIae q. 21, a. 4.

[45] *De virtutibus theologicis* (Rome, 1948), p. 359: "Some say that Saint Thomas is not a psychologist, but this article [*Summa theologiae* IIa-IIae q. 19, a. 1] suffices to prove the contrary. Against the nonsense of Reformed theologians, Jansenists, and Kantians, Saint Thomas employs optimally the sword of distinction."

ated tone seems oddly out of place after the Second Vatican Council's call for theological renewal and ecumenical sensitivity. Still, the student of theology would do well to heed his suggestion that Aquinas's discussion of Fear of the Lord warrants a close reading. Here we find an essay, representative of the classical period in moral theology, that furnishes an adequate and lucid account of the spiritual development of a Christian soul.

Like each gift of the Holy Spirit, Fear of the Lord represents the flourishing of a particular feature of the Christian virtuous life. But how can fearing God belong to the perfection and virtue of Christian life? The New Testament makes the point explicitly: "There is no fear in love, but perfect love casts out fear; for fear has to do with punishment, and whoever fears has not reached perfection in love" (1 Jn 4: 18). Still, Isaiah foretells that "the spirit of knowledge and the fear of the Lord" (Is 11: 2) will rest on the Messiah, and the Church numbers Fear of the Lord among the special endowments that belong to every baptized person in the state of grace.

Considered as a human emotion, fear belongs to the order of the irascible or contending emotions. These emotions take hold of a person who is confronted by a threatening evil that is (at least apparently) difficult to overcome. As fear represents an emotive response to evil, the theologian first of all needs to explain in what sense God, who perfectly possesses the sovereign good, can elicit fear. In order to make the required distinctions, Aquinas suggests that there exists a basic difference between fearing evil and fearing the person who has the power to inflict evil. The gift of Fear of the Lord concerns only the person who has the power to inflict evil. In this sense, Fear of the Lord attunes the believer to God, "who will repay according to each one's deeds" (Rom 2: 6).

In order to understand properly how this gift helps the Christian accurately contemplate an avenging God and thus aids the virtuous reliance on God's merciful love which hope provides, we must recognize the destructive power that sin itself holds. In other words, the proper use of the distinction between fearing evil and fearing the One who can inflict the evil of punishment requires an accurate theological analysis of the reality of sin. Otherwise, we run the risk of imagining God simply as an avenging Judge who stands ready to mete out punishment to those who have failed to discharge fully their moral obligations. But the authentic Christian notion of the gift impels us to discover a more penetrating and less anthropomorphic analysis of divine judgment.

According to the classical explanation, personal sin always involves two elements: the *malum culpae*, the evil of fault, and the *malum poenae*, the evil of punishment. In his treatise on Fear of the Lord, Aquinas recalls this distinction. First of all, he talks about sin as fault:

> Because the meaning of goodness always implies order to some final purpose,
> evil implies deprivation of this order; the only outright evil is one destructive of
> order to the ultimate end, and this is the evil of fault (*malum culpæ*). [46]

The evil of fault – *culpa* – represents the actual offense that sin effects against
the divine goodness itself, whether the sinful fault strikes directly against God
in the form of an offensive turning toward him, as happens with sins against
the theological virtues, or against God and neighbor, as happens with the sins
against the moral virtues. In the second case, we know that vicious actions
are constituted in their sinfulness precisely by a disordered turning towards
the creature (*conversio ad creaturam*) that necessarily implies a simultaneous
turning away from God (*aversio a Deo*). "Moral goodness and evil," explains
Aquinas, "consist chiefly in a turning to or a turning away from God." [47]

On the other hand, since it supposes a painful separation from certain created goods, punishment – *poena* – constitutes a different sort of evil. For within
the larger picture of the moral life, the only real and outright punishment is hell,
or the state of being fixed forever in a state of "turning away from God." And
yet, Aquinas explains how in our state as wayfarers the evil of punishment can
contribute to overall well-being.

> Punishment is indeed a genuine sort of evil, since it does in fact result in the loss
> of some particular good; nevertheless in the last analysis it is good, namely, in
> regard to its bearing upon the ultimate end. [48]

As bearing upon the final end, here and now punishments of any kind always
stand in a relative relationship to our reaching the goal of eternal beatitude. So
St Paul counsels the Galatians: "Bear one another's burdens, and in this way
you will fulfill the law of Christ" (Gal 6: 2).

According to Christian belief, everything that the human person experiences as burdensome and painful results from punishment for sin. But Christian faith also teaches us that suffering can be redemptive. Recall what Christian theology teaches about the present economy of salvation. Because of
the lack of original justice, every human person can experience appetitive
movements that incline him or her towards disordered behavior; as we know,
these disordered emotions continue even after sacramental incorporation into
Christ. [49] In addition, other psychological defects such as liability to anxiety,
slowness in learning, and weakness of personal resolve in important matters

---

[46]   *Summa theologiae* IIa-IIae q. 19, a. 1.

[47]   *Summa theologiae* IIa-IIae q. 19, a. 2, ad 1: "Bonum morale praecipue consistit in conver-
sione ad Deum, malum autem morale in aversione a Deo."

[48]   Ibid.

[49]   If this were not the case, people could find baptism attractive for the wrong reasons, for
instance, as a means to escape the debilitating effect of unruly emotions or some other
burdensome condition that marks the state of original sin. See *Summa theologiae* IIIa q. 69,
a. 3.

retain the character of punishment for human nature considered in itself. But for the person who lovingly bears such burdens, these same thorns in the flesh become the occasion for conformity to Christ's sufferings and the gradual reformation of the godly image in which we are all created. [50] Only our blessed Lady receives her salvation in another way, though the grace of the Immaculate Conception does not preserve her from sharing in the redemptive sufferings of her Son. The gift of Fear of the Lord helps believers to recognize that in the present economy of salvation, we must take St Paul's admonition seriously: "While we live we are constantly being delivered to death for Jesus' sake, so that the life of Jesus may be revealed in our mortal flesh" (Eph 4: 11).

The rich spiritual tradition that developed during the patristic period inspires Aquinas to distinguish four sorts of fear that figure in the Christian life: (1) worldly; (2) servile; (3) initial; (4) filial. Worldly fear obviously represents a spirit entirely opposed to Gospel values, whereas the development of servile, initial, and filial fear charts a course of growth in the spiritual life. We will examine in turn each of these kinds of fear.

1. Worldly Fear. Fear is born of love, says St Augustine, for one fears to lose only what he loves. [51] The worldly sinner loves only the things of this world. As a completely sinful disposition, this sort of fear has nothing in common with the gift of the Holy Spirit; rather it marks persons who remain sinfully entangled in the misuse of created goods. Those who never think about God's justice in the course of pursuing sinful conduct embody worldly fear. So worldly fear belongs to a person who remains hostile to the evangelical life. "Do not fear those who kill the body but cannot kill the soul," Jesus instructs his disciples, "rather fear him who can destroy both soul and body in hell" (Mt 10: 28). These words are addressed to the person who shudders at the thought of forfeiting one or another created good, even though he or she remains sinfully attached to it, that is, loves the created good outside of a due ordering to God.

2. Servile Fear. Fear of punishment remains for many persons the principal motive for maintaining some relationship with God, and so this psychological stance ordinarily plays a role in the development of the theological life. Aquinas distinguishes two modes of servile fear. The first is a mere servility, but the second is a fear of punishment that includes a proper recognition of the evil of sin. In his commentary, the American theologian William Hill summarizes this important distinction: Servility or slavishness, he explains, occurs

[50] See T. C. O'Brien, *Original Sin*, vol. 26 of the Blackfriars translation of the *Summa theologiae* (London, 1965), especially pp. 50–55. There O'Brien offers a profound commentary on Ia-IIae q. 83, a. 2: "Whether original sin is in the substance of the soul rather than in its powers."

[51] *De diversis Quaestionibus LXXXIII* Bk. 1, no. 23 (*PL* 40: 22).

when the avoidance of punishment is considered as a greater good than conforming to the divine will, in such a way that the proper motivation for the act lies in that very preference. Servility is, in effect, an inversion of the hierarchy of values, a refusal to acknowledge that the divine good is superior to one's own private good. As such, servility is always contrary to charity. [52] In servile fear that is free of such servility, or even in initial fear, the avoidance of punishment may predominate psychologically, i.e., here and now more intensely engage the attention, but implicitly it is evaluated as objectively subordinate to the greater evil of sin.

In order to understand correctly this important point, we must recall that punishment for sin lies in the disorder that the sinful action itself causes in a person's life. By reflection on the meaning of human life and, especially, by the experience of the self-destructive character of sinful behavior, the human person comes to realize that sin inflicts its own punishment. Indeed, every disordered desire, as St Augustine likes to remind us, carries with it its own punishment. Servility distinguishes those disordered persons whose very attachment to some created good, such as sexual gratification, high honors, or personal convenience, prevents them from conversion, from moving towards God. The person possessed of worldly fear simply gives no thought to God, whereas the servile person considers God but remains frozen in sin because he or she refuses to acknowledge that the divine good is superior to his or her own embrace of a created good.

Servile fear without the mark of servility characterizes the person who experiences the sense tugs and pulls towards disordered behavior of one kind or another but honestly acknowledges that to pursue created goods in this way would entail a painful separation from God. Still fear of punishment alone restrains such a one from sinning. As such, this attitude represents the spirit of the Old Law: "You who fear the Lord, wait for his mercy; do not stray or else you may fall" (Sir 2: 6 – 9). St Augustine even says that servile fear can exist along with willingness to sin. [53] So servile fear keeps a person from the love that characterizes initial fear; and for this reason, the believer who remains in this rudimentary disposition never becomes like the little child that the Gospels tell us will inherit the kingdom of heaven (see Mk 10: 13 – 16).

The graced Christian can remain with servile fear over a long period of time. For a person can maintain a self-regarding love by fearing the punishment that sin entails, and at the same time develop the proper kind of self-love that comes to perfection only with theological charity. This happens when, for example, a person painfully recognizes and accepts that the "punishment" of sin

---

[52] Hill, *Hope*, p. 56, note *b*.

[53] *De natura et gratia* 57 (*PL* 44: 280).

is of less moment than sinful separation from God. To put it differently, servile fear is not contrary to charity because through servile fear a sinner comes to appreciate that suffering the purification of disordered attachments no longer constitutes the maximum evil. Of course, this sort of spiritual growth requires that one accept at some point the objective truth about the moral life. "To regulate human life according to divine reasons [*rationes*] is in fact the work of wisdom," Aquinas teaches, "and the first indications of this ought to be reverence for God and subjection to him, with the consequence that in all things whatsoever a person will shape his life in reference to God." [54]

Take the example of the person who indulges in some form of unchaste conduct, whether in thought, words, or actions. To the extent that the fear of forfeiting delight in venereal pleasure restrains a man or woman from accepting divine truth, in this case about chastity, the unchaste person remains fixed in a state of servility. To put it differently, such a one abides outside the order of divine wisdom and love. And this implies that his or her life is not shaped in reference to God. But when a sinner experiences the true emptiness of unchaste activity in any form, and thereby comes to recognize the truth about the virtue of chastity, such a person begins to experience servile fear, i.e., he or she fears returning to the state of enslavement that this particular form of sinful self-gratification generates. "Servile fear is caused by love of self," says Aquinas, "since it is fear of punishment as detrimental to one's own well-being." [55]

In servile fear, the sinner recognizes the self-destructive character of sin, that is, its intrinsic punishment, and starts to look for ways to avoid it. Significantly for Aquinas, this happens only when the believer accepts the "first principles of wisdom," which Aquinas identifies as the "articles of faith." [56] The Church's role as a moral teacher is especially important at this stage of moral development. When this growth takes place however, reverence and submission to the heavenly Father replace a false regard for and slavish attachment to the creature. As the Old Testament wisdom observes, "The fear of the Lord is the beginning of wisdom" (Prov 1: 7).

3. Initial Fear. Substantially initial fear denotes filial fear, but in a mixed or imperfect way. For the motive that inclines a person to avoid alienation from God still involves fear of punishment, but with the dawning realization that to love God constitutes a good in itself. Aquinas makes the point with great clarity:

> Of itself initial fear is not concerned with punishment, as if this were its own proper object, but only to the extent that it has mixed with it the quality of servile fear. In its essentials, servile fear is compatible with charity, once the servility

---

[54]   *Summa theologiae* IIa-IIae q. 19, a. 7.
[55]   *Summa theologiae* IIa-IIae q. 19, a. 6.
[56]   *Summa theologiae* IIa-IIae q. 19, a. 7.

is put aside. Thus, servile fear continues to be operative, along with imperfect charity, in those instances where the motivation is not only love of rectitude but fear of punishment; yet such activity ceases with the coming of perfect charity, which, as 1 John says, "casts out fear which dreads punishment" (4: 18). [57]

There is a relationship between love and discipline: the weak person refuses discipline in as much as it seems a rejection; only the loved person can accept discipline as a means to grow closer to the source of love. In a certain sense, everyone remains a beginner in the spiritual life. And to that extent initial fear characterizes the lot of most Christian believers, for only the gaze of the saint remains so lovingly fixed on God that he or she possesses both the wisdom to discern properly the moral good and the will immediately to recoil from all evil.

4. Filial Fear. The gift of the Holy Spirit achieves in the believer the ability to reverence God and to avoid any alienation of ourselves from him. For this reason, filial fear grows to the extent that our charity increases. St Augustine writes that "chaste fear really means a will so disinclined to sin that we do not worry about falling from frailty, but rather shun sin in perfect tranquillity." [58] Those who reverence God as a true Father fear not the loss of disordered attachments to created goods, but only fear offending the Father whom they love as the source of all goodness. The Christian spiritual tradition repeatedly holds up the filial norm characteristic of a good child as the central feature of a holy life. As a matter of fact, as a way of identifying with Jesus who came among us as a little Child, the saints are known to cultivate devotion to the holy childhood. The 12th-century Cistercian Guerric of Igny throws light on the gift of filial Fear and the mystery of the Incarnation. In one of his Christmas homilies, he says: "When [Christ] manifested himself to mortals he appeared as a Child, a little one more lovable than terrible. Because he came to save and not to judge he preferred ways of inciting love to means of striking terror." [59]

Filial fear perdures even among the saints. "Evil for the rational creature lies either in becoming subservient to a lower creature out of disordered love, or in not submitting to God and instead in presumptuously rebelling against him and scorning him." [60] But even though this is not possible in heaven, the gift of Fear remains in the blessed. Fear of the Lord takes the form of awe, a beholding of the wonderful work of our salvation "his utter transcendence and incomprehensibility." [61] Christians anticipate this state of heavenly awe

---

[57]   *Summa theologiae* IIa-IIae q. 19, a. 8, ad 2.

[58]   *De civitate Dei* Bk 14, chap. 9 (*PL* 41: 416).

[59]   Guerric of Igny, *Liturgical sermons*, trans. by monks of Mt Saint Bernard Abbey (Spencer, MA, 1970).

[60]   *Summa theologiae* IIa-IIae q. 19, a. 11.

[61]   Ibid.

by living the beatitude of poverty of spirit. "A beatitude," explains Aquinas, "means an operation of a virtue in a state of complete perfection." [62] The one who lives poverty of spirit submits to God and therefore remains disinclined to seek glorification in his or her own person or in any other except God. The true experience of childlike dependency that marks the poor in spirit remains the best disposition for developing a life of Christian love. It should characterize not only the one who is perfect in charity, but also the person who is just coming to learn about moral rectitude and chaste fear.

---

[62] *Summa theologiae* IIa-IIae q. 19, a. 12, ad 1.

CHAPTER 3
THEOLOGICAL CHARITY AND COMMUNIO

1. CHARITY, THE REALIZATION OF FRIENDSHIP

In the course of its theological development, the Christian tradition again and again identifies the good of friendship among human persons as the single human experience best able to illumine specifically the meaning of divine love. The New Testament itself warrants the choice of friendship as a model for agapic love or theological charity. And so in their treatises, the Fathers and the medieval doctors sought to explain the important words that Jesus spoke to his disciples before his Passion: "I do not call you servants any longer, because the servant does not know what the master is doing; but I have called you friends, because I have made known to you everything that I have heard from my Father" (Jn 15: 15). In Christian life, says Aquinas, authentic and complete love implies "a sharing of man with God by his sharing happiness with us; and it is on this that a friendship is based."[1] Theological literature, especially from the Cistercian school, developed the New Testament teaching on *agape*[2] Two major elements in this analysis require further consideration: First, the *communicatio* or *koinonia* of beatitude; and second, *benevolentia*, the reciprocity of benevolent love.

The New Testament makes it abundantly clear that Christian life is ordered towards communion (*koinonia*): "What we have seen and heard, we announce to you also, so that you might be in communion with us; and we, we are in communion with the Father and with his Son Jesus Christ" (1 Jn 1: 3).[3] The

---

[1] *Summa theologiae* IIa-IIae q. 23, a. 1.

[2] For a study of the New Testament notion of charity, see Ceslaus Spicq, O.P., *Agape dans le Nouveau Testament* (Paris, 1958) [English translation: *Charity and Liberty in the New Testament* (New York, 1965), pp. 11–71]. Aquinas provides his commentary on this teaching in *Summa theologiae* IIa-IIae q. 23, aa. 1–8, where he first inquires about the nature of charity as a kind of friendship (a. 1), as a created reality (a. 2), and as a specific virtue (a. 3–5); then he turns to consider the relationship of charity to the other virtues, first by appraising its importance among the virtues (a. 6) and secondly by considering its role and influence (aa. 7, 8).

[3] See also, Rom 12: 13; 1 Cor 1: 9; 2 Cor 13: 13; Phil 2: 1. Texts such as these, moreover, have occasioned sharp differences of interpretation between Protestant and Roman Catholic authors.

possibility of this kind of communion lies at the heart of Christian revelation. "Charity is not any kind of love of God," Aquinas insists, "but that love of God by which he is loved as the object of beatitude [*beatitudinis objectum*] on which we are bent by faith and hope."[4] This brief definition captures and underscores the unique character of the love of divine friendship as well as its relationship to the other virtues of the Christian life. Charity is first of all a sharing in the very love of God himself.

While sharing in charity moves beyond the self-interested love of hope, it does not exclude the love of desire. The British theologian Thomas Gilby summarizes this important point of Catholic understanding about Christian love.

> Charity is more than the loving of the good-for-you, and more than loving the good for another; it is a loving shared by you and another of such sort that the terms "egoism" and "altruism" are irrelevant. It is the whole-hearted love of God but no more self-denying at the deepest level than the object in the union of knowledge and love spells diminishment for the subject.[5]

Because it establishes the believer in communion with God himself, theological charity represents a distinctive form of the love of benevolence or of friendship. Accordingly, the formal terminative object of theological charity is the good God who is to be loved above all other persons and things, and the formal mediating object, i.e., that which motivates us to love or that by which we achieve theological love, is nothing other than the identical divine goodness. Moreover, this love of God for his own sake provides the content of the communication that believers share with one another.

What human experience or relationship best illustrates the sharing of charity? The canonical Scriptures speak about the reality of the Church, whose soul is love, in a variety of images. "These have been taken," *Lumen gentium* explains, "from the life of a shepherd, from agriculture, from the construction of buildings, and even from the family and betrothal."[6] By using metaphors such as these, Christian revelation announces a sharing that exists at the most basic levels of human existence. For this reason, the theologian must probe a range of proper analogies that can serve, under the light of divine revelation, to illumine the nature of authentic Christian love. The ultimate significance that charity holds in the Christian life dictates that its analogues should be taken from the realities of nature and ordinary life, not from abstractions.

In *Familiaris consortio*, Pope John Paul II remarks on the foundational character of the human family for all other instances of human society: " 'Since the Creator of all things has established the conjugal partnership as the be-

---

[4]   *Summa theologiae* Ia-IIae q. 65, a. 5, ad 1.

[5]   Thomas Gilby, O.P., introduction to vol. 34 of the Blackfriars translation of the *Summa theologiae*, pp. xvii, xviii.

[6]   *Lumen gentium*, chap. 1, no. 6.

ginning and basis of human society,' the family is 'the first and vital cell of society.' " [7] And because of this immediacy with the order of creation, one theological tradition identifies the family as the best analogy for understanding the fellowship of divine charity. Why? In this kind of friendship one finds: "a fellowship rooted in nature; one of reverence in equality; a proportionate relationship of justice and love; a kind of excellence that arises from people loving each other and for these reasons it is judged to be the best expression of divine charity." [8] Just as the human family constitutes in the order of creation a kind of "community of friendship," so the Church includes all those who are bound together in the friendship of divine love. Christian catechesis even speaks about the family as the "domestic church."

The choice of the human family as a basic analogate for speaking about divine charity illumines the Christian conviction that grace does not destroy nature, but perfects it; or as the Second Vatican Council puts the same truth, that "sanctity is conducive to a more human way of living even in society here on earth." [9] While *Familiaris consortio* concerns more the fundamental mission of the family within the Church rather than the way in which the family naturally images (and prophesies) the *communicatio* of charity, the Holy Father points out the parallels that exist between human development in the family and growth in Christian maturity:

> Christian marriage and the Christian family build up the Church: for in the family the human person is not only brought into being and progressively introduced by means of education into the human community, but by means of the rebirth of baptism and education in the faith the child is also introduced into God's family, which is the Church. [10]

The New Testament records that Jesus himself favors comparing the superabundant love of his Father to the ordinary love that properly belongs within the covenant of the human family. "What father among you will give his son a snake if he asks for a fish, or hand him a scorpion if he asks for an egg? If you, with all your sins, know how to give your children good things, how much more will the heavenly Father give the Holy Spirit to those who ask him" (Lk 11: 11 – 13).

Not every form of communion with the transcendent realizes the communion of beatitude. For example, some hold that an undifferentiated communication of being that does not distinguish between the divine activity whereby God both creates and sustains the whole cosmic order and the personal union of grace with the blessed Trinity adequately accounts for what the New Testament

---

[7] *Familiaris consortio*, 3, no. 42.
[8] Cajetan, *In secundam secundae* q. 24, a. 1, no. 1.
[9] *Lumen gentium* chap. 5, no. 40.
[10] *Familiaris consortio*, 2, no. 15.

calls love. For Aristotle, love of God coincides entirely with contemplation of the First Mover, but he also concludes that no truly personal relationship could develop between mortals and the divine. It is important to note that on account of the Scriptures' clear teaching, Christians unequivocally dissent from this agnostic theism in whatever form it may appear. For as St Paul instructs the Romans, "All who are led by the Spirit of God are sons of God. You did not receive a spirit of slavery leading you back into fear, but a spirit of adoption through which we cry out 'Abba!' – 'Father! . . . But if we are children, we are heirs as well: heirs of God, heirs with Christ, if only we suffer with him . . . so as to be glorified with him" (Rom 8: 14 – 15, 17). In other words, the Christian tradition recognizes that the incarnation definitively changes the terms that establish our relationship with God, so that the only *actual* perfection for humankind lies in beatific communion with the blessed Trinity. [11] Moreover, the Church repeatedly announces the universal call to holiness in these Trinitarian terms: "In the different kinds of life and its different duties, there is one holiness cultivated by all who are led by the Spirit of God; obeying the voice of the Father and worshipping God the Father in spirit and in truth, they follow Christ poor and humble in carrying his cross so that they may deserve to be sharers in his glory." [12]

The Christian *koinonia* establishes the foundation for a rich relationship of mutual love, for *benevolentia*. Within the communion of beatitude, charity embodies a reciprocal benevolence; it is only with a friend, says Aquinas, that a friend is friendly – *amicus est amico amicus*. A theological commentator helps us realize the profound reality that theological charity encompasses:

> According to *divus* Thomas, the final, specifying *ratio* for charity abides in the very divine goodness itself as it is objective beatitude: not, however, insofar as we seek that goodness for ourselves, for that belongs to the love of desire, nor, if we speak in a most precise manner, as we wish that goodness to God, for that is included in the love of simple benevolence; rather, as we wish the good to God as to a friend with whom we are united and who communicates himself to us in beatitude. Thus God is loved in charity not with simple benevolence but with a reciprocal benevolence of friendship in the supernatural order. [13]

Christ instructs us that God is a Trinity of persons: "Do you not believe that I am in the Father and the Father in me?" (Jn 14: 10); and "the Paraclete, the Holy Spirit whom the Father will send in my name, will instruct you in everything" (Jn 14: 26). Accordingly, charity never implies love for an abstract ultimate reality or for a nameless expression of transcendental mystery.

---

[11] It is significant to observe that at this point in the *Summa theologiae* Aquinas does not digress about any purpose or end for the human person other than beatific union with God.

[12] *Lumen gentium*, chap. 5, no. 41.

[13] Cajetan, *In secundam secundae* q. 23, a. 5.

Since its nature includes the notion of relation to another who is Father, Son, and Holy Spirit, Christian charity achieves its perfection at the deepest level of personhood. Gospel truth accordingly excludes any real "friendship" with infra-personal creatures, for in loving a good wine, I am really loving myself drinking the wine. But in a true friendship, an *amicitia honesta*, one loves the friend precisely by wishing him or her the good and in that reciprocal benevolence lies the model for Trinitarian friendship.   •

Even Aristotle contended that some kind of *amicitia honesta* or virtuous friendship can exist among humankind. He held that in the love of benevolence, we esteem the "honest worth" of the friend, instead of the friend's usefulness or pleasurableness. [14] Neither Aristotle nor any philosopher ever dreamt, however, that human friendship could extend to God. Christ of course reveals precisely this, namely, that God himself is numbered among the friends that we can have. Moreover, he instructs us that God wants to be each person's First Friend, to bestow the beatitude that only a share in divine love communicates. Because of this free, divine initiative, divine charity enables a person to love God as God loves himself, *viz*, both on account of God's own self (or his "honest worth") and because of God's goodness. Moreover, since it is founded on the unlimited goodness of God, the communion of saints welcomes each new member as an occasion for increasing its joy and happiness, whereas useful or pleasurable friendships are limited by definition. Fra Angelico visually captures this expression of Christian *communio* in his painting, "Welcome into Paradise," where the multitude of saints from "all different kinds of life" greet each other with charity unfeigned. Since it relies on the supposition that true friendship rests on something finite, as if love might run out if too many people share in it, unholy jealousy signals something short of true friendship, a lack of the love of true benevolence.

When the theologian says that charity loves God as God loves himself, this means that charity is based on the absoluteness of divine goodness. God is perfectly good, meaning first that no created being can cause God to act in any way whatsoever, and second, that since the perfection of the divine nature excludes all potentiality, God needs nothing other than his own goodness in order to enjoy the most perfect measure of perfection. In a beautifully lapidary way, Aquinas expresses this truth about the absolute sovereignty of God's goodness.

> The ultimate end is not the communication of goodness, but rather divine goodness itself. It is from his love of this goodness that God wills it to be communicated. In fact, when he acts because of his goodness, it is not as if he were pursuing something that he does not possess, but as it were willing to commu-

---

[14]   See *Nicomachean Ethics*, Bk 8, chap. 3 (1156a7 – 1156b32).

nicate what he possesses. For he does not act from desire for the end, but from love of the end. [15]

God stands at the origin of all true friendship; he is the one Unbefriended Friend who in Christ befriends all those destined to share in Christ's glory. "For those whom he foreknew," St Paul instructs the Romans, "he also predestined to be conformed to the image of his Son, in order that he might be the firstborn within a large family" (Rom 8: 29). The great gift of holiness that Christ communicates to the members of his Body is motivated only by the goodness that belongs to God alone.

How, then, are creatures related to the goodness of God? In order to answer this question, we should distinguish between loving God in himself and loving God in his creatures. First, we can love God in himself, *in ipso*, simply by letting God be God, by delighting in the fact that he is God. Second, we can love God in his creatures, by wanting them to be rightly ordered to him and to work for his glory. One commentator expresses the reason for this distinction in the following terms:

> There are some goods, however, which more properly are said to belong to God than to be God's, for example, honor, kingship, obedience, and in short, everything which should be ordered to his glory. In charity we not only wish for God that these things be (as with the goods which are *in ipso*) but we are eager that they be and flourish. We do what we are able to do to ensure that these goods grow; we are happy when they thrive and sad when they fail; we fear lest they falter and are courageous against those things which impede them. [16]

This explanation of charity effectively provides a commentary on the Our Father, for when we ask that God's name be hallowed and that his Kingdom come we actually pray for growth in charity. Christ gives to his disciples a new personal consciousness with respect to their filial relationship with God, and as God's children we are impelled to a new sort of love. "The moral task of the Christian," explains von Balthasar, "is to accomplish this personal consciousness in a vigorous way. In this way the Church is open to the world, just as Christ is open to the Father and his all-embracing Kingdom (1 Cor 15: 24)." [17]

In his *Summa contra gentiles*, Aquinas offers some helpful indications of what constitutes this "personal consciousness of one another among the members" of the Church. [18] He emphasizes the following six personal qualities of friendship: First, exchange of personal knowledge, openness: "Now, it is proper to friendship that a man reveals his secrets to his friend: because friendship unites their affections, and of two hearts makes one; and consequently

---

[15] *Quaestiones disputatae de potentia*, q. 3, a. 15, ad 14.

[16] Cajetan, *In secundam secundae*, q. 23, a. 1, n II.

[17] Hans Urs von Balthasar, "Nine Theses," (2) p. 110.

[18] Bk IV, chaps. 21–22.

when a man reveals something to his friend, he would seem not to have taken it out of his own heart." Secondly, effective sharing of goods: "Now it is part of friendship not only that a man share his secrets with his friends, on account of the union of hearts, but the same union requires that he should share his belongings with him; because, since a man regards his friend as his other self, it follows that he will succor him as he would succor himself, by sharing his goods with him." Third, pardon of every offense: "Now, if a man becomes another's friend, by this very fact all offense is removed: since friendship is opposed to offense." Fourth, contemplation: "In the first place mutual inter-course would seem to belong to friendship in a very special manner... Since, then, the Holy Spirit makes us to be lovers of God, it follows that by him we are made contemplators of God." Fifth, interior joy: "It also belongs to friend-ship that a man delight in the presence of his friend, and rejoice in his words and deeds: also that he find in him consolation in all his troubles: hence it is especially to our friends that we have recourse in time of sorrow." Sixth, har-mony of wills: "It also belongs to friendship that a man consent to the things which his friend wills." Taken together, these six characteristics constitute the outlines of charity by which we are joined to God, Father, Son and Holy Spirit and to those who, with us, share in the *communio* – the friends of God.

Hans Urs von Balthasar insists on the Trinitarian significance of Chris-tian *communio* and the divine origins of all authentic love in the world; "love for one another," he writes, "which is the object of the new command that Jesus gave us to fulfill, is poured out into the hearts of the faithful (Rom 5: 5) antecedently in a more profound way through the outpouring of the Holy Spirit of the Father and of the Son as the divine 'We.'" And again we return to the central significance of the incarnation, for it is through Christ that we are drawn into this endless and perichoretic interplay of Trinitarian love: "For Christ, the Son of God, who with the Father and the Spirit 'alone is holy,' loved the Church as his bride and delivered himself up for it that he might sanctify it (see Eph 5: 25 – 26), and he joined it to himself as his Body and bestowed on it the gift of the Holy Spirit to the glory of God." [19] And within the Church, authentic eucharistic union with Christ realizes in each one of the members of his Body the qualities of life that represent the perfection of charity.

2. THE DISTINCTIVENESS OF CHRISTIAN VIRTUE

For Christian moral theology, the relationship of the theological virtues to the intellectual and moral virtues raises a significant question. For just as the Church develops out of the human family, the *habitus* of grace strengthens and enriches the *habitus* that actualize human nature. Because it takes seriously the

---

[19] *Lumen gentium*, chap. 5, no. 39.

affirmation that, even here on earth, the fullness of the Christian life conduces to a more human way of living, the Thomist tradition provides the grounds for extensive reflection on the relationship between the acquired and the infused moral virtues. Aquinas and his commentatorial tradition principally investigate two central questions about Christian virtue and human excellence. The first concerns the universality of charity: Is charity so much at the heart of the other virtues that without divine grace human virtue cannot even exist? And the second probes the mode of charity's influence: How does charity exercise its influence on the moral virtues, and even on the other theological virtues? In the technical language of theology, the second question inquires whether charity is the "form" of the other virtues?

In order to achieve excellence in the moral life, does a person require the infused virtue of charity? Why would charity add to the perfection of the moral virtues? In order to answer these questions, we need to adopt a position on the relationship between grace and nature. Historically, theological discussion about nature and grace vacillates between the Scylla of outright humanism and the Charybdis of positive reprobation. The first extreme, Pelagian humanism, identifies Christian life with the best that nature can achieve, and the second, ultra-Augustinianism, argues that the person living outside of grace and charity immediately falls into sinful disorder on every front. Against the first school of thought, the Church defines that nothing effectively meritorious for our eternal salvation either begins or comes to completion without the special help from God that we call divine grace. Against the second view, the Church repudiates the theses associated with the milieu of Michel Baius, namely, that every act of an unbeliever amounts to something sinful, and that human nature possesses no capacity whatsoever for realizing its inbuilt capacities and ends. Indeed the Church even recognizes that a person without charity can profess the Creed without hypocrisy. [20]

Within the dependable traditions of scholastic theology, two tendencies emerge with respect to evaluating the good that an individual human person can accomplish without the help of divine grace. First, there is the optimistic position represented in the work of the Jesuit commentator Francisco Suarez. This position holds that the wounds of original sin amount to only a mere privation of original justice, so that after the fall, Adam exists in what Suarezians refer to as a state of "integral nature." In many instances, the criticisms spawned by the mid-20th century European theological movement known as *la nou-*

---

[20] See Aquinas's illuminating remark on unformed or dead faith in *Summa theologiae* IIa-IIae q. 1, a. 9, ad 3: "The profession of faith contained in the Creed, which is for all believers, is delivered, in the person of the Church, and this is a loving and living faith, such as is found in all persons who worthily belong to the Church; ... those of the faithful who lack this loving belief should try to attain it."

velle théologie aim at this view of the "natural man," which formed the basis for standard instruction in many schools during the neo-scholastic era. Secondly, there is the fundamentally misanthropic position, represented by certain Augustinians, that the wounds of original sin effectively constitute a corruption of the good of nature, *viz*, a positive disordering of our capacities, so that any human good outside of grace would be accomplished, if at all, only with the greatest difficulty. Adherents of this school eschew natural virtue as the practical equivalent of "apparent virtue," and hold a dim view of anything that transpires outside of a clearly perceptible association with the sources of divine grace.

Neither of these exaggerated viewpoints adequately represent a proper theological perspective on the necessity of grace for authentic human conduct. First of all, the concept of a "pure [human] nature" is a chimera. It is flatly erroneous to suppose that, once Adam by sinning lost the endowments of grace for all humankind, there remained a purely natural "man," by which is understood human beings ready to pursue happily the ends for which their natural capacities endowed them. The Bible, to be sure, offers no grounds for such imagining. In addition, a correct philosophical conception of nature argues against the view. For by definition any nature implies activity; *natura* comes from *nativitas*, and implies being born to act in a certain way. Thus in the human being a "pure nature," *viz*, one that would entirely act on its own, could not long remain in either a pure or integral state. For once individual human persons began to engage the moral challenges that arise in a real world, they would encounter obstacles for which, relying only on natural resources, they possessed no effective moral resources. The privation of original justice means, in fact, that human nature is left bereft of what it requires to keep from becoming unglued in the world of actual moral decision and choice. And the more complex the moral situation, the more difficult it becomes for unaided nature to maintain its virtuousness. But this does not mean that without grace the human person can do nothing well; projects indispensable for human life such as – and these are Aquinas's own examples – planting vineyards and building shelters are surely possible. Aquinas, it should be noticed, singles out the elementary activities of *homo faber* to illustrate some of the things that a person can accomplish without the help of divine grace. We are not, however, invited to suppose that there exists a natural clone of the one vocation in which we are "all called to the fulfillment of the Christian life and the perfection of charity," so that outside of Christian culture a human person can actually achieve full moral excellence and happiness. [21]

---

[21] *Lumen gentium*, chap. 5, no. 40.

In fact when Aquinas asks whether without charity there can exist any true virtue, his response is quite nuanced. Recall that virtue represents a *dispositio perfecti ad optimum*, that is, an ordering of what is perfect to its maximum realization. In this, virtue differs from a mere disposition, for as true operative *habitus*, the virtues ready a man or woman for sustained morally virtuous conduct. The moral virtues differ in fact from the intellectual virtues in as much as the latter possess no ability to shape an overall good moral character, though they do make a person smart and, perhaps, even wise. Moral virtue shapes human character. Thus the standard definition insists that moral virtue makes both the doer and his or her actions good – "bonum facit habentem et opus eius bonum reddit." How much of this moral goodness can one achieve without charity?

The Christian tradition generally agrees that without divine charity a person cannot develop a complete life of authentic virtue. But Aquinas introduces an important distinction for the moral theologian. "Charity," he says, "comes into the definition of all the virtues, not because it is essentially identical with them, but because somehow they all depend on charity." [22] How do the moral virtues depend on charity, and still retain their individual character as true human virtues? As a model for theological explanation, Aquinas suggests the way that the intellectual virtue of prudence regulates and integrates the behavioral virtues in human life. [23] In any event, the human virtues still retain their identity and moral value in the person who enjoys the favor of divine love, such that theologians must distinguish between human virtue in itself and human virtue as it depends on theological charity. [24]

---

[22]   *Summa theologiae* IIa-IIae q. 23, a. 4, ad 1.

[23]   "There is a parallel here," Aquinas says, "with prudence which, as Aristotle points out, forms part of the definition of the moral virtues because they depend on it" (*Summa theologiae* IIa-IIae q. 23, a. 4, ad 1). In Aquinas's account of the moral life, any vicious *habitus* can threaten the equilibrium of prudence. P. T. Geach, *The Virtues* (Cambridge, 1977), p. xxxi, summarizes the classic argument for the dependence of the moral virtues on prudence as follows: "Corrupt *habitus* of action in any area destroy the *habitus* of prudence; but without prudence as a regulator no behavioral *habitus* is genuinely virtuous; so the loss or lack of any one behavioral virtue is fatal both to prudence and to all other behavioral virtues."

[24]   In an attempt to address the question, the 16th-century Italian theologian Cajetan distinguishes between the "essence of virtue," by which he means that a person possesses the form of the *habitus*, and the "state of virtue," that is, when a person actually puts the form into action. On the basis of this distinction, he suggests that without charity it would be possible for someone to possess an unconnected string of virtuous "essences," but not actually to live out the "state of virtue." Thus according to Cajetan, a person without charity could enjoy the radical "essence" of a virtue, but not incorporate this form into a complete life of virtuous conduct. What is more important, even this residual "essence of virtue" would in the course of time and under the pressures of everyday life break down into dishevelled bits of human behavior. Because the "essence of virtue" succumbs so easily to the existential temptations of life in the world, another commentator, John of St Thomas, gives no quarter

Because the one who believes in Christ enjoys the aid of divine grace in the actual living out of human life, we can make some helpful distinctions about charity as the form of the moral virtues. For example, without charity a person can act in accord with the simple natural dispositions of nature. (For example, Roger Milquetoast finds practicing chastity easy because he finds greeting any-one difficult.) But in the present economy of salvation, only charity can uphold the whole ensemble of authentic virtues, so that the human person achieves the freedom that the New Testament promises to those who remain united with Christ. Because Aristotle knew only about the power of human intelligence, he opined that prudence was required to maintain an ordered and integral life. The Gospel supplies another kind of wisdom, and this makes itself felt in the power of the Holy Spirit that is poured into the souls of the just. Von Balthasar insists that only the beneficiary of Christian revelation is invited to share in a type of freedom that comes from the supremely free God. [25] Human prudence alone may keep the wise person from committing major anomalies in a dis-ordered life, but only theological charity sustains a uniformly happy life and leaves the believer free to attain the highest Good.

Of course, one does not include among authentic virtues those counterfeit virtues that characterize the vicious, for example, the tenacity of the miser, the meekness of the drunkard, or the boldness of the rapist. But one can in-quire concerning such apparent moral oxymorons as the industriousness of the promiscuous businessman or the generosity that a criminal shows towards his family. Ought the Christian to regard such traits as authentic virtues? In other words, because of his after-working-hours vice, is it also vicious for the busi-nessman to apply himself dutifully to his professional work? Or does the per-son who lives at odds with the civil authorities do wrong when he legitimately provides for his family with abundance? Since these would-be "virtues" do not render either the businessman or the mafioso altogether good, it would seem not. Yet there is a sense in which persons such as these exhibit authentically virtuous actions, even though their lives taken as a whole obviously exclude naming these authentically good dispositions true and outright virtues. For just as without prudence the human virtues lose their proper direction and integrity, so when vice forms a significant part of a person's life, he or she remains frag-ile in the pursuit of perfection. Common experience shows this to be true. The lustful businessman can easily find himself turning away from honest business practices in order to finance his sexual liaisons, or the gang member may sub-

---

to the humanist position that human nature can take care of itself, and instead holds a dim-mer view of what human nature can achieve without charity. For John of St Thomas, even to achieve the essence of virtue requires that a person possess the ensemble of the virtues, and thus charity.

[25] "Nine Theses" (8), p. 119.

stitute lavish spending on his family for the more personal expressions of filial love that are proper to parenting.

There is still more that needs to be said concerning the role of charity in the moral life. Because the industriousness of the profligate businessman and the generosity of the racketeering citizen do not exist in a "state of virtue," that is, do not belong to the order of virtue that only charity can establish, these isolated virtues do not make the one who possesses them fully good and entirely happy. Even if one allows that some individual persons might develop all the natural moral virtues, these human beings would still fall short of achieving the destiny for which we are made. To put it differently, such "naturally" good persons would still miss the supreme goodness of God for which each human person enjoys the passive capacity; indeed, only the love that God bestows in theological charity can unite human beings with their ultimate true goal. Aquinas contends further that this rule holds true even if one grants the hypothesis that a person, e.g., the politician *qua* politician or a whole society could make building the City of Man an ultimate goal and even achieve a well-ordered human community. Von Balthasar reaches a similar conclusion. In the prebiblical natural order, he writes, "the goals of human activity remain partly political (within a micropolis or a macropolis), partly individualistic, and partly intellectualistic, since pure knowledge of the constant laws of the universe appears to be the most noble thing man can strive for." [26] Yet such nobility falls short of the ultimate good. For Christian believers "are citizens with the saints and also members of the household of God, built upon the foundation of the apostles and prophets, with Christ Jesus himself as the cornerstone" (Eph 2: 19,20). In sum, only Christ brings the stability of divine goodness into the fragility of human lives and makes the human person a participator in the divine life.

If by a truly virtuous life we mean to refer to a comprehensive account of the good and perfect life for men and women, then only charity can make this possible for each person. Only the theological virtue of charity ensures that everything that a person does reaches the optimum expression of our human capacities. This view does not require that one implement sharp and rigid distinctions between grace and nature; rather it recognizes what every Christian must accept, namely, that the justification of the sinner results only from God's gracious benevolence. The gift of grace alone perfects the human person so that he or she can reasonably expect to follow Jesus's command: "You, therefore, must be perfect, as your heavenly Father is perfect" (Mt 5: 48). Since human nature diversely relates to the immanent and transcendent ends that constitute its perfection, there is no "layering" of grace onto nature. "Personal and so-

---

[26]   Ibid.

cial fulfillment are harmonized only in the Resurrection of Christ," says von Balthasar, "who is the guarantee not only for the fulfillment of the individual but also for the Church community and through her for the whole world so that God, *without eliminating the reality of the world*, can be 'all in all.' "[27]

3. CHARITY, THE FORM OF THE INFUSED MORAL VIRTUES

It remains to discuss how charity affects the development of the human virtues. According to the classical theological tradition, charity constitutes the form of the virtues, for it exercises an influence on the other virtues principally in the line of efficient causality. In other words, charity explains why the other theological virtues of faith and hope and the cardinal moral virtues operate fully in the Christian life. Historically, some theologians have opted to describe the relationship of charity to the other virtues principally in terms of formal exemplary causality, but this only results in making every virtue look as if it were a species of charity. So while the proposal possesses its own sort of appeal, especially in light of the New Testament insistence on the primacy of love in the Christian life, it actually hampers the development of an adequate theological ethics. In other terms, the moral theologian needs to describe the Christian moral life by taking full account of the various life situations that require a specific virtuous response. At the same time, it is clear that final causality remains an important consideration for determining how charity relates to the other virtues. If charity addresses Christian morals at the most personal level, then this virtue must influence the world of personal intentions and meanings that shape a moral action in an ultimate sort of way.

Every moral action receives a relatively complete determination from its moral object – what moral theologians call its *finis operis*. But a moral meaning embodied in a particular action suitably defined also receives a second moral determination from the interior act of the will with which it is imperated or commanded. For example, to speak an untruth with the purpose of causing mental anguish to the person whom one deceives makes the action not only a violation of justice, but also of kindness. Again, for one to fast with the added purpose of praising God makes his or her action not only an act of temperance but also an act of the virtue of religion (*latria*). As an efficient cause that makes the virtues operate in a way that conforms entirely to the teaching and promises of the Gospel, charity transforms a virtuous deed from within. In this way, as Origen says, Christ becomes the very substance of the virtues.

---

[27] "Nine Theses" (9), p. 120.

Since it can imperate every human action towards the ultimate good of beatitude, charity effects this purposing in every one of the virtues. Just as any sin can take on an added negativity when it is done out of hateful malice for either God or man, so anything done for the love of God achieves a different dimension than otherwise would be the case. The Salmanticenses, a group of Discalced Carmelite theologians who taught at Salamanca roughly between 1600 – 1725, set forth the following account of the relationship or *ordo* of charity to the other virtues.

> Although this ordering (*ordo*) [of charity] lies beyond the species of a given virtuous act, which it receives from its object and proximate end, nonetheless it would be wrong to consider it as something sheerly accidental to virtue. Rather charity remains something that belongs to the heart of virtue (*per se*) and for which, moreover, the virtues themselves long.[28]

Christian life, in short, is the only real form of human life. The Carmelite theologians explain the place of infused virtue in theological ethics in such a way as to make it normative for human life. But note that even though Christian virtue makes one simply a lover of God, the virtue of charity itself remains formally distinct from the other moral and theological virtues, even if without charity there is no virtuous life in the full and unqualified sense of the term. So even if one granted the hypothesis that the human person could acquire the ensemble of human virtues on his or her own efforts, no person can unaidedly realize the *dispositio perfecti ad optimum*, the best that human nature can achieve in grace, for that is to be found only in beatific union with God. Cajetan supplies the following explanation of how charity forms the other virtues.

> Thus it is that the virtues possess this order to a "form-ed" action; the informing (*formatio*) is from charity as it alone orders the act of every virtue towards the ultimate end in an unqualified fashion. For this reason, charity is said to be the form of the virtues, namely, that it constitutes them in the full, existential possession in what true virtuousness consists (*tanquam constituens eas in esse virtutis simpliciter*).[29]

For the Christian believer, the life that the New Testament describes and enjoins upon us does not constitute one alternative among many for achieving a happy life. Nor does it amount to an illusory palliative for weak people, as Nietzsche suggests is the final result of Christian life and worship. The Christian life, animated by theological charity, provides the only way for the human

---

[28]   See Salmanticenses, *Cursus theologicus*, IIa-IIae, q. 23, a. 8, n 45.

[29]   *In secundam secundae* q. 23, a. 6, ad 2. See also ad 1 for Aquinas's account of why it is better to love things that are superior, e.g., man's love for the angels, even though in knowing things, the intentional reality of the known corresponds in dignity to the being of the knower. Thus, whatever is received is received after the manner of the recipient (see *Summa theologiae* Ia q. 84, a. 1).

person to reach the full perfection of human existence and to avoid the disin-tegrating effects of original sin. [30]

4. PERSONS IN THE *Communio*

We have seen that theological charity loves God above all things and on ac-count of his lovableness, but the Christian life involves others besides self and God. The New Testament makes it abundantly clear that Christian love by its very nature reaches out and embraces the whole order of creation: "And this commandment we have from him, that he who loves God should love his brother also" (1 Jn 4: 21). In *Summa theologiae* IIa-IIae q. 25, aa. 1 – 12, Aquinas undertakes a detailed discussion of what he calls the objects of char-ity. In this discussion which still merits close study, Aquinas distinguishes the classes of people who comprise the Church, so as to order them within the unity of the one bond of love. In other words, Aquinas identifies the classes of persons that concretely form the *communicatio* of charity. Indeed, the Gospel itself requires such an inquiry, for in imitation of her Lord, the Church as a whole must respond to the question, "And who is my neighbor?" (Lk 10: 29).

The New Testament unequivocally speaks about the primacy of charity in the life of the believer. This means that any person can authentically love only on account of his or her share in that unique *communicatio* which God estab-lishes within the human family through the incarnation of his only Son. But so that theological charity does not become indistinguishably conflated with other forms of human affectivity nor the Church mistaken for whatsoever hu-man community, the moral theologian must examine carefully what makes for divine charity. For this reason, Aquinas's method requires that we establish the membership of the *communicatio* strictly in terms of the *ratio formalis ob-*

---

[30] The 20th-century French theologian Henri de Lubac, in his *Brief Catechesis on Nature & Grace*, accuses the standard theology of the neo-scholastic period of reading Cajetan's language concerning the essence of virtue as if a natural human life could be sufficient for some persons. Thus de Lubac and those who followed him react strongly against any suggestion of layering the supernatural onto the natural. But *gratia perficit naturam* does not imply that human nature in itself forms a de-supernaturalized clone of the Christian saint. If we take Aquinas's moral theology in context, to be fully moral means to be on the way to God, on the way to beatific fellowship with God. A supernatural human act is an oxymoron, but a human action ordered by theological charity to the end of beatific fellowship is quite different. These charitable sorts of virtuous actions lead us to heaven, and at the same time they build up the unity of the Church on earth. There is a continuity between the process that grace begins here below and the love that, as St Paul tells us, abides forever: "And now faith, hope, and love abide, these three; and the greatest of these is love" (1 Cor 13: 13). For Cajetan, only this sort of life produces the "esse virtutis simpliciter," the outright being of virtue lived in the context of a full and happy life.

jecti of charity. In one of his sermons, St Leo the Great expresses the defining element of charity in this way:

> For the man who loves God it is sufficient to please the one he loves; and there is no greater recompense to be sought than the loving itself; for love is from God by the very fact that God himself is love. [31]

Only the good God then is the First Friend for every member in the *communicatio* of charity; and his unlimited goodness subsequently forms the radical ground for every manifestation of authentic friendship. First of all, charity embodies a befriended friendship. And since it represents the human person's limited participation in divine love, the virtue of charity always remains a created endowment.

At the same time, the gospels make it clear that even though God alone is the sole explanation for charity, other persons, whom the New Testament refers to as "neighbor," can enter into the *communicatio*. The new commandment explicitly speaks about these relationships when it enjoins that "you shall love the Lord your God with all your heart, and with all your soul, and with all your strength, and with all your mind; and your neighbor as yourself" (Lk 10: 27). And in his last discourse, Jesus himself says: "I give you a new commandment, that you love one another. Just as I have loved you, you also should love one another" (Jn 13: 34). Who are the neighbors that this fundamental gospel injunction requires that we love as ourselves; or to put it differently, which persons are included in the *communicatio* of theological charity?

While divine beatitude in itself imparts to charity its formal unity, the love of divine charity moves beyond the three persons of the blessed Trinity. In other words, the true love of charity does not stop with God; it embraces creatures as well. Historically, people have held diverse views on this subject. Some thinkers argue that nothing divine really infiltrates the created order, while others have upheld the opposite view, namely, that "divine" represents nothing more than the epitome of human consciousness. However, it is a distinctive feature of catholic doctrine to take analogy seriously. Even though there exists but one *ratio diligendi* for theological charity, i.e., God as the highest good, we know in Christian faith that this theological charity opens out to include all those whom God himself has predestined for glory.

The Christian believer loves everything simply because of God, not *as* God nor *as* much as God, but on account of the divine goodness. This means that divine charity must adapt itself to the specific situation of what in technical language we identify as its secondary material objects. But how does one's friendship with God become a love for all creation? The theological *habitus* of charity instrumentally accomplishes this effusion of divine love in the world

---

[31] *Sermon 92*, chap. 1 (*PL* 54: 454).

by shaping the affective movements of the charitable person to the way and degree that the "material object" participates in the *communicatio beatitudinis*. In other words, the virtue of charity makes it possible for us to love others according to the measure that God has made them loveable. Aquinas puts it this way:

> Charity loves God because of himself, and because of him loves all others in so far as they are subordinated to him. Hence, in a certain way we love God in all our neighbors, for to love another in charity is to love him because he is in God or so that God may be in him. But if we were to love our neighbor just for his own sake, and not for God's, this would belong to another kind of love, either based on natural ties, or on citizenship or on any of those loves which Aristotle touches on in *Ethics* viii, 3.[32]

Thus, the uniqueness of Christian charity lies in that it seeks above all to bring about the moment when, to repeat von Balthasar's phrase, "God, without eliminating the reality of the world, can be 'all in all.' "

Charity embraces in its affective movement both persons and things; however, only persons are loved as friends; things are loved in reference to persons, as goods wished to the friend. The embrace of charity directly involves all those who are called to share in the *communicatio* of beatitude. Aquinas supplies three reasons for why what derives from theological charity is confined to the human and angelic community. First, since one cannot will the good to a brute animal, the sub-human cannot encompass the *ratio boni*. Secondly, authentic fellowship requires intelligence or the spiritual dimension of life, but there is no context for such exchange among animals. Thirdly, one cannot identify in infra-rational creation the required proportion that must exist between the members in a *communicatio* that entails reciprocal benevolence.

Since persons constitute the only true terms of the love of benevolence, they alone are the true "objects" of charity. Three categories are to be considered: God, ourselves, and the neighbor. The proper and formal object of course is God, the Principal Friend to whom everything is referred; God alone remains the reason why we love ourselves and our neighbor. Next, each believer constitutes an object of charity for him or herself. Then, charity goes out to the neighbor, both angels and men, who either participate in or are called to participate in the fellowship of God's love (*communicatio beatitudinis*).

There are two distinct ways in which charity relates us to others: First, as a *friend* of God and, therefore, as our friend in sharing God's love, or alternatively, as an *object*, i.e., as God's *thing*, referred to God unto his honor and glory. In the final instance, the neighbor is not loved precisely as a person to whom one wishes the goodness of God, but as a "thing" that one wishes unto

---

[32] *Quaestio disputatae de caritate*, trans. John P. Reid, O.P. (Providence, 1960), a. 4.

God, for his honor and glory.[33] This last category includes the sinner who *de facto* is not a friend of God. Hell represents the state of a person permanently excluded from incorporation into divine friendship, reduced as it were to a "thing" whose punishment also reflects the divine attributes. Of course, before the final judgment we cannot say for certain that any particular human person exists in hell, so until the moment of judgment even the hardened sinner is to be loved so that he or she might again become God's friend.

Christian charity embodies an eminently personal reality, one, moreover, that exists according to diverse measures in each individual. Furthermore, because everyone is not equal by reason of his or her actual participation in beatitude, we need suitable distinctions when determining the following questions. First, how are we to love ourselves in charity? Next, how are we to love our neighbor? And among the neighbors to be loved, we must consider how believers move out in love toward sinners, their enemies, and even the spiritual creatures.

First, the gospel requires us to love ourselves properly. "Just as unity is presupposed to union," says Aquinas, "so our love for ourselves is the model and root of friendship; for our friendship for others consists precisely in the fact that our attitude to them is the same as to ourselves."[34] Aristotle remarks that "friendly feelings towards others flow from a person's own feelings towards himself or herself."[35] We should recall that charity surpasses mere egoism; authentic self-love never apes self-centered and egoistic love. When we love ourselves in charity, we love ourselves as befriended by God, for charity numbers us among his true friends. Aquinas identifies the ability to love oneself as the "root" (*radix*) and "model" (*forma*) of all charity. In an especially touching section of her autobiography, St Thérèse of Lisieux casts a different light on this important element of Christian teaching.

> This year, dear Mother, God has given me the grace to understand what charity is; I understood it before, it is true, but in an imperfect way. I had never fathomed the meaning of these words of Jesus: "The second commandment is LIKE the first: You shall love your neighbor as yourself" (Mt 22:39)… But when Jesus gave his Apostles a new commandment, his own commandment, as he calls it later on, it is no longer a question of loving one's neighbor as oneself but of loving him as He, Jesus, has loved him, and will love him to the consummation of the ages.
>
> Ah! Lord, I know you don't command the impossible. You know better than I do my weakness and imperfection; You know very well that never would I be able to love my Sisters as you love them, unless you, my Jesus, loved them in me. It

---

[33] Cajetan develops these points in his commentary on *Summa theologiae* IIa-IIae q. 25, a. 1.

[34] *Summa theologiae* IIa-IIae q. 25, a. 4.

[35] *Nicomachean Ethics*, Bk 9, chap. 4 (1166a1); also see, chap. 8 (1168b5).

is because you wanted to give me this new commandment since it gives me the assurance that your will is to love in me all those you command me to love!

Yes, I feel it, when I am charitable, it is Jesus alone who is acting in me, and the more united I am to him, the more also do I love my Sisters. [36]

This testimony helps us to see the proper ordering of God's love, namely, that first we know in faith that God loves us because he is good, not because we are; next that we love ourselves in hope and charity as people here and now being loved by God; and finally from this bond of charity, we can move to an authentic love of self that forms the basis for the expansion of the *communicatio*.

Proper love of self also directs us to love our bodies as belonging to the whole person; there is no room for a disguised Manichaeism in Aquinas's moral theology. At his death, St Francis of Assisi, recognizing that he had imposed difficult hardships on his mortal frame, asked forgiveness from his body, his "Brother Ass." Proper love of our bodies does not exclude penitential practices from the Christian life, which always includes a place for asceticism. Indeed, charity impels us toward asceticism; it makes us long to move away from the taint of sin and from the corruption of punishment that it brings.

As the gospel command reminds us, we are required not only to love God and self but also our neighbor. When applied to those who are one with us in the *communicatio*, this command remains relatively simple. But how can sinners, who by definition are those who have exchanged the good of beatitude for the apparent goods of finite capacity, fit into this conception of charity? For by definition, the sinner is not God's friend. Aquinas here introduces a helpful distinction: while it is true that sinners are not actual sharers in the *communicatio beatitudinis*, they still remain until death potential sharers in it. Charity urges us, then, to promote their return to God's goodness. This means that we should love them in such a way as to ensure that they come to participate fully in the mystery of Christ's love. Christ's own example and his teaching, especially in the parables of the lost sheep and the prodigal son, amply emphasize this central Christian concern. Moreover, Christ's death on the cross, as St Augustine explains, introduces a judgment of mercy into the world. In his commentary on the Gospel of John, the Doctor of Hippo writes:

If you pay attention, even the cross itself was a judgment seat; for when the judge was seated in the middle, the one thief who believed was freed (Lk 23: 43), the other who taunted was condemned. Now what would happen to the living and the dead was signified; some will be placed on the right, others on the left; the one thief is like those who will be on the left, the other like those who will be on the right. [37]

---

[36] *The Story of a Soul*, trans. John Clarke, O.C.D. (Washington, DC, 1976), pp. 220, 221.

[37] St Augustine, *Tractatus super Joannem* 31, c. 7 (*Pl* 35: 1642).

Of course, the love of charity makes the Christian believer insatiably thirst that every sinner would come to appreciate the divine favor, and, like the good thief, would turn to Jesus on the cross, saying, "Jesus, remember me when you come into your kingdom" (Lk 23: 42).

An incident in the life of St Dominic, his encounter with the Albigensian innkeeper, exemplifies the right approach to sinners. The story goes like this: By his willingness to eat and drink with a certain Provençal who had lapsed into heresy, St Dominic first shows his love for the innkeeper; then afterwards the saint stays up late into the night with the misled innkeeper to explain the truth of the gospel. Moreover, since sectarians frequently are involved in other sorts of immorality, we can suppose that the saint likewise rescued the innkeeper from errors about the moral life.

All sin entails activity that lacks the right ordering to the good ends of human prosperity and the ultimate end of divine beatitude. Therefore, St Augustine defines sin as "every word, action, or desire that goes contrary to the eternal law." [38] This means that, by sinning, the sinner actually turns away from embracing in an ordered way the goods that God's creative wisdom has constituted for the human person's own happiness. Theological guilt or the liability to punishment that abides in the very disordered act itself subsequently may generate a species of psychological guilt. But the full and corruptive reality of guilt involves alienation from what is truly good. Such alienation, moreover, is not overcome simply by learning to feel right or comfortable with behavior that by its nature (ex objecto) falls short of both embodying the good of human flourishing and reaching the measure of divine love. Because of the human penchant for self-deception, charity obliges the believer sometimes to rouse the sinner from his or her false complacency.

Sin wrecks tremendous havoc in a person's life. Indeed, because they are excluded from the communicatio of beatitude, sinners cannot love themselves. [39] Only the Christian gospel preaches the kind of dignity that is fulfill-

---

[38]   St Augustine, Contra Faustum Manichae Bk 22, chap. 27; see "Reply to Faustus the Manichean," trans. R. Stothert in Nicene and Post-Nicene Fathers, vol. IV (Buffalo, 1887), pp. 155–345.

[39]   But this truth is meant not only for confirmed sinners, and Cajetan in fact uses this text as the basis for a Dominican examination of conscience. "Guard in your heart the conclusions of this article [q. 25, a. 7]: first, that evil is a sort of thing that makes it impossible for sinners to love themselves; and secondly that there are five signs of authentic self-love that can be found only in good persons, namely, to want to live a spiritual life in accord with recta ratio; to want to develop within this life the good of virtue; to want to act so as to realize this; to be free of anxiety; and finally, to want to get along peacefully with others. Examine your conscience on these points if you want to know whether you are good or not, whether you truly love yourself, whether you truly are a friend to yourself. And do this frequently, at least once a day."

ing for human beings; those who place their confidence in some other god can discover no adequate and complete grounds on which to build an authentic self-love. "The work of the devil," writes von Balthasar, "shows itself above all in a proud gnosis without love, which pretends to be coextensive with the agape that is submissive to God, but actually 'puffs up' (1 Cor 8: 1)."[40] On the other hand, conversion and the experience of divine love through forgiveness beget true peace of mind.

The Christian must also love the neighbor who happens to be an enemy; an analysis of this issue requires another set of distinctions. For "enemy" can refer to personal enemies, or to the enemies of the communities to which we belong: the family, the fatherland, even the Church. The following conclusions illustrate some main points about loving an enemy: First, to love an enemy as such, i.e., *sub ratione inimici*, would be the same thing as to love a sinner as a sinner. Theological charity will not allow us to engage in moral persiflage of this kind. Still, we can recognize that there is a distinction to be made between a sinner and an enemy; the sinner remains someone who fails to keep God's law, but a person can become an enemy through no personal fault. One example is the soldier enlisted in the service of an enemy army. In this case, the *communicatio* of charity first requires that the offense be removed – in the example of the soldier, whatever precipitated the hostilities – by the guilty party. This occurs through making restitution or satisfaction, so that the grounds for loving are re-established. At the same time, the teaching of the gospel enjoins us to love the individual enemy, even with a predilection that exhibits the perfection of charity (see Mt 5: 43 – 48). Philosophical ethics may discover utilitarian reasons for overlooking past offenses, but only Christ makes it possible to love the enemy in a way that transcends self-referential love.

Sometimes the enemy is not at all ferocious, as this incident in the life of St Thérèse of Lisieux points out. Her personal experience lived in faith illustrates the profound significance and importance of the Gospel teaching about loving other persons.

> There is in the Community a Sister who has the faculty of displeasing me in everything, in her ways, her words, her character, everything seems *very disagreeable* to me. And still, she is a holy religious who must be very pleasing to God. Not wishing to give into the natural antipathy I was experiencing, I told myself that charity must not consist in feelings but in works; then I set myself to doing for this Sister what I would do for the person I loved the most. Each time I met her I prayed to God for her, offering Him all her virtues and merits. I felt this was pleasing to Jesus, for there is no artist who doesn't love to receive praise for his works, and Jesus, the Artist of souls, is happy when we don't stop at the exterior, but, penetrating into the inner sanctuary where he chooses to dwell, we

---

[40] "Nine Theses" (4), p. 112.

admire its beauty. I wasn't content simply with praying very much for this Sister who gave me so many struggles, but I took care to render her all the service possible, and when I was tempted to answer her back in a disagreeable manner, I was content with giving her my most friendly smile, and with changing the subject of the conversation, for the *Imitation* says: "It is better to leave each one in his own position than to enter into arguments."

Frequently, when I was not at recreation (I mean during the work periods) and had occasion to work with this Sister, I used to run away like a deserter whenever my struggles became too violent. As she was absolutely unaware of my feelings for her, never did she suspect the motives for my conduct and she remained convinced that her character was very pleasing to me. One day at recreation she asked in almost these words: "Would you tell me, Sister Thérèse of the Child Jesus, what attracts you so much to me; every time you look at me, I see you smile?" Ah! what attracted me was Jesus hidden in the depths of her soul; Jesus who makes sweet what is most bitter. I answered that I was smiling because I was happy to see her (it is understood that I did not add that this was from a spiritual standpoint). [41]

Christian maturity requires that we develop the proper kind of relationships, but only theological charity ensures that the full measure of Christ's love controls our perspectives. Christian teaching on love for the enemy and for the disagreeable comes from St Paul's strong insistence that the believer always seek first to overcome evil with good (Rom 12: 21).

The love that one renders to an enemy does not, by the very fact that she or he is an enemy, make the love a better one to pursue. In fact, all things being equal, to love a friend is both better and more meritorious. Cajetan makes clear this important point in the following text:

> The principal reason is because the object of such a love is both better [objectively] and more closely joined to us [appreciatively]. Hence it is the case that being nearer to God, the friend is better; being nearer to the one loving, a friend is closer. Therefore the love of a friend conforms best to the measure of caritative love. [42]

This viewpoint strikes a strange note for those who hold that the more difficult is always the more meritorious, as happens in some schools of spiritual theology that recommend that one even look out for ways to *agere contra*, to go against the bent of our natural inclinations.

Charity breaks down all barriers, of nationality, of race, of class, of culture, but it also transcends the more profound, ontological barrier between the orders of creation. The communion of the Church reaches beyond the limits of the visible world. We know that creation includes other personal beings in addition to those whom we encounter in the visible world. And since the perfection of

---

[41] *The Story of a Soul*, pp. 222, 223.

[42] Cajetan, *In secundam secundae* q. 27, a. 7.

charity achieves the ultimate realization of personal communion, the Christian reaches out to the angelic persons who also, we are told, inhabit the new and celestial Jerusalem. On the other hand, those who are definitively excluded from the company of the saints, the damned and the demons, cannot be loved as God's friends. Those in charity, however, may continue to regard them as God's "things" that are given over to God's honor which, in the case of the demons, at least, already manifests the divine justice.

Aquinas's commentary on the objects of charity reflects the classical teaching of the Western theological tradition, namely, that God, the self, the neighbor, and the person's body figure into the *communicatio beatitudinis*. In the *De doctrina christiana*, St Augustine wrote: "There are four kinds of things a man must love, one is above him, namely God; another is himself; the third is close by him, namely his neighbor; and the fourth is beneath him, namely his own body." [43] Like the other theological virtues, charity remains formally one virtue. It possesses only one formal object, the good God in himself. However, this perfection can attract other ends without losing anything of the divine simplicity.

As we have seen, this does not mean that God is simply one among these objects; he is always the First Friend, the eminent and principal Object of charity. From all eternity, God exists as the basic and original *communicatio beatitudinis*. For God abides as a Trinity of divine persons who know and love each other in that perichoretic relationship that marks the mutual "being-in" of one person in the other as well as their mutual relationships. Because of the Trinitarian exemplar, no authentic friendship exists apart from a relationship to the *communicatio* of charity. Again, the Little Flower summarizes the superintending role of divine charity in our lives.

> It is only charity that can expand my heart, O Jesus, since this sweet flame consumes it, I run with joy in the way of your NEW commandment. I want to run in it until that blessed day when, joining the procession of virgins, I shall be able to follow you in the heavenly courts, singing your new canticle (Ps 118:32) which must be LOVE. [44]

The realization of charity in the world constitutes the Church; where love is, there is God. Through the capital grace of Christ, God unleashes his divine love into the world. And in the person of Christ, the Church finds the source of its life. Von Balthasar puts great emphasis on the Church as *quasi una persona*: "The Church of Christ is nothing else but the plenitude of this one Person ... To the extent that Jesus' work of salvation was accomplished 'for all', life in his community is at the same time both personalizing and socializing." [45] In order

---

[43] Bk I, chap. 23, (*PL* 34, 27).

[44] *The Story of a Soul*, p. 226.

[45] "Nine Theses," (2), p. 110.

to benefit fully from so great a gift, the Christian lover needs to observe the right order of relationships that form the community of the Church.

5. THE PRIORITIES OF CHARITY

"The perfect fulfillment of the will of the Father in the Person of Christ," says von Balthasar, "is an eschatological, unsurpassable synthesis." [46] As a goal, every Christian strives to achieve this synthesis in his or her life. But even within the communion of charity, conflicting claims can be put on our loving. The Church's catechetical tradition, as I have said, recognizes four "objects" that charity must embrace: God, the self, the neighbor, and one's own body. [47] So it is important to have a clear idea of how these objects relate among themselves, and in the case of conflicting situations, which class of persons takes priority over another. As star differs from star, charity differentiates one person from another within the one Body. Caritative love then must observe an ordering. The Christian tradition recognizes both a dialectical discovery of the good in another and the gradual development of our appreciation of God's love in the members of the Church.

"God is love, and those who abide in love abide in God, and God abides in them" (1 Jn 4: 16). Charity for the neighbor brings our love for God to completion; it never spells its diminishment. This truth the New Testament makes quite clear: "Those who say 'I love God,' and hate their brother, are liars; for those who do not love a brother whom they have seen, cannot love God whom they have not seen" (1 Jn 4: 20). The following principles help to show how many and diverse persons fit into the communion of charity that, because God alone causes its realization, remains an "unsurpassable synthesis" of God's will.

The first criterion for determining how someone should be loved in charity depends on how a given person actually participates in the *communicatio beatitudinis*. This criterion specifies how anyone is to be loved *objectively* in charity. There also exists an order of charity that is determined by the way interpersonal relationships actually develop between individual friends, between an I and a Thou. This sort of affective relationship can of course occur in diverse ways. For example, affection increases when a believer comes to recognize and to appreciate how much the divine love of benevolence in fact shapes the character of a friend. Or again, affective friendship also occurs in nature, for example, among the members of a family. In any event, this intimacy and closeness establishes the basis for another sort of loving, namely, *appreciative* love or the love of intensity. Thus the second criterion for reckoning how one should be

---

[46]   Ibid.

[47]   Aquinas addresses this subject in *Summa theologiae* IIa-IIae q. 26, aa. 1–13.

loved in divine charity. Bearing in mind, then, the distinction between loving objectively and loving appreciatively, the following set of guidelines for exercising charity within the community of the faithful are applicable.

Because the formal object of charity is the divine goodness, charity first recognizes the absolute priority of divine love over all of the human participations in it. This holds true even though, as 1 John 4: 20 reminds us, the neighbor remains phenomenally more present to us than God. [48] It also means that charity gives priority to the divine love itself over an individual's own interests and worth. Why? The individual's worth depends upon his or her participation in the *communicatio benevolentiae*. This does not mean that by preferring the divine love to our own interests we become forced into a continual stream of self-diminishment, for we know that the person who loves God is drawn into the perfecting love of beatitude and is thereby "fulfilled" in the most radical sense. Thirdly, because the person is a *per se unum* composed of body and soul, charity establishes the priority of self-love over love of neighbor. In other words, the self embodies an ontologically strong reality, a unity, that surpasses the caritative union that exists between friends. This principle, however, rests both on the fact that the spiritual powers of the soul represent the human person's true dignity and that the spiritual powers of knowledge and love communicate to the whole rational supposit a special excellence. As a corollary to the principle that the self enjoys priority over the neighbor in charity, each person ought to love his or her body in true charity.

When Aquinas turns to consider the priorities that exist among the various members of the Mystical Body, he firmly rejects the hypothesis that love is egalitarian. [49] Christian love, in fact, displays preferences for one neighbor over the other. The preferential mode of loving takes into account both God and the person who loves, and "the nearer the 'object' is to either of these," says Aquinas, "the dearer it is." [50] On this account, God first loves the blessed Virgin Mary more than he loves the other saints because by reason of the grace that he gave her, she is the closest human person to God. God's preferential love for Mary, however, is not a "closed" love, for it establishes her at the center of the Church. "Mary is the archetype and first cell of the Church," explains von Balthasar, "and when the Church participates in Mary's disposition, the Church is the Body of Christ in full truth." [51] To take another example, St Paul instructs us "to work for the good of all, and especially for those of the family of faith" (Gal 6: 10). What reason can we assign for this preferential love, other

---

[48] See *Summa theologiae* IIa-IIae q. 26, a. 2, ad 1

[49] *Summa theologiae* IIa-IIae q. 26, a. 6: "Sed hoc irrationabiliter dicitur!"

[50] Ibid.

[51] Von Balthasar, *The Threefold Garland*, trans. Erasmo Leiva-Merikakis (San Francisco, 1982), p. 33.

than the fact that Christian faith unites one to another in what von Balthasar describes as a continuous movement toward the Church's own center, which, in Mary, already contains full reality. The order of charity, however, does not constrain love nor engender a sectarian spirit, for the "Church remains open to the world, just as Christ is open to the Father and his all-embracing Kingdom (1 Cor 15: 24)." [52]

Thus, when it comes to making a judgment about which persons are to be loved and according to what criteria, we must recall the distinction between *objective* loving and intense or *appreciative* loving. The objective love of charity looks to the specific goodness of the neighbor as this participates in the *communicatio benevolentiae*, whereas the intensive or appreciative love of charity flows from the felt closeness or intimacy that exists, based either on nature or acquired friendship, between two persons. The following general theses illustrate this paramount distinction according to the four categories of charity, God, the self, the neighbor, and one's body. First, God is to be loved both objectively and appreciatively above ourselves and our neighbors. Second, the Christian should love himself or herself more appreciatively than the neighbor, though objectively less if the particular neighbor shares more in the *communicatio benevolentiae*. Thirdly, the Christian should love the neighbor more than his or her own body, although one is required to sacrifice one's natural life only for the benefit of another's eternal salvation. St John Chrysostom reflects on these priorities when he tells Christians that you "must surrender everything but your faith: money, body, even life itself. For faith is the head and the root; keep that, and though you lose all else, you will get it back in abundance." [53]

Among the various neighbors that charity requires us to love, we can distinguish between common cases and particular instances. First, as a common rule, we should love objectively better people more than those who are close to us, even if we love more intensely our ungodly intimates than we do a holy stranger. Again, we should love more our family members, at least in those things that pertain to the natural bond, than we do those who are friends by election, e.g., through the vows of religion. Secondly and in particular, one should objectively love more a father and a mother, but children more intensely or appreciatively than parents. Aquinas goes on to propose that anyone in charity should objectively love fathers more than mothers and wives, even though a husband must love his wife with greater intensity and appreciation than his father or children. As the prime natural analogue for the *communicatio beatitudinis*, the right ordering of relationships within the family remains central to Christian revelation. The casuist theologians used the above classifications for

---

[52]   "Nine Theses," (2), p. 111.
[53]   St John Chrysostom, "Homily on Matthew" 33, 1, 2 (*PG* 57, 389 – 390).

solving practical questions that involved either/or decisions, but it is sufficient to recognize that the ordering of charity in the Church exists because of the ordering within the blessed Trinity. Charity represents the communication of the divine goodness to the human creature; neither the contractual principles of self-determination nor the unrealistic principle of secular egalitarianism can coerce the utterly free gift of God that brings salvation in Jesus Christ.

6. THE REALIZATION OF CHRISTIAN *Communio*

The full realization of Christian *communio* takes place within the sacramental and juridical structures of the Church. Christ transforms every expression of human love, so by responding to a series of little questions about loving we come to appreciate the extraordinary consequences that divine charity makes in our lives. Because friendship is founded upon a reciprocal loving, this fact immediately raises the question whether charity is more realized in loving actively or in being loved. Aquinas explains that *habitus* by their very nature are chiefly ordained to those sorts of activity that are perfective of the one who possesses the *habitus*. [54] Like the other theological virtues, charity conforms to this dynamic, so that charity first of all directs our loving, and only indirectly does it regulate our being loved. However, according to the text, "Let us therefore love God: because God first has loved us" (1 Jn 4: 19), it is the very experience of this divine love that enables every believer to begin to love. William of St Thierry discovers this truth at the heart of the New Testament: "So, Lord, as the Apostle of your love tells us, you 'first loved us' (1 Jn 4: 10); and you love all your lovers first." [55] Moreover, when God loves a creature, we know that the creature, not God, is perfected.

The love of charity is to be distinguished from simple benevolence or plain goodwill on two counts. First, insofar as love issues from a sense-passion, it is marked with a certain intensity or desire. But Aristotle says that simple goodwill "does not involve intensity or desire." [56] Again, charity's loving differs from simple benevolence which issues from the rational appetite, for the virtue of charity requires that one establish a certain affective union between the lover and the beloved, whereas benevolence enables us to wish another well without requiring any such union. From a psychological point of view, benevolence represents a more general kind of disposition in the person; and, to be sure, one that precedes charity. For although the psychological roots of theological love lie in benevolence, it never reaches the perfection that describes charity alone.

---

[54] See *Summa theologiae* Ia-IIae q. 49, a. 3.

[55] William of St Thierry, *On Contemplating God*, trans. Sr Penelope (Spencer, MA, 1970), no. 10.

[56] *Nicomachean Ethics* Bk 9, chap. 5 (1166b33).

Only charity establishes an affective bond between the lover and the beloved; only charity represents the sort of deep-seated emotion that is so charged with ecstatic energy that it produces a certain familiarity or connaturality with the beloved "object." In sum, then, simple goodwill can never substitute for divine charity. [57]

Charity loves God only because of his goodness; as I have said, even our love of God falls under the formal object of theological charity. In order to understand why one should love God for himself alone, we can investigate three lines of causality. First, in the line of final causality, the human person can discover no other or more ultimate motive for loving God than God himself. Why? No goodness exists other than what God himself possesses. Second, in the order of formal causality, we likewise recognize that the divine goodness cannot increase, so there exists no greater goodness that could provide a more compelling reason for loving God. Thirdly, in the order of efficient causality, we recognize that no cause of authentic loving exists other than what God makes possible for us in Christ. If we were to inquire whether the Christian loves God on account of anything besides God, then as far as these three categories are concerned, the theologian must reply negatively. Aquinas sums up the matter in this way:

> For, being himself the last end of all things, there is no other end to which God is subordinate; nor does he need any other form to make him good, since his very substance is his goodness and the exemplar of all other goods; nor does his goodness derive from another, rather is God the source of whatever goodness there is in everything else. [58]

However, there does exist a qualified way in which love for God is motivated by certain goods that are less than God himself, namely, when a person draws close to God as a result of hoping for the good things that he promises and of fearing the bad things that befall those who fail to make him their complete joy.

The love of benevolence (*amor benevolentiae*), or friendship, reaches out immediately to God. Even in this life, theological charity makes us directly and immediately adhere to God, and this without the benefit of any intermediaries. On the other hand, one can imagine reasons for thinking that theological love does in fact fall short of reaching God immediately. For example, one could argue that theological faith achieves knowledge of God only "through a glass in a dark manner" (1 Cor 13:12). But the will depends on the intellect for its illumination and direction, and so theological charity, since it remains a virtue of the will, cannot achieve a greater perfection than the faith that di-

---

[57] For an interesting application of this principle, see Dietrich von Hildebrand, *Man and Woman* (Chicago, 1966).

[58] *Summa theologiae* IIa-IIae q. 27, a. 3.

rects it. Again, sin weakens the human will so that we fall short in doing good to our neighbor. But loving God is a higher activity of soul, and so it seems unlikely that theological charity can reach God. Notwithstanding these kinds of objections, Aquinas contends that theological love must draw us immediately to God, for otherwise charity would not measure up to its full character as a love, but would exist only as an elaborate form of simple desire. And this sort of affective movement falls short of what the New Testament promises for full-bodied charity.

To affirm that the believer is capable of a full and immediate union with God in charity forms an important element of Catholic teaching on theological charity. By emphasizing the immediacy of charity, we do not in any way impugn the complete authenticity of those created instruments that help us to love God. The sacred humanity of Christ, the blessed Virgin Mary, the blessed sacrament of the altar and the other sacraments, the ministerial priesthood all contribute to building up the body of Christ. But when it comes to a believer loving God, none of these instruments stands as a medium between the lover and the God who is loved; or as von Balthasar insists, both Christ and Church " 'mediate' only in immediacy." [59] This point is especially significant since the truth of the Catholic faith obliges us to recognize that other creatures legitimately serve as necessary instruments for our salvation.

Consider two important examples for the everyday life of the Church: the roles of the blessed Virgin Mary and of the ordained priest. Neither Mary nor the priest "impede the immediate union of the faithful" with God in charity; rather, if one were to analyze these relationships correctly, God himself serves as the medium for our relationship with our blessed Lady and with the priest who acts *in persona Christi*. So, for example, the Second Vatican Council teaches that "all the saving influences of the blessed Virgin on humankind originate ... from the divine pleasure." [60] Through the power of the Holy Spirit, God constitutes both Mary and the ordained priest, though in diverse ways, as instruments of charity. Mary is made so through the grace of the Immaculate Conception and the priest by his sacramental configuration with Christ in Holy Order, "which equips and obliges him to be a living instrument of Christ the eternal priest and to act in the name and in the person of Christ himself." [61] Accordingly, each believer is established in a certain ordination to Our Lady and to the priests of the Church, so that the members of Christ's body are made proximately more receptive for growth in the divine love. This disposition does not imply that either Mary or priests serve as bridges between God

---

[59] "Nine Theses," (2), p. 111.

[60] *Lumen gentium*, no. 60, as cited in Pope John Paul II's *Redemptoris Mater*, no. 38.

[61] Pope John Paul II, *Pastores dabo vobis*, no. 20.

and the believer, for the charity of this life always adheres directly to God. It is extremely urgent that priests and confessors communicate this understanding in their preaching and direction, for everyone is able to love God immediately and to be loved by him in the same way; indeed, no way other than immediately loving God stands open for us.

The Cistercian tradition offers a rich suite of commentaries on the text of the Canticle, "I to my beloved, my beloved to me" (Can 2: 16). These monastic sermons point out that Christian joy remains bound up with the person's ability to make an act of love that draws him or her into an immediate union with God himself. On this basis, believers are said to love God wholly: that is, every person who forms part of the *communicatio benevolentiae* loves God with his or her full human energies. This is true even though our limited capacities impede us from loving God in an infinite mode as his infinite Goodness would deserve.

But is it not possible that, through the power of God, we are capable of infinite love? At the beginning of the 14th century, Duns Scotus made just such an argument to prove the necessity of Christ's creation. On his account, God would hope to possess in the incarnate Son a creature that was at last capable of returning the kind of love that marks the divine loving itself. [62]

But no creature can exist that would be capable of loving God wholly, for such a creature would have to be infinite, and that involves a clear contradiction. Although no creature, not even the human will of the incarnate Son, can infinitely love God, it is still incumbent on every creature to love God without measure. Aquinas interprets the long tradition on the question of how much one should love God by concluding that, since theological charity reaches God immediately, there cannot be a question of any "more or less"; in loving God, there is never a question of excess. As St Bernard remarks, "The cause of loving God is God; the measure is no measure." [63] Furthermore, the more prudently we love God, the better will our loving become. Even in the case of activities motivated by the theological virtues, prudence is required to ensure that we will duly observe the proper measures that our human limitations impose on us. So for example, people should not consider giving alms to the poor if they still have to meet unfulfilled contractual obligations, or attempt to offer a fraternal correction outside of the norms for its implementation.

The Christian tradition harbors no doubt that to love God is the most meritorious of all loving, and so this love deserves a great reward for its own sake.

---

[62] For further discussion of Scots's arguments, see "Duns Scotus, John" in *New Catholic Encyclopedia* 4 (New York, 1967), pp. 1102–1106.

[63] St Bernard, *De diligendo Deo*, chap. 1; see Bernard of Clairvaux, "On Loving God," trans. Robert Walton, in *Treatises II* (Cistercian Fathers Series, 13; Kalamazoo, MI, 1980), pp. 43–132.

The whole movement of divine love tends toward the enjoyment of God. This holds good even if loving God entails less difficulty than loving the neighbor. It is the goodness of what is loved, not the difficulty of loving, that determines merit and virtue. Loving what is more difficult, then, does not constitute a better form of love, unless the more difficult also instantiates the better. [64] "For this love to which we are called," writes von Balthasar, "is not a circumscribed or limited love, not a love defined, as it were, by the measure of our human weakness." [65] It is a love measured only by God's measureless desire to bestow it on us.

7. THE FRUITS OF CHARITY

The scholastics reserved the Latin term *diligere* specifically to designate the act of theological charity. As faith's proper action is believing and hope's proper action is hoping, so charity's proper act remains loving. Because Christian charity particularly extends to a number of special material objects, the theologian is able to distinguish certain activities that especially belong to the concrete practice of theological charity within the Church of faith and sacraments. Though each one of the activities that together make up the practice of Christian charity represents a whole range of virtues, the Christian tradition nevertheless identifies certain activities as particular expressions of *dilectio*. By reason of charity's formal object, *viz*, to love God above all thing on account of his very goodness, these good deeds comprise a single class or set of actions.

Theological charity particularly attends to the specific ways that *dilectio* realizes itself in the world. Because these activities especially represent the flourishing of divine charity, theologians traditionally have called these special activities the fruits of charity. [66] An examination of the fruits of charity is distinct from the consideration of charity as the form of the virtues; for the fruits indicate specific kinds of activity that mark both the internal disposition and the external comportment of one who seeks to extend and enlarge the *communicatio benevolentiae*. In the treatise on charity, Aquinas identifies three internal fruits of charity, namely, joy, peace, and mercy, and three external fruits, namely, kindness or benevolence, almsgiving, and fraternal correction. [67] Each of these special acts of theological charity likewise possesses its own sort of

---

[64]   See *Summa theologiae* IIa-IIae, q. 27, a. 8, ad 3.

[65]   Von Balthasar, *The Christian States of Life*, trans. Mary Frances McCarthy (San Francisco, 1983) p. 27.

[66]   For an historical study of the fruits of charity, see Odon Lottin, *Psychologie et Morale aux XIIe et XIIIe siècles*, t. I: Problèmes de Psychologie (Paris, 1942).

[67]   *Summa theologiae* IIa-IIae, qq. 28 – 33.

vicious deformities. Hatred, for instance, stands opposed to the very act of love; acedia and jealousy check the joy of loving; discord and schism thwart the peace that charity produces; and finally, offensiveness and scandal hinder the good that fraternal correction seeks to promote.

Charity creates order and balance in the world. In one of his homilies, St John Chrysostom wrote, "More than anyone else, the Lord knows the true natures of created things; he knows that moderation, not a fierce defense, beats back a fierce attack." [68] Because the love of benevolence makes a person secure in the possession of the good, moderation brings about a joyful spirit. Joy represents the fruit of charity in our lives and not one of its pre-conditions. The gospel offers no guarantee that the sinner will experience joy from the first moment that he or she turns to Christ, and so only poor counsel directs the behaviorally weak to wait until their behavior changes before they make an act of charity. Judgments based predominately on feelings or emotions, the Christian tradition holds suspect. Good spiritual instruction will encourage everyone to start loving God immediately, so that as a result of these acts of charity, the rest of the virtuous life will develop harmoniously. The resulting joy comes from loving God himself. Jesus himself counsels his disciples: "When a woman is in labor, she has pain, because her hour has come. But when her child is born, she no longer remembers the anguish because of the joy of having brought a human being into the world. So you have pain now; but I will see you again, and your hearts will rejoice, and no one will take your joy from you" (Jn 16: 21–22).

Joy also derives from beholding the glory of God that appears in his works, especially from loving the neighbor in theological charity, that is, a person who is both our friend and a friend of God. Because the believer in charity loves God, he or she also loves all that God has created. But this joy can suffer diminishment, for human creatures always remain subject to the evil of punishment (*malum poenae*) and the evil of fault (*malum culpae*). Still, the gospel instructs us to maintain hope that ultimately charity will reign; for God "will wipe every tear from their eyes" (Rev 21: 4). On that day, the saints will experience only the joy that comes from beholding God's mercy and his justice. But while the Church continues to labor on earth, it does everything it can to ensure that the saints rejoice more and more on account of God's mercy. So when a friend, for example, freely chooses a course of action that places him or her outside of the *communicatio benevolentiae*, the one who would exercise true Christian compassion will look for ways to draw the person back to the joy of loving God.

---

[68]   Homily 33, 1.2 (*PG* 57: 389–390).

Authentic self-love also produces a joyful and self-forgetting spirit. The 14th-century Dominican mystic John Tauler explains how the saints can esteem others as their betters and still remain joyful. In one of his sermons, he describes St Paul's ecstacy:

> If I love God, I love St Paul's rapture more in him than in me... And still, through charity that ecstacy also belongs to me. Charity does not suffer from sadness on account of the fact that it is not the first to experience something good. Rather it recognizes only the exultation that comes from knowing simply that one is before God, and that only by his gracious gift that lasts forever not only am I a glorious person, but also unique, singular, and privileged. [69]

Only the profound sadness of remaining in habitual sin inveighs against this sort of joyful disposition. Among the blessed, joy corresponds to the sure possession of the divine goodness in glory; in heaven all desire stops, though not even the saints merit strictly this joy. Rather God's supreme benevolence draws them into it: "Enter into the joy of your master" (Mt 25:21 & 23). Joy does not constitute a virtue distinct from charity, "but it is a certain act or effect of charity." And on this account, it is numbered first among the fruits of the Holy Spirit that St Paul lists in Galatians: joy, peace, patience, kindness, generosity, faithfulness, gentleness, and self-control (Gal 5: 22). [70]

In the strict sense of the term, peace does not qualify as a specific virtue; however, because charity produces unity among God and humankind, peace eminently belongs with charity. Moreover, the fruit of peace implies two kinds of unions: the first kind of peace brings the sum of a person's own desires into an ordered unity; the second establishes a union between one's desires and those of another person. Charity accomplishes this first by focusing our desires onto the love of God and, secondly, by making us want to do what pleases the neighbor as if to do so actually suited our own will.

Mercy appropriately belongs with charity because it flows from the desire to relieve the wants of another; and on Aquinas's account, this desire necessarily belongs to someone who is both noble and good. In a beautiful phrase, Aquinas expresses the special way that mercy pertains to God: "Love is the sole reason for God's mercy, for he loves us as something of himself." [71] Moreover, when true Christian mercy moves beyond mere sentiment and expresses the measure of right reason that guides the truth of life, *veritas vitae*, this fruit, unlike joy and peace, supplies the emotional balance that undergirds all human virtue. Aquinas combines his discussion of joy, peace, and mercy under

---

[69] John Tauler, *Sermons*, trans. Maria Shrady (Classics of Western Spirituality; New York, 1985).
[70] For Aquinas's treatment of the fruits of the Holy Spirit, see *Summa theologiae* Ia-IIae q. 70, a. 1.
[71] *Summa theologiae* IIa-IIae q. 30, a. 2, ad 1.

the heading of the internal effects of charity, for he considers these qualities of soul as the chief traits that mark the interiority of the Christian lover. Obviously, these traits affect the external comportment of one who loves, but only to the extent that they first adorn the soul of the one who belongs to the *communicatio benevolentiae*.

Charity also produces special sorts of fruit that pertain to external expressions of human behavior that transpires within the *communicatio benevolentiae*. Aquinas identifies three such specific acts: beneficence, or kindness, almsgiving, and fraternal correction. First, kindness represents a general expression of charity. Although any number of virtues ordain that one show kindness or act beneficently toward a neighbor, there also exists a more general sense of beneficence that we show to our friends, and that especially flows from our loving them. Secondly, this general sort of kindness includes eleemosynary acts that traditionally form part of the Christian life. For the medieval theologians, almsgiving includes a broad range of spiritual and material relief, not just the giving of money to the destitute or needy. [72] Thirdly, there is a specific form of spiritual assistance or alms that the tradition refers to as fraternal correction.

The New Testament itself speaks about fraternal correction as a service of charity (see Mt 18: 15 – 17). And St Jerome points out that "we ought to take a brother aside to rebuke him, for fear that, having once lost all sense of shame or modesty, he may persist in his sins." [73] Fraternal correction points an errant Christian toward the truth of God's wise providence, towards appreciating how God knows the world to be. The virtuous practice of fraternal correction urges hope and filial fear onto those who habitually act outside of conformity to moral truth. Since fraternal correction often implies exhorting the sinner to relinquish an apparent good to which he or she is attached in some vicious way, the task of gently urging knowledge of the truth through correction is at once both urgent and difficult.

Because we sin daily, we need correction from others who love the truth. But in correcting a brother or sister, the Christian believer must pay close heed to the promptings of the Holy Spirit. The believer accomplishes this through the virtue of infused prudence, especially as it is helped by the gift of Counsel. The theological tradition maintains that fraternal correction expresses true charity, but mediated by mercy; it is, in effect, a species of almsgiving. Aquinas relates the connection in this way:

> Accordingly, both charity and mercy dictate fraternal correction: charity in order that the one corrected might possess good the more; mercy in so far as the misery [of sin's disorder] might be removed the sooner. Charity principally commands

---

[72]   In *Summa theologiae* IIa-IIae q. 32, aa. 1 – 10, Aquinas takes the opportunity to examine specific questions related to the giving of alms.

[73]   *In Matthaeum* III, chap. 18, v. 15 (*PL* 26, col. 136).

fraternal correction, but mercy does so secondarily. However it is prudence that both directs and shapes the very act of admonishing so that it might achieve the desired end of bringing about a change of heart in the one corrected. [74]

From this it is clear that fraternal correction represents a particularly ecclesial action, for it combines the specifically evangelical qualities of mercy, charity, and prudence into the single exercise of a profound care and concern for the neighbor. For just as the gospel requires that we give to our brothers and sisters who are in material distress, so the same evangelical law enjoins those who participate in the love of benevolence that they relieve the members of Christ's body that suffer from the spiritual distress of sin. But this work of transforming love can only happen in union with the suffering Christ. "Even if it is true that the purpose of the rules of the Church is to free the believer from the alienation of sin and to lead him to his true identity and freedom," writes von Balthasar, "they may and indeed often must seem to be harsh and legalistic to the imperfect believer, just as the will of the Father appeared harsh to Christ hanging on the Cross." [75] The person who would correct another virtuously must first turn to Jesus, so that his love and compassion will shine through the words and gestures of admonition.

---

[74] Cajetan, *In secundam secundae* q. 33.
[75] "Nine Theses," (1), p. 109.

Part II

The Moral Virtues

CHAPTER 4
CHRISTIAN PRUDENCE AND PRACTICAL WISDOM

1. "BUT WE HAVE THE MIND OF CHRIST" (1 COR 2: 16)

"The end of a virtuous life," says St Gregory of Nyssa, "is to become like unto God."[1] Because the uniquely Christian virtues of faith, hope, and charity hold the preeminent place in the moral life of the Christian believer, the theologian gives these virtues first consideration in any treatment of the moral life. But as Proverbs reminds us, "The man of discretion watches how he treads" (Prov 14:15), and so the Christian believer requires other human virtues in order to lead a good life. And first among these, the tradition numbers prudence. Prudence opens up the human mind to the world of moral truth and value. Within the community of the Church, human prudence achieves an entirely new perfection. Von Balthasar speaks about the " 'opening up' to 'the Gentiles' (Gal 3: 14) that is effected in the gathering together of Jesus' followers and the bestowing on them of the Holy Spirit (through faith in him)."[2] The same kind of opening up takes place in the moral life through the graced transformation of the human virtues – what we call the infused virtues. Because Jesus promises the guidance of the Holy Spirit to all those who are gathered in his name, the Christian believer is a man or woman whose soul brims with a graced discretion that continues to develop during the course of a virtuous life. For as Origen rightly remarks, Christ loves the virtues.

In his *Summa theologiae*, Aquinas elaborates a particularly good schema for setting up a virtue-centered approach to the Christian life. He announces the broad outline of this schema as follows:

> The entire subject matter of morals being thus condensed under a discussion of virtues, these, in turn, are to be reduced to seven. Three are theological, and they must be the first topic; the other four are cardinal, and will be the second. As to the intellectual virtues, prudence is one of them and is included and listed among the cardinal virtues.[3]

---

[1] St Gregory of Nyssa, *Orationes de beatitudinibus*, 1 (*PG* 44: 1200).
[2] "Nine Theses" (5), p. 114.
[3] *Summa theologiae* IIa, prologue.

Altogether in the second part (*secunda pars*), Aquinas devotes 170 *quaestiones* to distinct virtues; in the same section, he also specifically relates these virtues to the particular vocations and special charisms that flourish within the Christian community. Of course, this syntagma of the moral virtues forms only the second half of Aquinas's entire treatment of moral matters. In the first section of the *secunda pars*, Aquinas develops the more general principles of Christian morality, among which he makes a point of identifying the ultimate *telos* of intelligent life as the blessed vision of God. In the Christian tradition, says Cardinal Ratzinger, "morality has its starting point in what the Creator has placed in the heart of every person: the need for happiness and love; [and so] human beings are like God because they can love and are capable of reason."[4] The prudent Christian man or woman has put on the mind of Christ, so that the power of Christ can transform the whole person in both mind and heart. The infused virtues not only bring Christian morality to its perfection but also ready the believer for the joyful vision of God.

2. WHAT IS CHRISTIAN VIRTUE?

We know that Aquinas in the *Summa theologiae* begins his analysis of virtue with the standard textbook definition of virtue that was common among 13th-century moralists: "Virtue is a good quality of mind, by which one lives righteously, of which no one can make bad use, which God works in us without us."[5] Following normal procedure, we can consider each element of the definition as Aquinas explains it within his general teleological view of the moral life. First, the formal cause: "Virtue is a good quality of mind." For Aquinas, virtue belongs to the generic category of quality; more specifically he places it within that kind of quality that Aristotle called *habitus*. As a philosophical notion, *habitus* signifies the perfection of a human capacity that enables a person not only to act, but to act well. Because the virtues really alter the particular substances in which they inhere, these good *habitus* modify or shape the psychological capacities of the human person. But this happens in a way that respects the virtuous person's ability to express a full range of creativity and human initiative. New Testament belief does not produce boring uniformity; rather the Christian experiences a kind of second-nature conformity to gospel values that makes living an upright life prompt, joyful, and easy. Since virtue is supple, the virtuous person can decide and act on moral issues that result from even the most complex circumstances of the moral life.

---

[4]   From Cardinal Joseph Ratzinger's presentation of the *Catechism of the Catholic Church* to the media; see *L'Osservatore Romano*, Weekly English edition, no. 50 (16 December 1992), p. 4.

[5]   See *Summa theologiae* Ia-IIae q. 55, a. 4,

Second, the material cause: Since virtue exemplifies a moral or spiritual reality, strictly speaking virtue has no material cause. Rather, for the purposes of analysis, we speak about the subjects in which the virtues exist as supplying for their material cause. These subjects include all the rational powers or capacities of the human soul: intellect, will (or the rational appetite), and the sense appetites. To possess human nature in itself does not suffice to cause virtue; rather, acquired virtue develops by some deliberate exercise of the human capacities or powers, *viz*, intellect, will, sense appetites. [6]

Third, the efficient cause: "which God works in us without us." While human actions can account for the development of the *habitus* that we call the acquired virtues, the definition envisages the infused virtues as sheer gifts of divine grace. That is, these virtuous forms come directly from the power of the Holy Spirit, who alone serves as the efficient cause of their coming to be and remaining in us. Because their origin and development depend on the divine agency, the infused moral virtues function only within the broader context of the theological life, of faith, of hope, and of charity.

Fourth, the final cause: "by which one lives righteously, of which no one can make bad use." As an operative *habitus*, the end or final cause of virtue remains the performance of the virtuous action itself. By definition, the exercise of virtue results only in the embrace of good objects. Each of the moral virtues formally marks off an area of human endeavor, but without specifying the exact shape that every good choice will take. The moral goodness that the virtues realize embraces the whole universe of moral objects precisely as these conduce to our possession of the supreme object of all human pursuit and desire. From a teleological perspective, there really are no general "basic human goods," for every virtuous act that is to be done in some way embodies a good basic or fundamental to the human flourishing of the person who acts.

Although there are some notable exceptions to this general rule, Christian theology today does not take much account of the distinction between the infused and the acquired virtue. Two factors account for this. The first emerges from discussions in the general area of theological anthropology, and especially the popular appeal that an inclusivist view of nature and grace has enjoyed during the period of post-conciliar theology. Many blame the Leonine neo-scholastic revival for its failure to meet every challenge that contemporary person-centered philosophies set forth, although 20th-century Thomists such as Jacques Maritain, for example, could well appreciate and develop the distinction between person and nature, both common and individual. Today, however, most Christian theologians are willing to consider only the individ-

---

[6] See *De veritate* q. 1, a. 8: "quaelibet virtus, faciens operationem hominis bonam, habet proprium actum in homine, qui sui actione potest ipsam reducere in actum."

ual person, and him or her precisely as a graced person, that is, as enjoying the benefits of an active personal relationship with the blessed Trinity. As a result, not much is said about the human person as a creature, precisely as one who possesses a created human nature. Nor has the claim that, in Christian theology, creation represents a properly theological notion made much of a difference in this respect. In my view, there is a connection between this vision of nature and grace and the fact that moral theologians have enjoyed a wide berth with their speculations about what does and does not perfect human nature, and why from both pulpit and podium we hear moralists hedge on, if not outrightly condone, some plainly immoral forms of human conduct. Because moral theologians lean toward describing the actual state of the believer exclusively in categories of grace and glory, they pay less attention to human nature with its specific capacities and built-in teleologies. To adapt St Augustine's description of the knowledge of the angels, theologians prefer to examine the moral life only in the light of the Word. But does this theological mood not risk creating some strange ambiguities? For example, to the extent that inclusivist views of nature and grace result in confusion about the moral responsibility of the person who participates in the life of Christ, we find ourselves confronted with antinomies, such as Catholic groups that advocate "abortion rights," or Catholic groups that condone the homosexual "lifestyle."

Secondly, there is the practice among moral theologians of establishing norms and rules for moral conduct. The Decalogue of course explains the Church's catechetical practice of using the commandments to instruct the faithful in the Christian life. I refer rather to the current fashion among moralists to speculate about the moral life in terms of normative conduct that is established exclusively by appeal to pure obligation of one kind or another. Both those who favor the formulation of absolute moral norms and those who want to provide a cushion for the contingencies of the real world by setting in place some contemporary equivalent of casuistry ironically share the same basic paradigm of norm-centered morality. What is important, however, is that those who develop a moral theology exclusively in terms of such moral norms, whether absolute or not, pay scant attention to the requirements of human nature and its real operative powers at work in the moral life. Rather they produce what I would describe as a morality of the head, in which natural law, if not entirely rejected, is portrayed principally as a product of human intelligence. It is especially true that revisionist moral theologians show little enthusiasm for talk about the virtues of the moral life. Because they fail to recognize both that *habitus* can serve as a real source of action in the human person and that prudence can grapple with the most complex of real life circumstances, the majority of these moralists agree that only some form of proportional reasoning can really assist the perplexed person who is required to make a moral choice.

When the theologian inquires what difference sanctifying grace makes for a life of virtue, the simple affirmation that the acquired moral virtues can develop within the setting of a call to supernatural beatitude and the sacramental practice of divine charity does not suffice. For this proposal offers only an extrinsic explanation, in which the Christian life merely provides an opportunity for instruction in virtue. But Aquinas and the tradition that follows him advance an integrated view of the infused virtues. Unlike those schools that consider theological faith and charity sufficient to account for the virtuous Christian, Thomistic ethics dares to consider the infused virtues as true forms that exist in the operative potencies of the nature that belongs to the individual Christian who loves God above all things and his neighbor as himself or herself. That the gifts of the Holy Spirit and the infused virtues together form the spiritual endowment of every justified believer is the clear teaching of Trent. These graces are not only the perks of the saints.

Virtue shapes the life of the Christian believer set on the path to beatitude. Thus, Aquinas explains the need for God's special action in the virtuous life in the following way:

> Besides the natural principles that humankind possesses for its perfection in the order natural to it, men and women need virtuous *habitus*... So also, besides the ... supernatural principles [of grace and the theological virtues], we are endowed by God with certain infused virtues which perfect us in the ordering of our actions to their end, which is eternal life. [7]

The universal call to holiness determines the reason for the existence of the infused virtues. Our behavior needs to be conformed to all that points toward eternal life, and neither charity nor faith in itself suffices to transform every feature of the moral life so that our choices become more and more centered on God and directed toward him. As the Letter to the Philippians puts it: "Fill your minds with everything that is true, everything that is noble, everything that is good and pure, everything that we love and honor, and everything that can be thought virtuous or worthy of praise" (Phil 4: 8).

The infused virtues describe the kind of life that is proper to the City of God, the heavenly city of grace. [8] While it remains perfectly legitimate to talk

---

[7] *De virtutibus in communi* q. 1, a. 10. The text that precedes this citation runs as follows: "There is infused into us by God, to enable us to perform acts ordered to eternal life as their end: first grace, which gives the soul a certain spiritual or divine being; and then, faith, hope, and charity. By faith the mind is enlightened concerning supernatural truths, which in their order stand as do principles naturally known in the order of natural actions. By hope and charity the will acquires an inclination to the supernatural good to which the human will, by its own natural operations, is not adequately ordered."

[8] See *La Vertu*, t. II la-2ae, questions 61–70, in *Somme théologique* (Editions de la Revue des Jeunes), ed. R. Bernard, O.P., esp. Appendice II "La vertu acquise et la vertu infuse," pp. 434ff.

about a perfection that exists for human nature itself, the ultimate perfection of each soul *simpliciter loquendo*, as the scholastics said, comes only from union with God. In a text from the *De veritate*, Aquinas again explains that "we do not need infused *habitus* for any other activity than that which natural reason dictates, but just for a more perfect performance of the same activity." [9] This means that the infused virtues, inasmuch as they operate within the life of faith, provide a safer and surer performance of the good actions that lead to happiness, even though in some cases they produce the same action materially considered, to wit, when both acquired and infused virtues of personal discipline moderate the impulse emotions and bolster the contentious emotions.

The Thomist commentatorial school further explains the difference between the acquired and infused virtues. The 16th-century renaissance commentator Cardinal Cajetan considers the difference according to the infused virtues' cause, formal object, and their relation to an end. First, the formal object: The infused virtues have a different formal object from the acquired virtues because the infused virtue operates according to a higher principle, namely, according to a divine measure – *secundum regulam divinam*. [10] The difference in formal object is realized diversely in the virtues of personal discipline, justice, and prudence. For justice and its allied virtues, a new formal object even changes the material cause of these virtues, that is, the very stuff which justice transforms, or as the Second Vatican Council expresses it "the material of the heavenly Kingdom." [11] On the other hand, the material element of the virtues of personal discipline, that is, the tempered or bolstered spirits in temperance and the sustained or strengthened forces in fortitude remain the same for both the acquired and infused virtues. Second, the difference in cause and end means that God remains both the origin and the end goal of the infused virtues. St Paul prays that every believer will reach "the measure of the stature of the fullness of Christ" (Eph 4:13). [12] As a category of the moral order, in-

---

[9]   *De veritate*, q. 14, a. 10. The fuller context for this remark is as follows: "One who is some distance from an end can know the end and desire it; however, he cannot engage in activity which directly concerns the end, but only in that which is connected with the means to the end. Therefore, if we are to reach our supernatural end, we need faith in this life to know the end, for natural knowledge does not go that far. But our natural powers do extend to the means to the end, although not precisely as ordained to that end."

[10] Special attention should be paid to *Summa theologiae* Ia-IIae q. 91, a. 4 ad 1, which discusses the relationship between natural law and divine law as distinct participations in the *lex aeterna*.

[11] See *Gaudium et spes*, no. 38.

[12] The infused virtues form part of the supernatural organism which makes up the Christian life. But virtue does not mean determinism. Stanley Hauerwas, *Character and the Christian Life: A Study in Theological Ethics* (San Antonio, 1975), for instance, emphasizes virtuedevelopment as a way to counteract various forms of social determinism. In his judgment, virtue underscores the role of freedom as an indispensable quality of the human person

fused virtue realizes in human conduct the unity of faith and knowledge about Jesus Christ that is promised to every one who embraces gospel truth.

As a real *habitus* of the person, Christian moral virtue never entails a repression of sense urges, but rather orders these inclinations of our nature according to the mind of Christ. [13] The infused virtues allied with cardinal temperance and fortitude differ then from continence and perseverance; these dispositions, even when they are found in the Christian, simply account for a willed enforcement of moderation in face of attractive things and of strengthening in the face of harmful ones. True virtue accomplishes more than a simple truce between unruly passions and the imperatives of a duly informed will; it impresses the measure of reason upon the passions themselves. However, because the infused or Christian virtues belong with the life of theological faith, hope, and charity, the Christian believer realizes this virtuous life only within the context of a living faith in Christ, of whom St Paul writes: "He is not weak in dealing with you, but is powerful in you" (2 Cor 13: 3). In one who believes in him, Christ supplies the full measure of virtue, "for he was crucified in weakness, but lives by the power of God" (2 Cor 13: 4). And, therefore, neither deformity of appetite nor weakness of intellect can frustrate the power of Christ in our lives. Since the theological virtues energize the infused moral virtues, the love of Christ opens up the way for the final perfection of each man and woman created in the image of God.

3. THE NATURE OF CHRISTIAN PRUDENCE

In order to explain the importance of prudence in a distinctively Christian but comprehensive moral teaching, the Christian tradition, and especially Aquinas, borrows generously from the classical notion of *phronēsis*, or practical reasoning. [14] But Christian prudence displays none of the restrictions inherent in philosophical systems of ethics that tend, as von Balthasar says, "to establish the human subject as his own legislator, as an idealized, autonomous subject

---

within the human community.

[13] By contrast, the voluntarist view that the human will alone ultimately achieves all virtuous conduct accordingly proffers grim prospects for harmony between reason and the affective life. Moreover, to view the virtues as heroic exercises of will power is to ignore a fundamental truth concerning human sense appetite, namely, that the lower appetites are born to obey reason. Compare *Summa theologiae* IIIa q. 15, a. 2, ad 1.

[14] See *Summa theologiae* IIa-IIae q. 47, aa. 1 – 16. In an unusually long *quaestio*, Aquinas sets forth a detailed description of prudence in itself. The material falls under four headings: (1) what kind of virtue is prudence (aa. 1 – 5); (2) what is its proper activity in the moral life (aa. 6 – 9); (3) what are is specific divisions (aa. 10 – 12); and, (4) what traits describe a prudent individual (aa. 13 – 16). For further information on this important matter, see the excellent and detailed commentary of R. A. Gauthier, O.P., *L'Ethique à Nicomaque*, vol. 1 (2d ed., Louvain, 1970), pp. 273 – 283.

who imposes limitations on himself in order to reach perfection." [15] By contrast, Christian prudence offers to the human person a means to participate in the wisdom of God, "in words not taught by human wisdom but taught by the Spirit" (1 Cor 2: 13). In order for this grace to work, however, prudence must rely on something higher than itself. The Christian tradition names the "something higher" eternal law. In his exposition of the eternal law, Aquinas unhesitatingly adopts St Augustine's definition: "That law which is named the supreme reason cannot be otherwise understood than as unchangeable and eternal." [16]

For the Christian theologian, eternal law represents nothing other than the divine wisdom that directs every created being to its proper end or *telos*. Infused prudence makes this eternal law available to every Christian believer whatever native intellectual abilities he or she may possess. [17] Because the Christian participates in the divine wisdom, he or she comes to know the truth about the moral life in accordance with the divine Word of creation. "As a consequence," concludes Cardinal Ratzinger, "the heart of all morality is love, and by always following this direction, we inevitably find ourselves encountering Christ, the love of God made man." [18]

The Christian conception of prudence takes full account of both classical philosophy's notion of practical reasoning, *phronēsis*, and the Christian realization that love constrains *amor meus, pondus meum*. From both of these sources, Christian moral theology is able to offer a full and compelling account of virtuous prudence as a nexus of knowledge and love: This takes on special importance in light of the usual connotations associated with "prudence" in modern usage. In today's common parlance, prudence implies that a person exercises right circumspection, whereas for the best of the Christian moral tra-

---

[15] "Nine Theses" (6), p. 115.

[16] See *Summa theologiae* Ia-IIae q. 91, a. 1, *sed contra*: " 'Lex quae summa ratio nominatur, non potest cuipiam intelligenti non incommutabilis aeternaque videri.' " See St Augustine, *De libero arbitrio* Bk 1, chap. 6 (*PL* 32: 1229; *CCL* 29: 220).

[17] In "St Thomas on Law," *The Etienne Gilson Series* 12 (Toronto, 1988), pp. 4, 5, James P. Reilly, Jr offers the following succinct account of Aquinas's view: "The Eternal law, then, is nothing other than divine wisdom as directive of the motions and acts of every created being. Consequently, all creatures are measured and regulated by Eternal law, and the natural tendencies or innate inclinations of all creatures to their proper acts or end are from Eternal law [cf. *ST* Ia-IIae q. 93, a. 5]. Since Eternal law is the governing idea in the ruler of the universe of being, the governing ideas in lower rulers and the obligatory force of these ideas are also derived from it [*ST* Ia-IIae q. 93, a. 3: "Cum ergo lex aeterna sit ratio gubernationis in supremo gubernante, necesse est quod omnes rationes gubernationis quae sunt in inferioribus gubernantibus, a lege aeterna deriventur."]. Therefore, Eternal law has a primacy with respect to every kind of law; and, correspondingly, whatever is–whether necessary, contingent, or free–is subject to divine governance [*ST* Ia-IIae q. 93, aa. 4 – 6].

[18] Ratzinger, *L'Osservatore Romano* (see note 4).

dition, prudence connotes the full and confident exercise of authentic love and practical wisdom. Moreover, both of these elements remain essential for prudence to operate well. Still, one-sided approaches to prudence exist. For example, certain traditions of moral intellectualism develop the view of John Duns Scotus that prudence represents a pure knowing, capable only of pointing out moral obligation. These theories stress prudence as a form of practical intelligence. From another perspective, Suarezian voluntarism neglects the important role that the human appetites play in actually achieving good conduct. [19] Voluntarist theories consider a loving will sufficient for achieving moral probity. Few ethicians advert to the fact that rational principles are unable by themselves to guarantee that human action will attain true moral good. And fewer still recognize that human appetites, though they contain what Aquinas calls the "seeds" of virtue, cannot in themselves supply a right moral measure for human conduct. [20] Because the virtuous life aims to make human conduct godly, the virtue that directs the whole moral life must shape the thought and touch the heart of the believer.

For pedagogical reasons, the ethicist ordinarily considers prudence in the form of what the tradition calls "monastic" or individual prudence. But the Christian moral teaching also addresses the need for the development of specialized prudences as these address the specific requirements of different social groupings. Thus for example, Aquinas talks both about a political prudence that specially guides the development of virtues that pertain to the common good, and an economic prudence that directs the development of those virtues required in various home-units within the *polis*. In short, the prudent person must engage in activities that aim at diverse ends such as one's own personal well-being, those of the household, and those of the larger political arena. [21]

---

[19] For further information on the particular emphases of the 17th-century Jesuit commentator Francisco Suárez, see John F. Treloar, S.J., "Moral Virtue and the Demise of Prudence in the Thought of Francis Suárez," *The American Catholic Philosophical Quarterly* 64 (1991), pp. 387–405. Stephen D. Dumont, "The Necessary Connection of Moral Virtue to Prudence According to John Duns Scotus Revisited," *Recherches de Théologie ancienne et médiévale* 55 (1988): 184–206, offers an interpretation of the position of Scotus.

[20] For a text that expresses the relationship of prudence to the ends of human appetites, see *Summa theologiae* IIa-IIae q. 47, a. 6, ad 3: "finis non pertinet ad virtutes morales tanquam ipsae præstituant finem, sed quia tendunt in finem a ratione naturali præstitutum... "

[21] In *Summa theologiae* IIa-IIae q. 47, a. 11, ad 3, Aquinas explains the relationship that exists between the different orders in which prudence operates. Thomas Gilby, *Prudence*, vol 36 of the Blackfriars translation of the *Summa theologiae*, p. 38, remarks that the text expresses "a thought characteristic of the author: subordination does not spell the obliteration of secondary principals or ends, or reduce them to the level of mere instruments and means to an end." In *Summa theologiae* IIa-IIae q. 50, Aquinas discusses types of prudence as "subjective" parts of the cardinal virtue: royal or political prudence; economic prudence; military prudence.

Prudence principally concerns the implementation of practical knowledge; this cardinal virtue strengthens human intelligence, the activity of the mind. We associate seeing with the human head. So the 7th-century etymological theologian Isidore of Seville suggests that *prudens* derives from *porro videns*, that is, "looking ahead." And in fact, the virtue of prudence is often represented in medieval sculpture by a figure with three faces, each one looking in a different direction. [22] St Augustine, however, offers a philosophically more satisfying definition when he says that prudence is love choosing wisely between the helpful and the harmful. [23] Aquinas clarifies the relationship between loving practical intelligence and prudent love: "Prudence is said to be love, not that of its nature it is a kind of love, but because its activity is caused by love." [24] Prudence points the believer in the right direction toward God. And this explains why Augustine further explains "that prudence is the love that well discerns between the helps and hindrances in our striving towards God." [25] Without the active direction of prudence, human conduct remains supine and prone to miss the mark; without true prudence, a person's actions inevitably manifest either excess or defect with respect to embracing the proper ends that compose human well-being. In short, prudence ensures that the believer possesses a complete moral culture and lives a well-ordered life, so that he or she easily reaches the goal of beatitude.

As the standard definition puts it, prudence establishes a *recta ratio agibilium*, a right norm or measure for human conduct. Because prudence immediately guides the judgment of conscience about the good to be done or the evil avoided, prudence seeks an end that lies outside the order of purely theoretical knowledge. Prudence shapes human actions in the concrete circumstances of the Christian life. "The prudent character," says Aquinas, "must needs know both the general moral principles of reason and the individual situation in which human actions take place." [26] But by itself, this practical knowledge never secures the order of execution, the actual being-there of a moral action. In fact, even the moral conscience cannot by itself account for making the transition from the order of moral knowledge to the real world of human activity. One has only to consider the common experience that some persons, in fact, act against the dictates of their conscience. So Aquinas points out that "deliberation is about what is to be done for the sake of an end." [27] In this context, end stands for the actual securing of the good things that con-

---

[22]   For example, the tomb of St Peter Martyr in the Basilica of S Eustorgio in Milan.

[23]   *De moribus ecclesiae Catholicae* Bk I, chap. 15 (*PL* 32: 1322).

[24]   *Summa theologiae* IIa-IIae q. 47, a. 1, ad 1.

[25]   Ibid.

[26]   *Summa theologiae* IIa-IIae q. 47, a. 3.

[27]   *Summa theologiae* IIa-IIae q. 47, a. 2.

cretely make up Christian perfection. Because prudence concerns the *agibile*, the do-able, the moral theologian needs to explain how this virtue exercises its directive role in achieving the good ends that comprise Christian *communio*.

In the performance of a good human action, the believer conforms entirely to what Pope Leo XIII called "that ordination of reason that one calls the law." [28] But universal knowledge, even practical moral principles that claim universality, such as the Kantian categorical imperative, cannot supply the immediate premises for human action. In other words, general maxims or principles do not suffice for human action. But while prudence depends on the eternal law, the prudent person must address the concrete singular, that is, the individual case. [29] Of course, to say that prudence concerns particulars does not mean that, in the final analysis, prudence is reduced to a form of casuistry. Because the uncertainties of the unexpected individual case pose a threat to prudence, philosophers sometimes depreciate the capacity of prudence to measure up to the scientific character of sure knowledge through causes. And in fact, because of the contingency of singular events, practical reason does fall short of the excellence that belongs to the theoretical sciences according to the Aristotelian notion of science. [30] From a purely human point of view, therefore, one reproaches the prudent person neither for failing in what reasonably cannot be foreseen, nor for failing to achieve mastery over the highly exceptional case. Prudence fulfills the definition of virtue inasmuch as it ensures that a prudent person will act well in the majority of instances. But Christian prudence aided by the gift of Counsel compensates for the limitations of practical reasoning through the action of the Holy Spirit.

Prudence differs from art, which is concerned not with the good things that a person does, but with the good things or artifacts that a person can make. Because prudence must produce good human conduct, only well-tempered passion ultimately ensures that one who knows the truth about moral conduct will act so as to achieve the good end of the moral virtues. To put it differently, only

---

[28] Leo XIII, "Libertas praestantissimum," citing Aquinas, *Summa theologiae* Ia-IIae q. 90, a. 1.

[29] Within the perspectives of a realist epistemology, particularization depends on the activity of the senses, but it belongs to the internal senses, especially the *vis cogitativa* or the *ratio particularis* to form the composite of the individual sensible object. For further information on these notions, see Thomas V. Flynn, O.P., "The Cogitative Power," *The Thomist* XVI (1953): 542–563.

[30] The many and varied contingencies of human life make it extremely difficult to ensure that prudence will achieve its appropriate goal: a good human action. Since human appetites do not observe the regularity that other physical bodies or mathematical entities do, ethics, and other life sciences in general, do not attain the same degree of certitude that one finds in the physical or mathematical sciences. Conscience merely applies the judgment of practical reason to particular circumstances, so even a well-formed conscience does not ensure that its "dictate" (*dictamen*) will *per force* result in a good human action.

well-formed rational and sense appetites can guarantee the truth-claim of the minor premise of a practical syllogism, for instance, "at this time, and under these circumstances, I should not now take *this* drink." Pure moral deontologies completely miss this point. "Kant's categorical imperative," explains von Balthasar, "has not escaped the danger of unbending harshness, for his formalism made him place abstract 'duty' over against the natural 'inclination' of the sensible part of our being." [31] Prudence then must involve the shaping of both intellect and appetites. As an intellectual virtue, prudence seeks to establish objective truth in the context of the here and now moral situation. But as a virtue of the practical intellect, prudence also relies on the rectitude of the appetites, with the result that whatever judgment prudence makes concretely fulfills the finalities of human nature. This is why prudence qualifies as a virtue *simpliciter*; it renders a person outrightly good. By themselves, the intellectual virtues only achieve some formal aspect of human perfection, such as truth. In simpler terms, excellence of mind and excellence of character constitute different realities; as a moral virtue or *habitus*, prudence makes its possessor good and renders good what he or she does. But as a *recta ratio agibilium*, prudence specifically concerns the actual performance of good human acts.

The Christian tradition especially associates prudence with watchful solicitude. According to the Latin Vulgate version, First Peter urges us: "Estote prudentes, et vigilate in orationibus," that is, "Be prudent, watching out for your prayer life" (1 Pt 4: 7). Christian prudence requires care about the important matters of life and even a right measure of disquiet when opportune. Aristotle describes the magnanimous person as one who maintains an easy-going posture and enjoys leisure. [32] Aquinas modifies this overly confident description; he describes the person who lives according to Christian prudence as one who remains tranquil, "not because she or he is not solicitous about anything, but because the prudent person is not over-anxious about many things, but remains confident and unworried over matters where one ought to have trust." [33]

4. PRUDENCE AND THE MORAL VIRTUES

Prudence signifies a perfection of human intelligence applied to action. The rectitude of prudence lies in its bearing upon the true, ultimate end of human existence. Prudence supplies a "word"about human action, a moral *logos*, that establishes a ground or condition for acting. Thus, prudential action always

---

[31] "Nine Theses," (7), p. 118.
[32] See *Nicomachean Ethics* Bk 4, chap. 3 (1124b24).
[33] *Summa theologiae* IIa-IIae q. 47, a. 9, ad 3.

leads to the end of human growth and perfection.[34] But how does prudence effectively guide the other moral virtues?

First of all, prudence helps the believer settle upon the right means to achieve a good moral objective. In one text, moreover, Aquinas remarks that "prudence directs the moral virtues not only in making a choice about the means, but also in appointing the end."[35] In the here and now situation, prudence points the person toward the concretization of the good ends that constitute human flourishing. The proper operation of prudence thus requires that all of a person's appetitive powers (especially the sense appetites) bear on the complex of good ends that compose the well-being of an individual. Because human appetites can reach out only for the good, prudence depends on the moral virtues.

We need to make an important distinction about prudence and the ends of human life, about how prudence develops human nature with its specific capacities and built-in teleologies. The directive function of prudence does not mean that it actually establishes or appoints (*præstituat*) the particular end or *telos* that formally defines each of the moral virtues. Rather, as Aquinas puts it, prudence "arranges our activities which serve to reach [these ends]."[36] In the order of intention, ends function as starting points, not merely as goals. Each human person possesses an instinctive understanding of the principles of practical action; the scholastics called this capacity *synderesis*.[37] In a particularly illuminating passage, Aquinas explains the relationship that exists between prudence, which develops out of *synderesis*, and the ends of the moral virtues:

> The end of the moral virtues is theirs, not as though they themselves appoint it, but because they stretch out to it as set for them by natural reason. In this they are helped by prudence, which opens the way and arranges the steps to be taken. We are left with the conclusion that prudence ranks above and charges the moral virtues; still *synderesis* moves prudence, rather as insight into principles advances into scientific knowledge.[38]

In this text, Aquinas compares *synderesis* to the direct grasp of first principles in any science through the power of insight. Prudence so develops these principles that the prudent person's actions serve to achieve and realize the end of

---

[34] For further background to this notion, see Joseph Owens, C.Ss.R., "How Flexible Is Aristotelian 'Right Reason'?" in *The Georgetown Symposium of Ethics. Essays in Honor of Henry Babcock Veatch* (Lanham, MD, 1984), pp. 49–65.

[35] See his treatment of the relationship of the intellectual virtues to the moral virtues and *Summa theologiae* Ia-IIae q. 66, a. 3 ad 3.

[36] *Summa theologiae* IIa-IIae q. 47, a. 6: "Et ideo ad prudentiam non pertinet praestituere finem virtutibus moralibus, sed solum disponere de his quae sunt ad finem."

[37] For further information, see *Summa theologiae* Ia q. 79, a. 12 and *De veritate* q. 16, a. 1.

[38] *Summa theologiae* IIa-IIae q. 47, a. 6, ad 3.

the moral virtues. Such a construal of the moral life reflects a long-standing Christian tradition; indeed Aquinas develops the rich suggestion of the late-fifth-century Christian author Pseudo-Dionysius, namely, that "even before the external distinction appeared between the virtuous man and his opposite, the ultimate distinction between the virtues and the vices existed long beforehand in the soul itself." [39] Aquinas phrases it with greater succinctness, "the ends of the moral virtues pre-exist in reason." [40]

What is the significance of the fact that the ends of the moral virtues already exist in some fashion in human reason itself? For a person concretely to discover the mean of any moral virtue denotes that he or she actually attains the end or *telos* of the virtue. But in any individual and contingent action, such an attainment requires more than what a simple grasp of first principles provides. Recall that prudence principally constitutes a form of reasoning. In particular, this virtue involves discursive reasoning in search of practical truth through collecting and appreciating all of the contingencies that mark a given situation. The moral theologian distinguishes between the virtuous mean in the formal sense and in the material sense. The formal mean of any virtue signifies the actual definition of the mean, that is, the right reason that universally defines the end of a moral virtue; the material mean of a virtue signifies the same rational measure as actually realized in a concrete circumstance. Whereas ethical theorists can identify and specify the formal mean of a moral virtue, only the proper exercise of discursive prudence achieves here and now the moral good as actually determined by right reason for a particular situation. [41] Critics of virtue-centered moral theory sometimes suggest that, while narrative accounts or depictions of virtue may describe moral character, virtue in itself does little to help a person make a moral choice. [42] Such criticisms fail to grasp how prudence concretizes the moral good.

Prudence puts right reason into human emotion. Between the first glint of *synderesis* and the proper act of prudence that is command, the mature moral person develops a well-defined structure of practical reasoning. Moral philosophers distinguish at least three distinct moments within this development: first, a stage of universal moral reflection, the pre-scientific grasp of

---

[39] *De divinibus nominibus* chap. 4 (*PG* 3: 733), trans. C. E. Rolt, *The Divine Names and The Mystical Theology* (London, 1920), p. 112.

[40] *Summa theologiae* IIa-IIae q. 47, a. 6.

[41] In his commentary on the *secunda secundae*, q. 47, a. 7, no. II, Cajetan writes: "... formaliter, pro ipsa medii ratione ; materialiter, pro re denominata media... Primo modo est bonitas rationis ; secundo modo est res bona bonitate rationis. Primo modo est finis moralis virtutis, secundo autem est id quod est ad finem."

[42] For example, see Raphael Gallagher's review of Servais Pinckaers, *L'Evangile et la morale* (Fribourg/Paris, 1990) in *Studia Moralia* 29 (1991): 484–488.

moral principles; second, the appearance of moral science or ethics;[43] third, the act of conscience, or a practical judgment made by applying moral knowledge to a particular act, that is either about to be done or already accomplished. The scholastic theologians accordingly interpreted prudence after the model of a demonstrative syllogism. Speculative discursive reasoning involves at least two operations of the intellect: (a) the seizure of first principles of speculative reason through the quasi-*habitus* of understanding (*intellectus*), and (b) subsequent acts of judgment and reasoned demonstration that develop the conclusions of a particular science. In this way, human intelligence develops its potential or capacity for true moral knowledge. Unlike the syllogism of the speculative intellect, the practical syllogism of prudence entails a movement from the order of intention (*actus signatus*) to the order of execution (*actus exercitus*). In other words, the person of purely speculative learning can choose whether to act in accord with what he or she knows or not, but the prudent person who chooses to act must always act prudently, that is, in accord with the principles of proven moral science. It is important to note that, even though the judgment of conscience concerns a particular case, this judgment still remains *in pura cognitione*, that is, purely in the order of cognition. Only prudence ensures that the right judgments of conscience move a person to accomplish *virtuous actions*.

As an intellectual virtue, prudence shapes the individual moral conscience in harmony with authentic human ends, and from this synergy of right reason and moral virtue, a person's conscience receives its executive power. As so many unhappy cases illustrate, any person can suffer from an ill-formed conscience. Take the case of assisted reproduction that involves artificial insemination. A spouse may think that a given set of (extraordinary) circumstances permits a man to masturbate in order to obtain semen samples; and today, given the encouragement and counsel of medical personnel, the same individual arguably remains in a state of invincible ignorance. However, in a moral analysis that takes virtue seriously, the casuist concern for subjective responsibility or culpability in fact retains a quite peripheral place. Although the husband may conscientiously hold the view that masturbation for the sake of obtaining semen constitutes a permissible exception to the mean of chastity, because chastity always excludes the auto-erotic behavior, such a person unfortunately abides in moral error. As long as it accurately reflects the eternal law, right practical reasoning can never validate a judgment of conscience that particular circumstances allow for masturbation. Moreover, the Church's Mag-

---

[43] Recall that the contingency and uncertainty of human events makes the science of ethics more of a reasoned opinion than a sure science, but the grace of Christ establishes its own sort of certainty in the moral life that allows theological ethics to lay claim to a sureness that our natural resources fail to provide.

isterium in *Donum vitae* explicitly teaches otherwise. Accordingly, even when the invincibly ignorant husband masturbates, the action remains a bad action and carries with it the inherent punishment that abides in all disordered activity. [44] In sum, an erroneous conscience can never provide the basis for an action that furthers the perfection of the human person. The believer who is shaped by prudence is saved from an erroneous conscience through his or her personal knowledge of moral truth.

Prudence aims at shaping the character of Christian believers so that they can participate fully in the communion of charity that abides in the Church. In the moral life of each person, the virtue of prudence must both conform and be conformed: prudence must be conformed to moral wisdom, i.e., to all that human intelligence can learn about a given subject. Prudence also learns from divine truth. In turn, prudence conforms human behavior, so that human action lies *ad finem*, that is, in accord with the right direction that the ends or goods of human nature stipulate. Prudence brings us into a right conformity with the "thing" or *res*, with reality as God knows the world to be. Unlike the good musician who may "know" how to play a false note, the prudent person is unable voluntarily to commit an imprudence, even though, as we have seen, involuntary error may produce a false conscience and a special kind of moral situation.

Prudence moves the human person to action; the prudent man or woman actually behaves in a virtuous way and does not simply deliberate about how to act. Whereas imperative decision constitutes the chief act of prudence, the Christian tradition nevertheless distinguishes three moments in the realization of a prudential act: counsel, judgment, and command. Counsel involves a rational deliberation about means to an end. This process of seeking counsel requires that the prudent person already enjoy the rectitude of appetite that bears upon the end of the moral virtues. Otherwise, disordered emotions would inevitably unsettle the deliberative process, with the result that such a person would be inclined to seek counsel from those who share his or her own disordered bent. In the traditional scheme, counsel is to be distinguished from "consent" (*consensus*), or the affective settling onto means that effectively moves the person to the second act of prudence, which is judgment. Judgment involves a rational determination or decision that strengthens the affective settling onto means that "consent" achieves. The judgment of prudence responds to the question: "What am I to do now?" The virtue of prudence ensures that this judgment makes a determination that falls within the legitimate ambit of moral virtue; but as I have said, a poorly formed conscience can frustrate the effective realization of this judgment.

---

[44]   On this, see the teaching of *Veritatis splendor*, no. 63.

To make a well-reasoned judgment about what is to be done here and now never guarantees that a person acts upon the judgment; human action requires an imperative motion from the intellect. As the principal act of the virtue of prudence, command transforms the judgment of conscience into an imperative: command accounts for the existential coming-to-be of the virtuous action. In a realist view of human action, the act of command (*imperium*) remains an intellectual act, not an act principally associated with the will. [45] But because command carries this imperative note, prudence is to be distinguished from a simply intellectual virtue. For this cardinal virtue, as I have said, enters into the formal act of a moral virtue, namely, to choose the good *simpliciter* or outrightly. In this view, *recta ratio* intervenes in the behavioral virtues at a point where the inclination of appetite meets the act of choice or election that prudence brings to completion by its act of command. The true exercise of Christian prudence corrects the Socratic fallacy that identifies virtue with simple knowledge of the right things to do. Instead it endows the believer with the full power of the Holy Spirit to accomplish "whatever is true, whatever is honorable, whatever is just, whatever is pure, whatever is pleasing, whatever is commendable" (Phil 4: 8). [46]

5. THE ELEMENTS OF PRUDENCE

For each of the cardinal virtues, the scholastic theologians identified three classifications of parts. These classifications help us to organize the variety of virtues that are clustered around the cardinal virtue. The basis for the distinction lies in the various ways that philosophers divide a whole: an integral whole, a subjective whole, and a potential whole. Like the integral parts of an organic body, there are the component parts of a virtue; whatever belongs essentially to the constitution of a virtue is called an *integral part*. Like the species contained in a genus, there are the specific types of a generic virtue; these are its *subjective parts*. Like the various active powers of a living substance, there are the virtues accessory or allied to the principal virtue; these are called its *potential parts*. Take the rational soul as an instructive example of a potential whole: the other capacities or *potentiae* of the human soul, *viz*, its vegetative and sensitive functions, participate to the extent that they are able

---

[45] See *Summa theologiae* Ia-IIae, q. 17.

[46] Prudence forms the basis for good spiritual direction. Although certain classical schools advise that one obey the directives of a spiritual director, this does not conform to the view of Aquinas. Rather one should seek as a "spiritual director" a man or woman of prudence, on whose virtue one can rely to shape one's counsel. For this reason, Dominican obedience, while it requires that one ordinarily obey a superior without good counsel (that is, an incompetent person), never requires that the subject modify his or her thinking (i.e., prudence) so as to conform to the ill-advised counsel or judgment.

in the rationality of the human soul. The following schema summarizes the standard teaching on the three different parts or classes of sub-virtues that fall under the four cardinal virtues.

Schema Of Parts

1. *Integral Parts*: These parts of the moral virtues represent the characteristic activities or psychological dispositions that any moral virtue requires in order to accomplish its proper act; as component parts, these traits or characteristics do not constitute distinct virtues.

2. *Parts That Realize The Same Formal Type*:

 A. *Subjective Parts*: These virtues represent the different species of a cardinal virtue; as real virtues (*habitus*), they possess the full and univocal realization of the virtue in question. What qualifies any virtue as a subjective part of a cardinal virtue is that the virtue fully realizes the generic definition of the cardinal virtue.

 B. *Potential Parts*: The potential parts of a cardinal virtue, though they constitute real virtues in themselves, realize the formal type of the cardinal virtue only in an analogous, i.e., restricted, way. While an allied virtue represents a diminishment of the full cardinal virtue as a type, it can happen, as in the case of the relationship of religion to justice, that a potential part of a cardinal virtue represents a more noble expression of human behavior than the cardinal virtue to which it is allied.

5.1. THE INTEGRAL AND SUBJECTIVE PARTS OF PRUDENCE

The integral parts of prudence are its component elements. While prudence needs the moral virtues in order to function properly, the prudent person also needs a variety of qualities or traits so that he or she can undertake the distinctively discursive reasoning that marks prudence. The Christian tradition names eight integral parts of prudence; together they provide a psychological sketch of the character type that can both recognize and enact moral truth. It can happen that in a given person, these qualities are phenomenally uneven, but the *habitus* of prudence compensates and corrects for any extreme irregularity. As an intellectual virtue, prudence requires: (1) memory; (2) intuition (insight/intelligence); (3) docility (teachableness); (4) sagacity (acumen); (5) reason (reasoned judgment) and as an imperative or prescriptive virtue, (6) foresight; (7) circumspection; (8) caution. [47] Consider the example of a driver approaching an intersection.

---

[47]   The Latin terms are variously translated into modern languages; for further information on English usage, see vol. 36 of the Blackfriars translation of the *Summa theologiae* IIa-IIae q. 49, aa. 1–8.

I approach a familiar intersection [memory] and am alerted to what practical wisdom may immediately provide about dealing with intersections [intuition], some of which I may have learned during the driving lessons that cost dearly [docility]. Sizing up the actual situation of the moment [sagacity], I come to a decision about how to proceed through the intersection [reason]. However, at this moment, I am still at the stop sign. Now, with the recognition that the stalled vehicle on the other side of the road will not impede movement through the intersection [foresight], and with due regard for other possible impediments to free movement [circumspection], I *move to* put my foot to the gas and proceed, though still with a certain wariness that an on-rushing car may yet appear in an instant [caution].

The example stops at the point of command, for at that moment, the virtue achieves its perfection, and human action comes to rest in its appropriate term.

The subdivisions or subjective parts of prudence include not only the prudence needed to govern one's own life (monastic prudence), but also that required for special undertakings, such as the military life, or for assuming the burdens of civil governance that is ordained to promote the well-being of the common good. Thus, statesmanship and lawmaking belong to those who hold authority in self-contained communities. Political prudence differs from individual prudence, and because of the former's role in directing the common good, it enjoys a certain excellence over individual prudence.

5.2. THE POTENTIAL PARTS OF PRUDENCE

The potential parts of prudence aid the first two acts of prudence: counsel and judgment. Since the principal act of prudence, *imperium*, belongs to the cardinal virtue itself, no allied or potential part strengthens the principal act of the virtue. However, there is a principle which claims that whenever there exists a distinctive end, there also exists the need for a distinct virtue. Aquinas states the principle this way: "A distinction of the various virtues should be drawn according to the distinction of activities which are not to be resolved into the same cause." [48] So the other acts of prudence do require strengthening by allied or potential virtues. Good counsel, *eubulia*, strengthens the act of counsel; whereas judiousness (*synesis*) and farsightedness (*gnome*), both strengthen the act of judgment.

Aquinas maintains Aristotle's Greek term *eubulia* for the virtue of good counsel or well-advisedness in investigation. This activity is not resolved into the same cause as prudence. (This is evident in the fact that some people excel in offering good counsel to themselves and to others, and still remain congenitally unable to move beyond this point.) *Eubulia*, then, promotes a particular

---

[48] See *Summa theologiae* IIa-IIae q. 51, a. 3.

good end, namely, to enable a person to develop the practice of seeking and giving good counsel. [49] Likewise, the virtues of *synesis* or judiciousness and *gnome* or farsightedness constitute special virtues; for they too strengthen a person to achieve distinctive goals within the larger scope of a prudential life. In the case of these virtues, the particular activity that requires the strength of distinctive *habitus* is judgment. *Synesis* is sound judgment about ordinary matters. It differs from prudence, for, as Aquinas again explains: "Sometimes it happens that a well-judged deed is put off or done carelessly or improperly. And so, to crown the virtue of sound judgment, a principal virtue is needed, which is well and truly imperative: such is prudence." [50] *Gnome* signifies sharp-sightedness or perspicacity of judgment in the face of circumstances other than what constitutes the normal routine. Aquinas observes that some people excel in this virtue; moreover, because to judge rightly about extraordinary matters in every circumstance betrays a mark of divine providence, such persons are rightly called wise men or women. [51]

6. THE VICES OPPOSED TO PRUDENCE

By definition, a virtuous action achieves an authentic or true moral good through the instrumentality of well-regulated reason. In this way, virtue perfects a person by making, as Aristotle puts it, both an action and the one who performs it good. Vice, on the other hand, generates actions that are not in conformity with the rule of right reason, so that, either through excess or by defect, all vicious actions instantiate a definite form of evil. As a matter of fact, the mean of a particular virtue often resembles one vicious extreme more than another; or, to put it differently, certain vices more easily masquerade as virtue than others. For instance, insensitivity frequently appears more like true temperance than the excess of debauchery does or, to some persons, foolhardiness might resemble fortitude more than the defect of timidity. Generally speaking, the virtues attached to temperance more closely resemble their defective forms and those associated with fortitude more their excessive forms. The defective forms of prudence, imprudence and negligence, deform one or another of prudence's distinguishing acts: counsel, judgment, and command. By contrast with these flawed forms of prudence, there also exist several species of counterfeit prudence, that is, a prudence that is ordered to a dishonest end.

---

[49] For further information, see *Summa theologiae* IIa-IIae q. 51, aa. 1, 2.

[50] See *Summa theologiae* IIa-IIae q. 51, a. 3, ad 3. Because in matters of exceptional cases one needs to invoke certain unique principles, the wit to judge the cases of this kind differs from ordinary *synesis*

[51] See *Summa theologiae* IIa-IIae q. 51, a. 4.

6.1. IMPRUDENCE

Just as prudence plays a guiding part in all moral virtue, so imprudence is at work in all sin and vice. In particular, imprudence covers a number of sinful actions that alter the poise that prudence requires to achieve its goal of a good moral choice. Precipitousness or undue haste in taking action obstructs the virtue of *eubulia* or good counsel. Inconsideration or thoughtlessness impedes the virtue of sound judgment. And the sins of inconstancy and negligence strike at the heart of prudence itself, by weakening the person's resolve to follow through on the command or *imperium*. Because of the architectonic role that prudence plays in the moral life, these sinful dispositions and actions affect, as I have said, every aspect of the virtuous life.

Consider for example the person who acts with precipitation, *viz*, the truly inconsiderate person. Though it is not virtuous to deliberate endlessly about a course of action, still less does it become a person not to reflect at all on his or her behavior; recall the Proverb, "The man of discretion watches how he treads" (Prov 14: 15). But because many persons consider themselves to be their own best friend and since even more persons cherish a false notion of personal responsibility and autonomy, men and women more often than not are reluctant to take counsel from anyone other than themselves. The inconsiderate person proves that the unexamined life is not worth living. The best remedy for an inconsiderate attitude consists in seeking conscientiously the counsel of mature men and women, especially in the important areas of life. For the Christian believer, the Magisterium provides an authentic source of good counsel.

Imprudence further manifests itself when a person makes superficial judgments or when someone judges according to standards that are entirely subjective. On the other hand, a firm attachment to perpetual reflection also impedes the making of sound judgments; this happens in those persons who foster a never-ending state of hesitation about a proper course to follow. If we consider conscience as an act of particular judgment that applies moral principles to specific circumstances, imprudence effectively distorts the judgment of conscience. Contrary to what moral subjectivism holds, an individual conscience does not form an infallible guide for realizing a good life. [52]

Finally, the vices opposed to prudence include inconstancy or the affective blocking of prudent directions. Inconstancy results in giving up on a decided course, "for a person is called inconstant when reason fails to carry out ef-

---

[52] See the very illuminating section of *Veritatis splendor*, no. 62 which explains why though non-culpable error of judgment may not be imputable to the agent, the evil done still does not cease to be an evil, a disorder in relation to the truth about the good.

fectively what he or she has thought about and decided upon." [53] The vice of inconstancy manifests the unity of the moral life which is based on the inescapable relationship between sound judgment and rectified appetite. And although inconstancy ordinarily stems from an appetitive source, it is principally a failure of the mind to follow through upon a resolve. [54] Even Aristotle reckoned the power of pleasure to impair the judgment of reason. In the Christian life, Gregory the Great specifies that unchastity or lust most frequently fosters imprudence. [55] "The lustful person," says one spiritual author, "will usually be found to have a terrible hollowness at the center of his life, and he is agitated to fill it, not daring to desist, lest he should have to confront the desert he has made of himself." [56] In this perpetual state of agitation lies one of the root causes of the sins against prudence.

Aquinas defines negligence as "a certain slackness of will which results in the reason's not being solicitous about coming to effective decisions on things that ought to be done and how they ought to be done." [57] The Christian tradition considers such negligence as a special sin against prudence. The casuists, who were very concerned with subjective responsibility, expended much energy discussing the conditions for due knowledge and culpability. However, if one can judge from the modest treatment that Aquinas gives to the topic, it seems that the patristic tradition of morality that he interprets and mediates adopts an entirely different emphasis about negligence. A person can lack sufficient energy for gaining the necessary knowledge required for good behavior or, on the other hand, fail to put into execution a good proposal that is already decided upon. The sinful attitude that negligence describes represents less a particular vice and more a psychological attitude or state that fosters different vices. Since imprudence never occurs in isolation from other moral faults, the negligent person remains prone to further sin. This proclivity to rest in unhappy ignorance accounts for its particular viciousness.

6.2. COUNTERFEIT PRUDENCE

The distortions of prudence frequently result from unchastity, but other moral faults produce counterfeit versions of prudence. For prudence can also appear in false guises. This happens either when a person develops prudence-like qualities in order to achieve an end that does not conduce to true happiness (for

---

[53] *Summa theologiae* IIa-IIae q. 53, a. 5.

[54] See the interesting description in *Summa theologiae* IIa-IIae q. 53, a. 6, ad 3 that Aquinas gives of continence and perseverance as forms of constancy in the reason, where there also exists inconstancy.

[55] For Aristotle, see *Nicomachean Ethics* Bk 6, chap. 5 (1140b13 ff.) and for Gregory the Great, see the *Moralia* Bk 31, chap. 45 (*PL* 76: 621).

[56] Henry Fairlie, *The Seven Deadly Sins Today*, (Notre Dame, IN, 1978), p. 187.

[57] *Summa theologiae* IIa-IIae q. 54, a. 3.

instance, when one makes bodily comfort an ultimate goal), or when a person wittingly adopts improper means in order to achieve a good goal. Because persons with uncontrolled wants easily substitute their own providence for the guidance that reflects the eternal law, the tradition names avarice as the capital vice responsible for turning a person away from the designs of divine providence.

The first species of counterfeit prudence is carnal or fleshly prudence. The person who possesses this imitation of virtuous prudence pursues the disordered interests of his or her own self; as a form of exaggerated egoism, the carnally prudent person looks after created goods first and last. Carnal prudence belongs, for example, to the miser who masters every possible way to gain a profit or to the Don Juan who masters every form of seduction that leads to sexual gratification. Authentic prudence of course does look after material things, but within an ordered hierarchy of goods, as when one maintains a careful diet in order to study better (Aquinas's own example!). [58] For prudence regulates a person's embrace of the goods of human flourishing so that they remain ordered within the context of a complete and good life and, in the case of infused prudence, the virtue ensures that these goods conduce to the perfect happiness of the saints, *beatitudo*.

Cunning, guile, and deception describe those circumstances "when in pursuit of some end, whether right or wrong, a person takes ways that are not genuine, but feigned and specious." [59] The cunning, guileful, and deceptive person pursues resourceful ways to hide from himself or herself as well as from others the evil means taken for accomplishing an objective. The goals may be respectable in themselves, but because of the deceitful approach that such people take to achieve them, the moral action is vitiated. If words are used to perpetrate the deceit, we call the counterfeit prudence cunning or guile; if the duplicity involves actions, then it is cheating. This form of false prudence usually reveals the presence of a deeper spiritual disease; Nietzsche spoke about the penchant in the modern era for people to turn false before themselves, to serve as their own self-executioners. Those unable to love themselves properly are most tempted to fall victim to sham prudence. Since spiritual orphans lack the conviction about their self-worth, they experience difficulty in being honest about how they pursue even their worthwhile goals. The cunning person attempts to live a double life. For it can happen that a cunning person wants to please God in some areas, but to please himself or herself inordinately in others.

---

[58] *Summa theologiae* IIa-IIae q. 55, a. 2.
[59] *Summa theologiae* IIa-IIae q. 55, a. 3.

As a remedy for the duplicity that marks cunning, guile, and deception, the New Testament repeatedly urges the believer to trust that God will provide whatever good things are necessary for life. False prudence effectively subordinates a loving confidence in divine providence to care for one's temporal life; this vice shapes a person to appreciate those things that are less important for human fulfillment and to depreciate or to ignore completely those things that remain indispensable for perfect happiness. Again, Christian wisdom warns that lust and covetousness foster imprudence and mock prudence.

St Gregory the Great develops an instructive list of the fruits that accompany the capital vices of avarice and lust:

> From avarice there spring treachery, fraud, deceit, perjury, restlessness, violence and hardness of heart against compassion. ... From lust are generated blindness of mind, inconsiderateness, inconstancy, precipitation, self-love, hatred of God, affection for this present world, but dread or despair of that which is to come. [60]

Since the person who sins against prudence mocks the counsels of God, these vices strike directly at the heart of what is required for biblical faith conceived as a trusting confidence in the care of the heavenly Father. The person without prudence becomes self-absorbed in a disordered love of self, with the result that he or she loses the spiritual capacity to perceive the reality of divine providence and to appreciate the gratuity of the divine love. Such a person remains stunted in the life of faith, for he or she has not yet learned how to say authentically the prayer that distinguishes the disciples of Jesus from all others, to address God confidently as Father.

Since it transcends the narrow limits of personal self-interest, truly virtuous prudence represents the highest achievement of the spiritual life. Recall that "one cannot serve God and mammon" (Mt 7: 24). Trust in the providence of the heavenly Father sets the standard for a proper solicitude about the things of this life. The Christian tradition, in sum, recognizes in the prudent person one who looks at the birds of the air and considers carefully the lilies of the field (see Mt 7: 25–34). No other attitude lies open for the man or woman who would rely fully on divine truth as the ultimate rational measure for living a happy life. [61]

7. THE GIFT OF COUNSEL

In his general introduction to the gifts of the Holy Spirit, Aquinas makes a curious reference to the insight of the ancient philosophers: "Aristotle," reports Aquinas, "says that it is not good for those who are moved by a divine prompt-

---

[60]   Gregory the Great, *Moralia* Bk 31, chap. 45.

[61]   For a profound study of the relationship of asceticism to the prudent life, see L.-B. Geiger, O.P., *Philosophie et Spiritualité* (Paris, 1963), pp. 318–322.

ing to take counsel according to human reason; but that they should follow their interior prompting, because they are moved by a better principle than human reason." [62] Aquinas is not suggesting that the divine promptings of the gifts are adequately understood by pagan philosophy. Rather, he indisputably centers his general teaching on the gifts around the virtue of charity. "The gifts of the Holy Spirit," he writes, "are connected with one another in charity, in such wise that one who has charity has all the gifts of the Holy Spirit, while none of the gifts can be had without charity." [63] While it may seem odd for Aquinas to introduce so distinctively Christian a reality as the gifts of the Holy Spirit by referring to classical philosophy, we can appreciate how this text suggests the special help that the gift of Counsel brings to prudence.

The general rule that explains why any virtue requires the assistance of a gift holds true for the virtue of prudence. There remains a real lack of proportion between what any virtue, even an infused moral virtue, can achieve in a person and the final end of the Christian life that lies in *beatitudo*. In his treatise on the *Flight from the World*, St Ambrose expresses this disproportion in distinctively Christian terms.

> We have died with Christ. We carry about in our bodies the sign of his death, so that the living Christ may also be revealed in us. The life we live is not now our ordinary life but the life of Christ: a life of sinlessness, of chastity, of simplicity and every other virtue. [64]

To observe St Ambrose's language, the gift of Counsel subordinates the *imperium* or command of infused prudence to the new life of Christ that belongs to every believer. Because prudence enjoys a directive role in the moral life, Counsel also enjoys a certain priority over the other moral virtues and the gifts that assist them. Accordingly, Counsel directs the virtue of justice, with its gift of Piety; the virtue of fortitude, with its gift of Courage; the virtue of temperance, with its gift of the Fear of the Lord.

Because of its fundamentally probative character, even infused prudence requires the aid that the gift of Counsel brings. Since the practical reason operates in a discursive manner, there exists a variety of ways for the practical reason to fail in grasping or discerning the moral good. The ordinary counsel-taking and deliberation that prudence requires withstands only with great difficulty the conglomeration of unsettling factors, especially the commotion that

---

[62] *Summa theologiae* Ia-IIae q. 68, a. 1.

[63] *Summa theologiae* Ia-IIae q. 68, a. 5. The tradition correctly emphasizes that the gifts of the Holy Spirit work their effect on the moral life through the theological virtues, so that everything the Christian believes and hopes for plays an active role in the faithful exercise of Christian virtue.

[64] St Ambrose, *On Flight from the World*, chap. 6, 36; chap. 7, 44; chap. 8, 45; chap. 9, 52 (*CSEL* vol. 32, pp. 192, 198–199, 204).

disordered passions cause. And such factors can tilt prudence's effective operation. Moreover, since even virtuous counsel naturally follows the measure of
human reasoning, the soul's journey to God requires a special guidance from
the Holy Spirit. This guidance, however, does not amount to the bestowal of
new information, as if a gift of the Holy Spirit supplies the believer with personal revelations. Rather, counsel works by conaturality; that is, it develops
out of a familiarity with divine things that grace gives to the human person.
Aquinas explains the relationship of prudence to the gift of Counsel in the
following way:

> Prudence or *eubulia*, whether acquired or infused, directs us in our searchings
> into matters that our minds can grasp, and enables us to be of good counsel for
> ourselves or for others. Still, because of our mind's inability to grasp all individ-
> ual and contingent events that can possibly happen, it happens that "the thoughts
> of mortal men are fearful and our counsels uncertain" (Wis 9: 14). Consequently
> we need in our searchings the guidance of God, who knows all things. This
> comes through the gift of Counsel, whereby we are guided by the advice, as it
> were, of God, rather as in human affairs those who are not sufficiently qualified
> to work things out for themselves require the counsel of wiser persons. [65]

This text makes explicit that the light of the Holy Spirit helps infused prudence
to discover the just mean for human actions in a way that harkens willingly to
the salvific instruction that we discover in the Church.

Prudence involves a complex of virtues that strengthen the acts of command, judgment, and counsel. The acts of judgment and counsel, it is true,
already rely on the special virtues of *synesis*, *gnome*, and *eubulia* But the act
of counsel especially requires divine assistance, for "it conveys the notion of
the mind being moved to ponder under the influence of another's advising." [66]
In the case of Christian prudence, God serves as the principal Other who advises those who seek to know the truth that makes one free (see Jn 8: 31). In
Aquinas's view, since "the eternal law provides the supreme rule for all human
rectitude," the truth that Christ communicates to his disciples reveals in human
terms the hidden mysteries of the eternal law. [67] "With all wisdom and insight,"
says St Paul, "God has made known to us the mystery of his will, according to
his good pleasure that he set forth in Christ, as a plan for the fullness of time,
to gather up all things in him, things in heaven and things on earth" (Eph 1:
8 – 10). As a pledge of abundant divine pleasure and with confident assurance,
the gift of Counsel aids prudence, provided that the believer remains open to
the good advice of others, and, in the final analysis, of God himself.

---

[65] *Summa theologiae* IIa-IIae q. 52, a. 1, ad 1.
[66] *Summa theologiae* IIa-IIae q. 52, a. 2, ad 1.
[67] *Summa theologiae* IIa-IIae q. 52, a. 2.

In the Christian life, all require instruction. The gift of Counsel effectively helps the believer remain in the Church as a learner. In the state of fallen nature, the human person ordinarily finds it easier to set his or her life in motion than to suffer being set in motion; but this propensity for moral autonomy falls short of the mark set by Christian revelation. While the tension that arises in the believer who must continually depend on the work of the Holy Spirit for perfecting good counsel disappears in the saints, Aquinas maintains that the wayfarer who lives according to the gift of Counsel especially imitates the saints in heaven who remain in a state of a simple turning toward God – *simplex conversio ad Deum.* [68]

Instead of the legalistic minimum associated with the fulfillment of obligation, the life of the virtues and gifts achieves the maximum of Christian perfection. So since the time of St Augustine, the Christian tradition in moral theology associates one of the New Testament Beatitudes with each of the cardinal virtues and gifts. The Beatitudes represent the fullness of Gospel life. St Augustine names the fifth Beatitude, "Blessed are the merciful, for they will receive mercy" (Mt 5: 7), as the beatitude that best manifests the virtue of prudence and the gift of Counsel. He does so because the person who remains attentive to the counsels of the Holy Spirit above all heeds the important New Testament injunction to show mercy. But good Counsel ensures that the believer knows how to show mercy in a way that is neither sentimental nor mawkish. In other terms, well-counseled mercy never accompanies false compassion nor does it follow upon presumption about God's forgiveness. Mercy kisses truth and justice, as the Psalmist reminds us. Counsel abets mercy to the extent that it renders a believer docile to the eternal norm for all moral truth. In his commentary on Psalm 19, Aquinas summarizes the Christian perspective on the role of the gift of Counsel in the moral life.

> Firstly, "May he grant you your heart's desire," is interpreted to mean what you will, as it bears upon the end, as if the Psalmist were to say, may he lead you to the end which you yourself intend. The end is God, as Proverbs [10: 23] has it: the desire of the righteous ends only in good.
>
> Secondly, "Fulfill all you plans" is interpreted to mean those things which are pointed toward the end [*his quae sunt ad finem*]. Because we are unable to foresee everything, our counsels remain feeble, as Wisdom [9: 14] puts it: the reasoning of mortals is worthless, and our designs are likely to fail. God, however, wants to confirm us toward the Good and this in a twofold way: (1) by directing our counsels which should be concerned with actively seeking eternal life, as in John 16: 24: hitherto you have asked nothing in my name, ask, and you will receive; that your joy may be full; and (2) by his giving us what we need in order to pursue our good counsels toward the joyful possession of himself. [69]

---

[68] *Summa theologiae* IIa-IIae q. 52, a. 3.

[69] *In psalmos* xix, no. 2 (Vivès edition, vol. 18, p. 336). Aquinas composed the *Postilla super*

Because of his gracious love and concern for every human person, Jesus especially promises that the Counsel that comes from the Holy Spirit will never disappear from the Church. "I still have many things to say to you," the Gospel of John records Christ saying, "but you cannot bear them now. When the Spirit of truth comes, he will guide you into all the truth" (Jn 16:12, 13).

Psalmos toward the end of his life, *viz*, 1272 or 1273. He is using the Gallican Psalter of the Vulgate, which then was proper for Dominican liturgical usage. Psalm 19, verse 5 reads: "May he grant you your heart's desire, and fulfill all your plans! [... *tribuat tibi secundum cor tuum omne* concilium *tuum confirmet.*]"

CHAPTER 5
CHRISTIAN JUSTICE AND HUMAN SOCIETY

1. "BUT STRIVE FIRST FOR THE KINGDOM OF GOD AND HIS JUSTICE" (MT 6: 33)

In her call for a just social order, the Church urges us to consider the ambit of justice as co-extensive with the global community of nations. In *Gaudium et spes*, we read:

> The increasingly close interdependence which is gradually encompassing the entire world is leading to an increasing universal common good, the sum total of the conditions of social life enabling groups and individuals to realize their perfection more fully and readily, and this has implications for rights and duties affecting the whole human race. [1]

If, as the Council further requires, "any group must take into account the needs and legitimate desires of other groups and the common good of the entire human family," then a thorough treatment of the concrete issues involved in the virtue of justice would require much scientific investigation and analysis. [2]

In his *Summa theologiae*, Aquinas devotes sixty-six questions to this important topic of justice, and so helps us understand how best to develop and maintain human life in community. [3] This fact alone once led the English philosopher Peter Geach to remark that "justice is an immensely problematic concept: there are, in old jargon, many parts of justice – there are many strands plaited together, and each strand carries many knotty problems." [4] Since the end of the 19th century, the Church has especially articulated Christian social teaching, and so we are better able to interpret the problems of justice in the light of the gospel. In his encyclical letter that marked the centenary of Leo XIII's *Rerum novarum*, Pope John Paul II again underscores the Church's mis-

---

[1] *Gaudium et spes*, chap. 2, no. 26.

[2] Ibid.

[3] In Aquinas's conception, justice forms part of a larger view of the moral life. Thus, his view on justice itself remains partial unless one considers such themes as natural law, the various forms of communities that can exist within the Church (see *Summa theologiae* IIa-IIae qq. 183 – 189), and the more general discussion of justice and virtue that Aquinas gives in the *prima secundae*.

[4] Peter Geach, *The Virtues* (Cambridge, 1977), p. 110.

sion to address the many complicated problems that arise from a concern for justice.

> The Church, in fact, has something to say about specific human situations, both individual and communal, national and international. She formulates a genuine doctrine for these situations, a *corpus* which enables her to analyze social realities, to make judgments about them and to indicate directions to be taken for the just resolution of the problems involved.[5]

This means that the Christian theologian and other members of the Church rightfully confront social justice issues, but always with an eye to the larger perspectives of the *sacra doctrina*. As Jesus himself teaches, "But strive first for the kingdom of God and its justice, and all these things will be given to you as well" (Mt 6: 33).

In a broad but radical sense, justice constitutes a true virtue because other persons exist in the world; and so every truly responsible person must take account of the neighbor. For no individual, even if he or she lives alone, can escape from being involved in some form of human relationships. Cardinal justice, as *Gaudium et spes* reminds us, principally concerns one of the primary givens of human experience, namely, "otherness" – the *ad alterum*. The Sacred Scripture continually speaks of an active commitment to the other, the neighbor, and demands that each of us share responsibility for all of humankind. The virtuously just person, then, demonstrates an active concern for bettering the reciprocal relationships that comprise the moral universe of human society.

Above all, the Christian believer should in no wise feel obligated to yield to the secularist practitioners of political science when it comes to issues of public and private justice. Justice remains a true virtue of the Christian life. However, since democratic forms of government, by distinguishing sharply between the public and private sectors, more and more repudiate the role of custodian of human morality, there exists a new urgency for promoting a fully Christian participation in the social order. Because he developed St Augustine's doctrine of the "Two Cities," the contribution of Aquinas to a theological analysis of justice remains especially rich. The classical principles that Christian theologians have established since the patristic era still provide an indispensable source of wisdom for public discourse about justice; indeed these principles remain relevant to an assessment of the problems and ambiguities associated with the specifically modern phenomena of the "Social Assistance State." Today, then, the Church must render a theological service to human society "by preaching the truth about the creation of the world, which God has placed in human hands so that people may make it fruitful and more perfect through their work; and by preaching the truth about the Redemption, whereby the Son

---

[5]   *Centesimus annus*, chap. 1, no. 5.

of God has saved mankind and at the same time has united all people, making them responsible for one another." [6]

While the application of the principles of justice requires that the just man or woman take account of actual social circumstances, the success of this social analysis entails first an understanding of the nature of justice as a real virtue. For every interpersonal relationship develops from and involves an exchange among human persons, and, like any human activity, this civil conversation requires a measure of virtuous regulation. But what is more important, justice forms a truly behavioral virtue; as a *habitus* of character, then, justice really shapes the personal dispositions of the human subject so that he or she experiences the inclination to act justly. Pope John Paul II makes this point clearly: "The way in which man is involved in building his own future depends on the understanding he has of himself and of his own destiny. It is on this level that the Church's specific and decisive contribution to true culture is to be found." [7] In the final analysis, the transformation of the world is accomplished in the hearts of those who accept the gospel of truth.

2. THE *Justum*, OR THE RIGHT

Because it upholds the view that justice possesses a purely objective foundation, Aquinas's notion of justice differs radically from most political theories that derive from Enlightenment thought. Indeed, for the Christian tradition as a whole, the virtue of justice rests upon what the Latin theologians called a *jus*. Unfortunately for realist moral theology, the English language translates *jus* as "right." But, in this context, the denotation of *jus* does not fully coincide with what the Anglo-American tradition normally understands by "right" in a politico-juridical sense. As contrasted with "positive" right, *jus* signifies something essentially inherent in a subject, not posited by legislative will or customary agreement. The appeal to a pre-juridical and fundamentally creation-centered notion of right distinguishes Roman Catholic natural law morality from all forensic conceptions of justice. To speak of a natural premise for justice does not imply a crass empiricist view of human nature and the world, as if the laws of justice ultimately lay hidden in an arcane cosmology or a metaphysical biology. Rather, it simply points up that there is an objective interest in justice that lies outside of the conventions that a people or government may devise for safeguarding the well-being of a community.

Unlike the virtues of fortitude and temperance, to realize the virtuous mean of justice does not directly depend on the particular dispositions that exist in the virtuous person. In justice the mean is called a "mean of the thing" – *medium*

---

[6]   *Centesimus annus*, chap. 5, "State and Culture," no. 51.

[7]   Ibid.

rei, an impersonal measure determined by nature, law, or contract. For example, justice clearly requires that one pay a debt in full, whatever the particular feelings or attitudes the debtor may harbor toward her or his creditor. By contrast, it is impossible to conceive of a temperate action, for example, with respect to food, without knowing the particular capacities and dispositions of the abstemious person. For this reason, the Christian tradition holds that the objective interest of the virtue of justice lies in rendering voluntarily the due with an eye toward the common good. In other terms, one can make a concrete moral judgment concerning what is the just thing independently of rectified sense appetites, even if the person who lacks the other moral virtues appears as an unlikely candidate for fulfilling the requirements of this moral virtue.

Aquinas defines the *justum* as "that which is due another with equality." [8] Justice requires that in social relations whatever is done matches, or fits evenly to, or balances with the rights of others. So the proper characteristic of justice is rightly to govern the human person in his or her dealings with others, whether in dealings between persons or between persons and their community. Both "otherness," the *ad alterum* that makes justice possible, and equality, the *ad æqualitatem* to which justice reaches out, belong by definition to an integral notion of justice. So much is this the case that relationships are not measured by justice properly speaking if a true otherness does not exist between the concerned persons, as happens, for example, in the "one flesh" relationship between husband and wife and, by extension, within the immediate family. By the same token, if there is no chance of achieving equality in rendering the debt owed, as between God and intelligent creatures, justice survives only in an analogical form. Isidore of Seville, called *Hispalensis,* maintains the classical distinction between *fas* and *jus*: what is *jus* pertains to human affairs and what is *fas,* following classical Latin usage, refers only to divine law. [9]

Justice discovers its objective ground in a *jus.* How does the theologian identify a *jus*? Aquinas, and with him the main lines of the Christian tradition, acknowledges two fonts or sources for the *justum,* the just thing. These are natural *right* and positive *right.* Natural right, as I have said, arises from the basic goods of human flourishing such as human life, bodily integrity and human reproduction, good reputation, community life, communication in truth, and so forth. Positive rights, on the other hand, stem from convention, usually formalized in law; a worked-cut system of justice, therefore, represents a distinctive evolution of human culture and civilization. Thomas Gilby comments on the main divisions of right and law as these appear in classical theological sources:

---

[8]   See the discussion in *Summa theologiae* IIa-IIae q. 57, a. 1.
[9]   Isidore of Seville (d. 636), *Etymologiarum Libri* Bk 5, chap. 2 (*PL* 82:198).

First, natural right and positive right. Natural right is not confined to a hypothetical state of pure nature, but is present throughout the activities of human nature under the reign of grace; the natural law corresponding to it is not a code. Second, positive law is divided into divine law and human law. Divine law is here taken to refer to the legislation of the Old Testament. Human law is subdivided into civil law and canon law: ecclesiastical law occupies a territory between these two. All these divisions are of abstractions; in fact and history their respective commands may overlap and intermingle.[10]

Natural right corresponds to divine truth insofar as it is communicated through the natural law. The Christian view of justice assumes that the eternal law – that is, "how God knows the world to be" – provides the ultimate foundation and norm for human action. Indeed, every authentic instance of human virtue ultimately reflects the eternal law. But because of its correlation with the eternal law, Christian justice differs from the positive law theory of justice as developed by Enlightenment philosophers such as Thomas Hobbes and John Locke. According to their view, human reason alone undergirds and determines right order in a just society. The Church, however, must preach the truth about creation, and about the order of creation, the *ordo rerum*, and now this has an impact on moral truth.

Although a fully-developed theory of international law developed only in the 16th century, especially in the work of the Spanish Dominican Francisco de Vitoria (c.1485 – 1546), the Christian tradition from at least the seventh century recognized the existence of a *jus gentium*. The universality of the *jus gentium* rests on the view that some rights (along with the laws and conventions that guarantee them) lie so close to what the natural law requires that such agreements merit universal application. In fact, some situations such as the treatment of prisoners of war, safe conduct for diplomats, and other matters of this kind warrant such widespread agreement among civilized peoples, that their governance can claim the equivalent status of natural right. Aquinas considers that this *jus* or right, along with the rights that belong to the heads of households and even to those who hold positions of authority in extended domestic units, lie somewhere between pure legal convention and natural law.[11] In certain ways, the recognition and development of these domestic rights approximate modern social good theories of justice, though without reducing the virtue of justice to a mere disposition of benevolence.

---

[10] Thomas Gilby, *Justice*, volume 37 of the Blackfriars translation of the *Summa theologiae* (2a2ae 57–62), pp. 8–9.

[11] See *Summa theologiae* IIa-IIae q. 57, a. 4 for a discussion of the *jus paternum* and *jus dominativum*.

3. THE VIRTUE OF JUSTICE

When Aquinas begins his treatment of justice, he starts with a definition of the virtue whose provenance derives from Roman law. [12] The Roman jurist Ulpian defined justice as the lasting and constant will of rendering to each one his right. [13] Because he considers all virtue as operative *habitus*, Aquinas modifies this definition so that it fits his psychological theory of virtues and vices. "Justice,"he underscores, "is a *habitus* according to which a person is said to be active by choosing what is right." [14] And Aquinas further observes that this formulation more closely resembles what Aristotle has to say about justice in the *Ethics*. [15] Still, we should note carefully that realist philosophers and jurists are likely to define justice with diverse emphases. Since the jurist remains concerned with the external relationships that bind men and women together in community, the juridical definition of justice chiefly looks to regulation and equity. But when Aristotle defines justice, he emphasizes the traits that characterize the just person, the one who chooses rightly with respect to what is owed to another – *ad alterum*. And so along with the philosopher, the theologian must concentrate on what shapes the just person.

Since the justice of the New Law begins with a rectification of the human person's own operative capacities, the philosophical emphasis better serves the purposes of theology. Aquinas analogically compares moral justice with evangelical justification that comes from belief in the gospel. "The justice that works in us by faith," he says, "is that through which the ungodly are justified; ... it lies in the due order of the parts of the soul." [16] This evangelical rectitude belongs to justice in its metaphorical sense and implies a broader theological understanding of justice, such as the one that figures in Aquinas's account of Christian satisfaction. For alongside the juridical model that emphasizes Christ's rendering something due to God, Aquinas places an "evangelical" understanding of justice, one that he succeeds in relating to the human model with greater success than that found in St Anselm's famous attempt in the *Cur Deus homo?*

---

[12] In his treatise on justice, Aquinas addresses five central questions: (1) how to define justice; (2) whether justice abides in the rational appetite; (3) to what objects justice extends; (4) what is its act and (5) its place among the other virtues. For a brief treatment of Aquinas's position, see the work by Alasdair MacIntyre, *Whose Justice? Which Rationality?* (Notre Dame, IN, 1988), chap. 11 "Aquinas on Practical Rationality and Justice," pp. 183–208.

[13] *Summa theologiae* IIa-IIae q. 58, a. 1.

[14] Ibid.: "justitia est habitus secundum quem aliquis constanti et perpetua voluntate jus suum unicuique tribuit." In presenting the virtue of justice, the *Catechism for the Catholic Church* adapts this definition (no. 1807).

[15] *Nicomachean Ethics* Bk 2, chap. 4 (1105a31).

[16] *Summa theologiae* IIa-IIae q. 58, a. 2 ad 3.

Both philosophical and evangelical notions of justice share the *ratio* of "rectus ordo" or "rectitudo." The latter term, however, more clearly indicates that the performance of the just deed proceeds on a prior divine initiative and that it consists formally in the subordination of the human person and his destiny to God in love. It is the restoration of this same evangelical justice that constitutes the inner motive of Christ's satisfactory work. This salvific purpose and love of Christ determines the several ways in which satisfaction has a personal relevance to each person's individual destiny and to the establishment and prolongation of a communal salvation-history. Because charity and justice lie so close to the heart of the Christian life, St Anselm contends that justice shapes the will. "Justice," he says, "is rectitude of will preserved for its own sake." [17] In sum, Christian justice is never a matter of simply knowing what is the right thing to do; the virtue also entails the steadfast accomplishment of what is right. This steadfastness develops only in one whose capacities for action have been shaped by the grace of justification.

Justice, then, principally concerns operations – it is *circa operationes*. Because justice involves willed activity, this virtue immediately depends on the actual rendering of what is owed to another, rather than on feelings of benevolence toward others. "Justice is not about the whole field of moral virtue," Aquinas continues, "but only about external deeds and things, and these under a certain aspect, namely of the due co-ordination of one person with another." [18] Because of the unity of the human person, we should not draw too sharp a distinction between the virtues that are *circa operationes* and those that are *circa passiones*. Indeed "doing justice," that is, the actual accomplishment of a just deed, comes easily for the person who possess a well-tempered and steady emotional life; thus, justice also relies on the virtues of personal discipline. "Accordingly," says Aquinas, "our actions as bearing on external things are put right by justice, but as originating in our feelings they are put right by other moral virtues, which are about our emotions (*circa passiones*)." [19]

In his *De officiis*, St Ambrose describes justice as "that which renders to each what is his or hers, and claims not what is another's; justice disregards one's own profit in order to maintain a common equity." [20] This means that the exercise of true justice achieves a virtuous mean in objective reality. Aquinas clearly explains in his commentary on Aristotle's *Nichomachean Ethics* the

---

[17] St Anselm, *De veritate* chap. 12 (*PL* 158: 482): "justitia est rectitudo voluntatis propter se servata."

[18] *Summa theologiae* IIa-IIae q. 58, a. 8.

[19] *Summa theologiae* IIa-IIae q. 58, a. 9, ad 2. For further information on the distinction between virtues of operations and virtues of the emotions, see *Summa theologiae* Ia-IIae q. 60, a. 2.

[20] St Ambrose, *De officiis*, Bk 1, chap. 24 (*PL* 16:62).

important difference between the mean of justice and of the virtues of personal discipline.

> Justice is not a mean in the same way as the other moral virtues. Their mean lies between two vices: liberality is a mean between parsimony and extravagance. But justice is not a mean between two vices. However, it can be called a mean by reason of its effect inasmuch as it constitutes a mean, since its act is a just operation which is a mean between doing what is unjust and bearing the unjust. The first of these, active injustice, pertains to a vice of injustice which is a *habitus* of extremes in as much as it takes too many goods and too few evils. But the other, i.e., the toleration of the injustice is not a vice, but a suffering. [21]

Because the text relates suffering to the establishment of a just order, Aquinas helps us to relate the practice of justice to distinctively Christian perspectives of human life.

3.1. PERSON AND COMMUNITIES

In order to explain the virtue of justice, the theologian must gain a clear comprehension of how parts relate to wholes. For justice within the community depends on recognizing the distinctive relationship between an individual human person, endowed with the full dignity that belongs to one created as *imago Dei*, and the common good of the body politic. [22] The underlying basis for the uniqueness of each human person lies in the fact that individuals are distinguished materially from the species because of the particular human flesh and bone that belongs to each member of the human species. Still, the human species grounds a certain form of general friendship. Aquinas remarks that "in some general sort of way, every man is by nature a friend of every man – in the way that *Ecclesiasticus* talks about 'every animal loving its own.' " [23]

In order adequately to examine the several relationships that exist within the human community, it is necessary to introduce the distinction between a human individual and the person. By their preoccupation with the "self" as a particular center of consciousness and volition, the philosophers of the Enlightenment broke with earlier philosophical traditions and their way of accounting for the individuality of each human being within the species. Because of the theology of the incarnation, Christian thinkers had always upheld the distinction between an individual instance of human nature and the human person; for whereas Christ possesses two individual and concrete natures, in the mys-

---

[21]   *Sententia libri Ethicorum* Bk 5, 1. 10: C 992, trans. C.I. Litzinger, *Commentary on the Nicomachean Ethics*, 2 vols. (Chicago, 1964), p. 430. For further information on the distinctiveness of the mean of justice, see *Summa theologiae* Ia-IIae q. 64, a. 2.

[22]   For an interesting catena of texts from Aquinas on the inter-relationship of parts and whole, see Marcus Lefebure, *Injustice*, vol 38 of the Blackfriars translation of the *Summa theologiae* (London/New York,1975), pp. 271–274.

[23]   *Summa theologiae* Ia-IIae q. 114, a. 1, ad 2.

tery of the hypostatic union, he remains one divine Person. And so the Christian tradition developed (at least since the 5th-century Council of Chalcedon) a heightened awareness of the unique dignity that belongs to human personhood. Christian doctrine accordingly recognizes that the human person signifies more than a singular instance of the human species. In speaking about the care and responsibility that the Church takes for humankind, Pope John Paul II reflects this appreciation when he says that "we are not dealing here with man in the 'abstract,' but with the real, 'concrete,' 'historical' man. We are dealing with each individual, since each one is included in the mystery of the Redemption, and through this mystery Christ has united himself with each one for ever." [24]

Scholastic theology especially developed appropriate ways to speak about created personhood as that which represents the most noble feature of all God's creation. In an important essay on this topic, *The Person and the Common Good*, Jacques Maritain observes that "the human being is caught between two poles; a material pole, which, in reality, does not concern the true person but rather the shadow of personality or what, in the strict sense, is called individuality, and a spiritual pole, which does concern true personality." [25] Maritain holds, moreover, that while the individual *qua* individual can be subordinated to larger societal interests, the individual *qua* person enjoys an excellence that surpasses that of the whole human social order and, because of the divine design, finds rest and perfection only in union with God. Some authors have criticized Maritain's distinction between individual and person as overly influenced by the Cartesian split between *res extensa* and *res inextensa*. But at least his argument asserts that there is a formal difference between the individual human being and the person. Apart from the metaphysical interest which such a distinction raises, the difference between person and individual also opens up issues for Christian ethics. For example, does a human being considered simply as an individual member of the species enjoy certain prerogatives, such as the freedom to marry, that even the state, for its own legitimate interests, cannot restrict? In any event, for the decisive and practical questions of moral theology, the Church affirms the unique place that the human person occupies in the community: "The origin, the subject and the purpose of all social institutions is and should be the human person, whose life of its nature absolutely needs to be lived in society." [26]

The important connection between the human person and the common good raises a number of important questions such as subsidiarity. The Church considers a social community as an "ordered whole" that can exist in diversely

---

[24] *Centesimus annus*, chap. 6, no. 53.

[25] Jacques Maritain, *The Person and the Common Good*, trans. John J. Fitzgerald (New York, 1947), p. 33.

[26] *Gaudium et spes*, chap. 2, no. 26.

interdependent ways; at the same time, it is important to recall that subordination does not spell obliteration. The principle of subsidiarity affirms that "a community of a higher order should not interfere in the internal life of a community of a lower order, depriving the latter of its functions, but rather should support it in case of need and help to coordinate its activity with the activities of the rest of society, always with a view to the common good." [27] When considering the human community as a whole, the Christian theologian must take two factors into account: first, the ordering of the whole to the common good, and second, the achievement of diverse ends within the same community. Radical individualism corrodes the due ordering of human society; totalitarianism trammels on the personal dignity that each member of a community ought to enjoy. True social justice aims to establish a human community that is readied for participation in the beatific communion of the saints, one which, because of the infused virtue of justice, already appears in some ways among those who belong to Christ.

By looking at three forms of human community, we can discern the diverse relationship between justice and charity in each one. First, the natural family represents the whole that in the created order best realizes the divine design; as the domestic church, the family finds its deepest origin in the sacramental bond between wife and husband. Since it arises from natural processes, however, the unity of the family whole excludes the "otherness" that justice requires, though not the exercise of charity that, according to St Paul, Christian marriage represents in a symbolic way. Secondly, the political community constitutes a perfect expression of human society whose end is the *bene vivere humanum*, the good of human prosperity for the community. [28] "If every community is ordered to the good," says Aquinas, "it follows that the chief community is the one that aims at the chief human good that exists." [29] Justice is a virtue of the "City." Of course, the achievement of a just political order lacks the ultimate perfection that consists in loving God above all things, but as an authentic secondary end, the human *polis* embodies its own degree of perfection that the universal call to sanctity must respect. Pope John Paul II expresses it this way: "The Church respects the legitimate autonomy of the democratic order and is not entitled to express preferences for this or that institutional or constitutional solution." [30] Thirdly, the Church constitutes the "new community" of the elect that arises from the distinctive bond that charity establishes among the members of the Body of Christ. In this community that supersedes every form of

---

[27] *Centesimus annus*, chap. 5, no. 48, citing Pius XI, Encyclical Letter *Quadragesimo Anno*, I.
[28] St Augustine's *City of God* is the classic Christian text that expresses all that is implied in the *bene vivere humanum* and the "City" in which it transpires.
[29] *Sententia libri Politicorum* Bk 1, lect. 1.
[30] *Centesimus annus*, chap. 5, no. 47.

human community, the new law of evangelical justice reigns, so that within the Church the end of all order is *beatitudo*, the blessed repose of the saints in God.

Each of these communities represent various "common goods" that provide, as it were, the arenas in which the virtues of justice and charity are to be exercised. Aquinas shares Aristotle's optimistic view "that there is as much of a natural impetus to live in the community of the state as there is for virtue in every man or woman." [31] At the present time and in the majority of cases, the Nation-State exemplifies the political community that authors traditionally referred to as the *polis* or "city." And while these realities often coincide in actual practice, the notion of a state, a country, and a government remain formally distinct ones. To cite one example of the practical importance of this distinction, the virtue of general justice governs activities within a state and government, whereas a potential part of justice, namely, the virtue of piety or patriotism, governs our respect for a native land or country (*patria*).

3.2. GENERAL OR LEGAL JUSTICE

Commenting on Aristotle's *Politics*, Aquinas remarks: "The end of natural things is their nature. But the state is the end of the subordinate communities which we have mentioned [i.e., household and township] and which we have shown to be natural. The State is, therefore, natural." [32] Because it possesses a distinct formal object, namely, the human community ordered towards the common good as such, general justice represents an authentic form of justice. Just as a hand naturally defends the whole body-person, so a virtuous citizen defends and promotes the good of his or her "city," the state. Christian social justice seeks to set forth a balanced view of the relation between the individual and the common good: "Any part naturally loves the whole more than itself. And any individual thing naturally loves the good of the species more than its own individual good." [33] General justice regulates the obligations that members of the political community have towards the common good; since a political community rests on an established order (instead of the natural ties that bond

---

[31] See *Sententia libri Politicorum* Bk. 1, lect. 1: "Now it is clear that the state includes all other communities, for the household and the township are comprised in the state, so that the political community is the chief community. Since it aims at the common good which is better and more god-like than the good of an individual, the state, as Aristotle states at the beginning of the *Ethics*, aims at the chief human good. And Aristotle concludes by saying that there is as much of a natural impetus to live in the community of the state as there is for virtue in every man or woman. At the same time, just as virtues are acquired by exercise, as the Second Book of the *Ethics* makes clear, so states have been instituted by human industry."

[32] *Sententia libri Politicorum* Bk 1, lect. 1.

[33] *Summa theologiae* Ia q. 60, a. 5 ad 1.

the family), general justice applies particularly to the well-being of the *polis*. Aquinas defines the act of general justice simply as each member of the *polis* contributing his or her due to the common good. Because general justice lacks the specific determinations that particular things and operations provide for the various forms of particular justice, positive law or convention usually determines the *ad æqualitatem* that justice requires. For this reason, the tradition sometimes refers to this general form of justice as legal justice.

In a broad but certain sense, general justice embraces the whole of human life, the *conversatio civilis*; and so even the virtues of personal discipline such as fortitude and temperance and whatever else remains indispensable for the well-being of human life in the city pertain in some way to this kind of justice. Because the Church distinguishes between the virtuous realization of the common good and exaggerated nationalism, theologians need to bear in mind that there exists a proper order of individual members, the citizens of a modern state, to the common good that the state embodies. For the Church has uniformly and repeatedly condemned the theoretical and practical alternatives to a just social order. These take the shape either of rankly individualist political theories that minimize what the state should do for its citizens or of oppressively socialist ideologies that restrict the legitimate liberties of citizens. [34] As a true perfection of the human person, legal justice shapes an individual toward a virtuous respect for law, thereby removing a servile fear of authority, and at the same time guards against a dismissive attitude toward proper statutes and good laws whose neglect can only cause harm to the common good. Obviously, the definition of legal justice approaches what today the Church defines as social justice, although as a comprehensive category for all kinds of justice, a complete definition of social justice would include elements of both general and particular justice. For true Christian social justice, says Pope John Paul II, must "situate particular interests within the framework of a coherent vision of the common good." [35]

Because the end or goal of legal justice embodies an ultimate perfection in the temporal order, there exists a certain similarity between general justice and theological charity. Indeed, Aquinas inquires whether general justice essentially represents every virtue. For charity imperates the other virtues so that they reach the properly supernatural goal of *beatitudo*. "The life which men seek to live well here on earth," says Aquinas, "is ordered to the blessed life we hope to live in heaven as to its end." [36] However, legal justice orders all

---

[34] "Socialism considers the individual person simply as an element, a molecule within the social organism, so that the good of the individual is completely subordinated to the functioning of the socio-economic mechanism" (*Centesimus annus*, chap. 2, no. 13).

[35] *Centesimus annus*, chap. 5, no. 47.

[36] *De regimine principum* Bk 1, chap. 15.

other virtuous activity toward an end or goal that is not found in any particular one of them. On account of this preeminent objective, general or legal justice, to the extent that it respects the requirements of the natural law, achieves the justification of the human city in a preeminent way. Thus the Church endorses "the principle of the 'rule of law,' in which the law is sovereign, and not the arbitrary will of individuals." [37] This endorsement assumes, of course, that constitutional law and statutory enactments remain in conformity with the eternal law.

The Thomist writers on Christian virtue further speak about *infused* general justice, which they define as the virtue that conduces toward the material upbuilding of the Church, "the holy city, the new Jerusalem" (Rev 21: 2). [38] Since Christian eschatology teaches that the "City of God" involves a true transformation of the "City of Man," infused justice must differ not only formally but also materially from its acquired counterpart. "Whoever welcomes you welcomes me," Jesus tells his disciples, "and whoever welcomes me welcomes the one who sent me" (Mt 10: 40). Infused justice works toward realizing the original unity that, by divine plan, belongs to all of creation. So although everyone is required to keep in good standing with just political authority, the Christian believer never serves just the political order. Charity and the infused virtues perfect the exercise of political responsibility. "The Christian upholds freedom and serves it, constantly offering to others the truth which he or she has known (see Jn 8: 31 – 32), in accordance with the missionary nature of the Christian vocation." [39] Because this represents an authoritative teaching, Christian citizens of every state must strive to fulfill this vocation.

3.3. PARTICULAR JUSTICE

Like general justice, the several forms of particular justice have as their proper activity to render to each his or her own. [40] "Now each person's own," explains Aquinas, "is that which is due to him in proportion to making things even. That is why the proper activity of justice is none other than to render to each his or her own." [41] Moral theologians further divide particular justice into two specific parts: distributive and commutative justice. In brief, distributive justice regulates what an individual receives from the common good and protects the rights that a member enjoys by reason of belonging to a specific community. Commutative justice, on the other hand, regulates the exchanges that transpire

---

[37] *Centesimus annus*, chap. 5, no. 44.
[38] In the same way, infused political prudence directs the activity of the Church as a political reality.
[39] *Centesimus annus*, chap. 5, no. 46.
[40] See *Summa theologiae* IIa-IIae q. 58, a. 11.
[41] Ibid.

between individuals or moral persons and protects the rights of one person in relationship to another. Because it involves establishing equality between one person and another, the proper act of commutative justice necessarily involves restitution. [42]

Commutative and distributive justice regulate the actions of a just person in diverse ways. The equality that commutative justice seeks is an arithmetical *ad æqualitatem*; in other words, the due is established, not on the basis of some proportional equality between one person and another, but according to the *res* or what is objectively owed. Distributive justice, on the other hand, achieves a different kind of equality, *viz*, a geometrical proportionality, that is, a likeness between two or more proportions: "In so far as one person exceeds another so also what is meted out to him exceeds what is meted out to another." [43] Since we are dealing with a virtue, it is important to recall that the quantitative measurements that Aquinas borrows from Aristotelian categories actually represent qualitative determinations. [44] As a genuine *habitus* or quality of character, virtue represents degrees of personal excellence. The principle of equality that both distributive and commutative justice regulate and promote is easily applied when a just person deals with concrete things, such as money, artifacts, or labor; but it is more difficult to make a determination when justice concerns the human word, a gesture, or a particular operation, such as job descriptions, public recognition, and so forth. In these latter instances, the intangibility of the exchange often makes it more difficult to assess the requirements of justice; this holds especially true in cases of commutative justice.

Does distributive justice differ from commutative justice in the subject matter that it treats? By pursuing this line of investigation, moral theologians seek to emphasize that both distributive and commutative justice regulate the same kinds of things, namely and first of all, human persons themselves, but also a person's real or intangible property as well as words and gestures. However, distributive and commutative justice engage these various realities in different ways. As the name suggests, distributive justice concerns distribution; it regulates how one in authority takes from the whole, or the common good, and gives to the parts of the whole in accord with each one's dignity and with complete respect for the well-being of the community at large. For this reason, real discriminatory actions thwart the realization of distributive justice. Just authority should distribute goods, honors, and spiritual benefits on the basis of proportionate need and merit, and not on account of other personal qualities.

---

[42] For the appropriate text, see *Summa theologiae* IIa-IIae q. 61, a. 1.
[43] *Summa theologiae* IIa-IIae q. 61, a. 2.
[44] See *Nicomachean Ethics* Bk 5, chap. 3, 4.

Unfair discrimination, then, establishes a vicious state of affairs within any commonwealth. [45]

Commutative justice regulates exchange; it seeks to establish an objective equilibrium between individual persons or corporate entities, who enjoy a sort of equality within commutative justice; for justice requires that one consider persons impartially, that is, without regard for other conditions in an individual's life. Moral theology views exchange in a very broad way. Indeed, some exchanges even involve dealings with an unwilling party. [46] In short, unjust exchanges between persons include deeds that directly prejudice the good of another's person – such as happen in voluntary homicide (the greatest injury one can do to the neighbor), abortion, bodily mutilation, beatings (that exceed the right measure of proper discipline), unlawful imprisonment – or actions taken against a person's property such as happen in theft and robbery. By extension, justice also governs actions taken against one's own person – such as unauthorized mutilation, suicide, and euthanasia. Likewise, unjust exchange includes those words or gestures that depreciate the good of another's personal worth, such as unjust speech, especially those exchanges governed by judicial structures, i.e., courtroom perjury and judicial execution of the innocent, and the unjust exchange of words within a community and the larger society. The latter category includes a long list of vicious activity that constitute serious harm for the well-being of both Church and society, such as defamation (openly taking away from someone's character), detraction (privately taking away from someone's reputation), [47] whispering (to speak or converse quietly and maliciously about a person), ridicule (to heap insult publicly on another), and cursing (to utter evil against someone either by ordering it or wishing it). Because each of these actions involves an element of objective personal hurt to another person as well as to the community of persons, a simple return or reciprocation does not suffice for establishing the full measure of justice. Thus, the judgment on theft, for instance, involves not only restitution but also a penalty

---

[45]   In *Summa theologiae* IIa-IIae q. 63, a. 1, Aquinas distinguishes between the giving that is regulated by justice and the giving that is governed by a potential part of justice, liberality, "which is a matter of freely giving to another something that is not his due." Aquinas compares the gift of divine grace with liberality; because grace is a free gift, God is not required in justice to give it his bestowing it on humans, therefore, resembles liberality.

[46]   Aquinas considers the various examples of unjust exchanges that involve an unwilling partner in *Summa theologiae* IIa-IIae qq. 64 – 76. He says that such non-voluntary transactions occur when somebody inflicts injury on another against his or her will, and this can be done in two ways, namely by deed and by word.

[47]   In *Summa theologiae* IIa-IIae, q. 73, a. 1, ad 3, Aquinas cites fours ways in which one can depreciate another's reputation: (1) by attributing what is false to him, (2) by exaggerating his sins, (3) by exposing secrets, (4) and by saying that good actions have been motivated by evil intentions.

of some sort; "Consequently," says Aquinas, "in exchanges the equalization of what is done and what is undergone in return requires a certain proportionate standard of measurement." [48]

The proper act of commutative justice is restitution. In order to restore the equality of commutative justice, restitution is required both when a person unjustly holds onto another's property (*res aliena accepta*) and when a person unjustly appropriates another's goods (*injusta acceptio*). [49] Because injustice so widely pervades the world, the theology of restitution engages the best energies of the moral theologian and the confessor. In practice, many of the conclusions that the casuist epoch developed for dealing with the extraordinary cases involving restitution still provide helpful guidelines and insights into this highly complex issue. But even before the rise of the casuist hegemony in moral theology, theologians dealt with the practical questions of restitution – for example, its purpose, the lawful recipients of restitution, those who are bound to make restitution, and the suitable time for making it. *Res clamat domino*, as the Roman legal principle puts it. Thomas Gilby offers the following succinct account of the place that restitution maintains in the scheme of justice.

> Restitution [involves] giving back something to its owner and/or making reparation for a loss or injury inflicted, so restoring the balance, *æqualitas*, of commutative justice. The putting right of other relationships, e.g., of charity, friendship, religion, or even of general justice and distributive justice is not directly a matter of restitution in the strict sense of the term, but of paying what is owed or of offering satisfaction or making a proper apology. The obligation is no less, but is not rendered in terms of commutative justice as narrowly defined. [50]

Common usage restricts the term restitution to those cases that, as instances of non-voluntary or unwilling exchanges, entail the commission of an injustice, but strictly speaking it also applies to voluntary exchanges, *viz*, fraud committed in the course of buying and selling or usurious interest on loans.

Christian theology distinguishes between restitution and satisfaction. As with justice itself, restitution principally engages an objective interest, or what is due, as when a judge orders an offender to pay a fine or to return some property to its just owner. In this circumstance, the judge is not primarily concerned with the personal attitude of the offender, for instance, whether the person expresses sorrow or not, but only that he or she make recompense. Since satisfaction includes restitution, but also compensation for the hurt that is caused, it aims to achieve a bigger goal. Restitution, then, chiefly involves restoring external goods that have been unjustly taken; it restores an equilibrium somehow disrupted, for instance, by the theft of property or assault on a person. Satis-

---

[48]   *Summa theologiae* IIa-IIae q. 61, a. 4.
[49]   See Thomas Gilby, *Justice*, p. 101, note b.
[50]   Ibid., pp. 104 – 105, note a.

faction does not principally concern such external goods, but seeks to redress the actual actions and attitudes that accompany an injustice. Aquinas even envisions the possibility that satisfaction can occur without restitution, as when someone who is unable to make full restitution still humbles himself before the neighbor hurt by some contumacious word or deed. We can also envision the opposite scenario when someone, for instance, who has violently robbed his neighbor makes restitution by restoring the illgotten goods, but refuses to satisfy for the personal hurt caused by the brutal act of robbery.

4. THE VIRTUES ALLIED TO JUSTICE

Because it regulates the interpersonal relationships that flourish within the human community, the cardinal virtue of justice governs significant areas of human life. It comes as no surprise, then, that Aquinas devotes more than forty questions to the virtues that are allied to justice. According to his schema, these virtues, which we will catalogue in this section, fall under two main headings: the virtues of veneration and the virtues of civility. While on the one hand, justice ordinarily aims at establishing a certain, definite equality (*ad æqualitatem*) between individuals of the same rank, the virtue can also extend to what transpires among non-peers. Broadly speaking then, the first group of virtues, *viz*, the virtues of veneration, regulates relationships between inferiors and superiors. On the other hand, justice also covers those circumstances in the human community when the requirements established by either general justice or a form of particular justice do not pertain. The second group of virtues, *viz*, the virtues of civility, regulate and direct interpersonal transactions of this kind among people who share life in the same society.

In scholastic terminology, both the virtues of veneration and the virtues of civility make up the different potential parts of justice. [51] This means that,

---

[51] T. C. O'Brien, *Virtues of Justice in the Human Community*, vol. 41 of the Blackfriars translation of the *Summa theologiae* (London/New York, 1972), p. 328 provides the following résumé of the scholastic teaching on the parts of virtue (*partes virtutis*): "The cardinal virtues attend to certain primary and more urgent objectives of human activity. When the act of one of these virtues is conceived of as a whole involving certain integrating steps in the attainment of its objective, St Thomas speaks of *integral parts* or *integrating parts* of the virtue, e.g., the steps needed to form the integral act of prudence. When within the objective of the cardinal virtue there are specifically diverse interests, the virtue is conceived of as a remote species, a subjective whole, and it has *subjective parts*, more specific virtues corresponding to the more specific objectives, e.g. as temperance includes the specific virtues of abstinence, sobriety, chastity. When there are virtuous objectives that, while not being more specific instances of the objective of a cardinal virtue, do have some resemblance of affinity to it, the cardinal virtue is considered to be a 'potestative whole', the virtues concerned with these related objectives, its *potential parts*. Thus the meaning of the cardinal virtue is verified more or less of its potential parts ... The potential parts are not inferior virtues, but

though the virtues of veneration and civility realize the purposes of justice, they do so only after a fashion. With the virtues of veneration, the analogical character of the potential parts of justice involves the notion of equality, or the *ad æqualitatem* that forms an essential element of the cardinal virtue. This circumstance occurs when someone receives from a person of greater status or dignity goods or benefits that exceed the inferior's capacity to repay. As a result, such relationships never realize the full equality that characterizes cardinal justice. In the virtues of civility, moral reasoning is at a loss to establish the debt of virtue by reference to a definite *res*; for there exists no legal debt determined either by positive law or by a private contract that morally and legally binds the debtor. [52] Instead, in the case of these virtues, the equality of justice is determined by less exact criteria.

Since a person realizes the cardinal virtue of justice only when he or she fully renders the debt owed to another – *alteri reddatur quod ei debetur secundum aequalitatem* – every other circumstance that entails operations such as distributions or exchanges among persons involves one of the potential parts of justice. These allied virtues are real virtues, for they shape and regulate the actions of the just man or woman. On the basis of this analysis, the Christian tradition recognizes two categories for the potential parts of justice: (1) virtues that regulate relationships in which there is inequality of condition (*deficit a ratione æqualis*) and (2) virtues that govern right conduct in circumstances where there is inequality of debt (*deficit a ratione debiti*). In the first category, we number the virtues of religion, piety, and respect (or observance) that regulate human actions, respectively, toward God, our parents, and lawful authority. In the second category, we include first of all legal debt, which, since it concerns the relationship of parts to a whole, remains governed by the cardinal virtue itself, and secondly, the various instances where, because of a lack of a clearly definable *jus* or right, it is appropriate to speak about a "moral debt."

When Christian theologians speak about a "moral debt," they do not mean to insinuate something optional or superfluous. A "moral debt" can oblige a person to act in a certain way, e.g., in human conversation and interaction, we "owe" truthfulness to the persons with whom we are engaged. In such situations, the virtue of truth or *veritas* establishes a mean between indiscriminate self-revelation and projecting a false image of oneself. [53] Again, "moral debt" can stipulate responsibilities toward others in circumstances that are difficult

---

often, as in the case of religion, superior to the cardinal virtue."

[52] Aquinas devotes a single question to equity or *epieikeia*, the special form of justice, which, since its objective is an order of justice not fully covered by positive law, actually consists of a subjective part of general or legal justice. For more information, see *Summa theologiae* IIa-IIae q. 120.

[53] See *Summa theologiae* IIa-IIae q. 109, a. 2.

to gauge. In the latter case, if the moral debt arises in return for a benefaction, a person exercises the virtue of gratitude, but if the debt results from some evil that a person has unjustly suffered, he or she can rely on the virtue of vengeance. Still other virtues that fulfill a moral debt contribute to an ampler form of virtuous living and therefore are necessary for the *bene vivere humanum* of the human community. In this category, we place the virtues of liberality and friendship or affability. [54]

4.1. THE VIRTUES OF VENERATION

The virtues of veneration share a common feature insofar as they regulate the conduct of inferiors to superiors. For there exists an inequality of condition or status between the religious, pious, and respectful person and those persons to whom he or she remains obligated. The virtues of veneration do not first of all impose a relationship that entails duty and obligation. Instead, the relationship of "veneration" requires a radical transformation on the part of the virtuous person who remains subject to another. In other words, even though they seem principally to determine certain particular acts that a person ought to perform, these virtues in fact constitute true operative *habitus* and, therefore, shape the moral character of those who possess them.

In the case of the virtue of religion, the grounds for the inequality lie in what distinguishes the Creator from the creature. This distinction, moreover, arises from a fundamental principle of causality, namely, the dependence that a particular effect owes to the universal principal cause of its being. God remains the source and the conservor of everything that exists and the governor of all that acts. As the first cause of all that exists and all government in creation, God alone abides as the ultimate *causa causarum*, the supreme cause of causes. But religion is not the only virtue of veneration. For God has not ordained that he alone exercise every authority, but that even created persons share in authority in various ways through a particular causal activity. Those who bring forth new human life and those who execute governance in the civil order stand in a special position with respect to those whom they beget and those whom they govern. Because parents procreate children, mothers and fathers enjoy a special bond with their offspring, and because legitimate superiors can lawfully direct others in specific areas of life, civil administrators hold a place of distinction within the human community. Specific virtues of veneration regulate these important relationships.

Like every virtue, the virtues of religion, filial piety, and respect enable the person who possesses the good *habitus* to exercise joyfully, promptly, and easily certain defined activities. And since the virtues of veneration develop

---

[54] For Aquinas's own presentation of the potential parts of justice, see the single article of *Summa theologiae* IIa-IIae q. 80.

psychological dispositions that suit a particular person's station in life, these virtues also regulate our bearings in other important areas of the Christian life. For instance, they facilitate the development of traits such as reverence, humility, submission, reverential fear, and thankfulness. As a general trait of character, reverence holds a special place in the dispositions that characterize a virtuous Christian life, for it disposes a person to practice the theological virtue of hope. Reverence, we know, even forms the psychological analog for the gift of Fear of the Lord.

The Christian tradition teaches that all of these virtuous attitudes are included in the single virtue of honor or *dulia*. This virtue readies a person to be conformed to a superior precisely as a source of good for the individual and, as a result, inclines a virtuous person to heed the will of the superior, instead of preferring his or her own will. Like all true virtue, *dulia* or honor aims to embody some particular good that belongs to the perfection of the human person. In the same way, the virtue of obedience governs the actions of the pious person, who obeys God, the author of divine precepts, fathers and mothers, who command through parental directives, and superiors, who may issue orders appropriate to their office. This virtue of obedience holds a place within the larger virtuous formation that cardinal justice develops; however, it does not account, as casuist and deontological models suppose, for the effective principle of the whole moral life.

Aquinas expresses the spirit of the virtues of veneration when he remarks about the character of those who bear authority in the world: "Now a person who has some authority stands as a source of guidance in regard to some special endeavor... and all such people can be called fathers because of a resemblance in the way they care for us."[55] While such a view about the importance of paternity in human life nowadays may give some moment for pause, Aquinas, it should be noted, establishes a structure for the virtues of veneration with the view in mind that all authority originates in the supreme goodness of the heavenly Father. In other words, Aquinas's suppositions are theological more than anthropological; they represent his prayerful reflection on St Paul more than his cultural circumstances. Because Jesus reveals a heavenly Father who knows only how to treat his children well, the Christian dispensation casts a new and transforming light on all social conventions. And so St Paul warns, "Masters, treat your slaves justly and fairly, for you know that you also have a Master in heaven" (Col 4: 1). Just as religion concerns ordering the creature's relationship with God, so the other virtues of veneration develop a religious sense in every person who is subject to authority in the world.

---

[55] *Summa theologiae* IIa-IIae q. 102, a. 1.

4.2. THE VIRTUES OF CIVILITY

The second division of the potential parts of cardinal justice includes the virtues that regulate and ensure a courteous life in the well-ordered human community. These virtues moderate the actions of persons who share the same status and condition – in other words, who are peers within the larger social grouping. Aquinas, however, does not draw a sharp distinction between the virtues of veneration and the virtues of civility. Indeed, the religious man or woman, one who respects authority, is best prepared to manifest a civil spirit toward others.

The virtues of civility themselves form two classes. First, there are virtues that remain indispensable for common life because they regulate those exchanges that make up authentic human *communicatio*. Secondly, there are virtues that contribute to living a happier experience of everyday life, or that simply develop more pleasant living. The first group includes the virtues of truth, gratitude, and vengeance, whereas the second group includes the virtues of liberality and friendship or affability. This first group of virtues – again, truth, gratitude, and vengeance – more fully realizes the essential component of justice, that is, they regulate activities that one can recognize as legitimately due to other people. The other virtues of civility include the virtue of thankfulness or gratitude, which governs how to acknowledge a benefaction; the virtue of vengeance, which controls the forms of retribution for harm done by another either to oneself or to a friend; a *habitus* of true friendliness, instead of a quarrelsome or meretricious spirit, that makes life within the human community more pleasant and joyful; and finally, liberality, instead of an avaricious or prodigal spirit, which measures the proper way that a person should acquit himself of debts that form no part of strict justice.

As an example of the dynamics of virtuous civility, we will consider the virtue of truth. In the strict meaning of the action, as when drawing up a contract or commenting about another's character, the obligation to speak the truth flows from and is governed by commutative justice. But there also exists a broader conception of representing the truth that constitutes a potential part of the virtue of justice. Aquinas names this virtue *veritas*, the simple virtue of truth. As with the virtue of religion, *veritas* likewise holds a greater eminence in the moral life than does the cardinal virtue of justice itself. For the virtue of *veritas* embodies a more profound and extensive meaning of virtue than what either the general or particular forms of justice can realize. When he addresses the Pharisee Nicodemus, Jesus points out the authoritative place that the virtue of *veritas* holds in the Christian life: "But those who do what is true come to the light, so that it may be clearly seen that their deeds have been done in God" (Jn 3: 21). Within a realist epistemology, truthfulness denotes a kind of fidelity that occurs when there is an adequation between a mental concept or spoken word and what these signs represent in reality. When this notion is applied to the moral virtue of truth, the fidelity applies not only in the cognitive order, but in the personal order as well. In other words, there exists a basic personal honesty or straightforwardness that characterizes the person who lives in the truth about his or her own worth. Aquinas puts it this way: "Like everything else, one's life is called true on the basis of its reaching its rule and norm, namely divine law; by measuring up to this, a life has uprightness. This is the kind of truth, i.e., uprightness, common to every virtue." [56] The person whose life reflects this truthfulness will, among other honorable actions, "speak the truth about himself or herself, sticking to the middle ground between one who speaks boastingly of self and one who speaks slightingly." [57]

As an infused virtue, the virtue of truth represents a particularly apt expression of Gospel values. Recall the distinction that St Paul makes between the old self and the new self, or the unspiritual self and the spiritual self (Rom 7: 22–23). Again, the Second Vatican Council describes the Church as at once on its pilgrim way and as the spotless bride of Christ. Because the Church "is at one and the same time holy and always in need of purification," the member of Christ's Body must move to the fullness of the heavenly banquet only with true simplicity of heart. [58] Aquinas holds that "simplicity takes its name in opposition to the duplicity by which a person holds one thing inwardly and outwardly expresses something else." [59] The moral virtue of truth abides no such duplicity, even though it frankly acknowledges the tug and pull of the believer's fleshly nature against the resolve to live a holy and truthful life. In this circumstance, St Paul recalls his own experience: "Three times I appealed to the Lord about this, that it would leave me, but he said to me, 'My grace is sufficient for you, for my power is made perfect in weakness.' So, I will boast all the more gladly of my weaknesses, that the power of Christ may dwell in me" (2 Cor 12: 8–9).

5. RELIGION

As the first of the virtues of veneration, the Christian tradition essentially defines religion as rendering to God the whole honor that is his due. [60] A complete discussion of the virtue of religion involves treatment of its definition, its proper actions, and the vices contrary to the practice of true religion. So

---

[56] *Summa theologiae* IIa-IIae q. 109, a. 2, ad 3.
[57] Ibid.
[58] See *Lumen gentium*, chap. 1, nos 7–8.
[59] *Summa theologiae* IIa-IIae q. 109, a. 2, ad 4.
[60] See *Summa theologiae* IIa-IIae q. 81, a. 1.

among the potential parts of the virtue of justice, the virtues associated with religion and worship form one of the most significant treatises in the theological disciplines. Moreover, since the New Testament presents Christ as the genuinely and supremely religious man, the virtue of religion provides important background for other theological topics such as the priesthood of Christ, the sacraments of the new law, and the efficacy of Christ's life, death, and resurrection. [61]

The virtue of religion consists in that *habitus* of the will that shapes a person to render carefully and permanently to God the supreme honor that is his due. Etymologically "whether [the term] religion is derived from frequent re-reading [*relectio*], from a repeated seeking of something lost through negligence [*reeligere*], or from the fact that it constitutes a bond [*religare*], religion," says Aquinas, "implies a relationship to God." [62] As a quality of character, religion concerns the interior and external worship that humankind offers to God as the creator and governor of the universe. But while religion elicits its own proper acts such as adoration and sacrifice, it can also command the actions of other virtues. In this way, the virtue of religion potentially relates to every good deed that a person might perform.

Religious worship represents an expression of reverence for God's majesty and pays a debt of honor to God. However, because religion turns us toward the divine majesty under a specific formal object, *viz*, as creator and governor, the *habitus* constitutes a special virtue. On this account, the virtue of religion can serve as a unifying principle for the various practices that embody true religion. As the source and support of all that exists, God possesses an unparalleled excellence, whereas the creature enjoys only contingent status. The ground for the debt that the creature owes to God lies in the very *actus essendi, viz*, the act of existence itself. This ontological debt results in a form of justice that exceeds what exists between natural parents and their child, for the disparity between parent and child does not approach that between creator and creature. Moreover, if one abstracts from the universal call to salvation that is realized in divine charity, the relationship between God and the creature does not imply a kind of friendship. Rather it is a relationship of the contingent to the necessary. This explains why religion continues to bind even a person who is brought into the *communicatio benevolentiae divinae*, that is, elevated to supernatural charity. Even the personal friendship between God and the creature that we call created grace does not alter the structure of religion, so that the favor of divine friendship never excuses one from rendering to God what is his due.

---

[61] For an interesting study on the relationship of priestly spirituality to the virtue of religion, see Eugene A. Walsh, *The Priesthood in the Writings of the French School: Bérulle, De Condren, Olier* (Washington, DC, 1949).

[62] See *Summa theologiae* IIa-IIae q. 81, a. 1.

In sum, the virtue of religion, as an allied part of justice, maintains a certain distinctness and possesses a special and unparalleled excellence even within the framework of the Christian life of grace.

It is important to comprehend why the Thomist tradition steadfastly distinguishes the moral virtue of religion from the theological virtues. In the technical sense of the term, a theological virtue establishes the human person in a direct and personal relationship with God; faith unites us with God as highest Truth, whereas hope and charity unite us to God as supreme Goodness. On account of this extraordinary bestowal of divine grace, the theological virtues of faith, hope, and charity together effectively constitute the human person as a true knower and real lover of God. But the virtue of religion establishes no such personal relationship between God and the creature; rather, as a moral virtue, religion regulates human conduct. As a potential part of justice, religion guides the worship and praise that the human person and community offer to God. Religion treats human obligation; charity signifies the free bestowal of divine love.

Like all created goods, the specific acts of the virtue of religion remain means to an end, not the end itself. Still, among the moral virtues, religion holds a special place of eminence and primacy, for this *habitus* is able to command a whole range of virtuous actions in the name of divine worship. For this reason, some commentators suggest a helpful comparison of religion with the virtue of legal or general justice, which, in a certain sense, governs all the activities of the moral life. John of St Thomas, for instance, favorably compares the just person and the religious person on the grounds that the latter demonstrates the principal Christian qualities of mercy, humility, penitence, and obedience. From this point of view, Christian authors often legitimately consider the virtue of religion as representing a certain summit of the moral life.

Like every moral virtue that shapes some aspect of human conduct, the virtue of religion profoundly affects the interior life. "Because he possesses perfect glory to which creatures can add nothing," writes Aquinas, "we do not give honor and reverence to God for his own sake, but rather *for our own sake*, because when we do so our mind is subjected to him and in this our perfection consists." [63] And Cardinal Cajetan further explains that we should interpret the words "for our own sake" as the *terminum utilitatis*, that is, the practical result of the virtue, not its formal object. The formal object or the good to which religion "is directed is giving honor to God." [64] But even if its exercise fulfills a debt of honor and reverence toward God, the virtue of religion contributes to

---

[63]   See *Summa theologiae* IIa-IIae q. 81, a. 7 (emphasis added).

[64]   *Summa theologiae* IIa-IIae q. 81, a. 4.

our personal sanctification. In a book about St Francis de Sales subtitled "The education of the will," a French spiritual author, François Vincent, summarizes the two poles of Christian spirituality with respect to their attitude concerning the virtue of religion: "The Benedictine [monastic] soul sanctifies itself for the sake of prayer, while the Salesian soul prays in order to achieve personal sanctification." [65] Within the Church, these two spirits complement one another.

The classical spiritual writers stress the bodiliness of religion and the importance that rightly ordered external comportment plays in establishing a religious spirit. In one especially important passage from his commentary on Boethius's *De Trinitate*, Aquinas summarizes the essentials of what the Christian tradition holds on faith, religion, and bodily worship.

> Religion consists in an operation by which the human person honors God by submitting to him; and this operation ought to be in harmony with him who is honored and with the one offering homage.
>
> Now since he who is reverenced is a spirit, he cannot be approached by the body, but only by the mind; and so worship of him consists chiefly in acts of the mind by which the mind itself is ordained to God. These acts are principally those of the theological virtues; and in accordance with this, Augustine says that God is worshiped by faith, hope, and charity, to which are added also the acts of the gifts ordained toward God, such as those of wisdom and of fear.
>
> But because we who honor God are also possessed of bodies and receive our knowledge through bodily senses, there is the necessity that certain physical actions accompany the worship of God, not only that we may render service to God with our whole being, but also by these bodily actions we may arouse in ourselves and in others acts of the mind ordained to God. Wherefore Augustine says in his book, *De cura pro mortuis habenda*: "Those who pray make the members of their bodies conform to their acts of supplication when they genuflect, extend their hands, or prostate themselves upon the ground, or perform any other visible action; and although it is their invisible will and the intention of the heart that is known to God, it is not unseemly that the human soul should so express itself, but rather by so doing the human person stirs himself or herself to pray and to lament his sins the more humbly and fervently." [66]

Cajetan, nonetheless, speaks a perennial and sober truth when he says that while all the saints are religious people, not all those who practice the virtue of religion are holy. Why? One can call religious whosoever occupies himself with ceremonies, sacrifices, and things of this sort; but the saints, Cajetan insists, are those who devote their whole being to God. [67] This sample of 16th-

---

[65] François Vincent, *S. François de Sales, directeur d'âmes. L'éducation de la volonté* (Paris, 1932): "L'âme bénédictine se sanctifie pour prier; l'âme salésienne pour se sanctifier."

[66] See *In Boethii De trinitate* q. 3, a. 2.

[67] See Cajetan's *In secundam secundae*, q. 81, a. 7: "Ex hac differentia patet quod multi sunt religiosi qui non sunt sancti, omnes autem sancti sunt religiosi. Qui enim cæremoniis, sarificiis, et huiusmodi vacant, religiosi vocari possunt; sancti autem nequaquam, nisi semetip-

century spiritual direction has not lost its original power to challenge consecrated persons to maintain an authentic life.

6. THE ACTS OF THE VIRTUE OF RELIGION

When treating the acts of the virtue of religion, we customarily distinguish between internal acts of religion, such as devotion and prayer, and the external or public acts of religion. This second category includes those actions whereby the human person offers or renders something to God, such as a sacrifice, oblations, or tithes, as well as those whereby a person promises something to God, for example, through pronouncing a vow.

6.1. SACRIFICE

According to Aquinas, to offer sacrifice reflects the natural law. In other words, this obligation rests on a *jus* or right that stems from the very order of creation, especially the natural finality that directs creation toward a particular end. However, the scholastics taught that because sacrifice does not belong to the primary ends or inclinations of the natural law, which concern the preservation of human life, proper comportment in sexual activity, and the communication of human truth, not every person would recognize immediately the place that sacrifice has in human life. Only the inescapable human experiences of dependency and contingency gently lead the human person to recognize the need that everyone has to offer special service to God. For the Christian believer, sacrifice consists principally in the internal action of the creature who inclines toward God as "the principle of its creation and the goal of its happiness." If indeed some internal action did not specify the act of sacrifice, every slaughterhouse would become a temple. So every act of true sacrifice must be ordered to a common objective or end. Aquinas describes this end as toward the divine reverence – *in divinam reverentiam,* and it is this attention to the divine reverence that distinguishes generic acts of sacrifice from those that truly belong to the virtue of religion.

Properly speaking, sacrifice requires that "something is done to the thing offered to God." [68] The general notion that sacrifice involves reverencing God allows the theologian to call any virtuous action a sacrifice provided that it fulfills this condition. Because of the dignity of the person who is both victim and priest, the sacrifice of Christ possesses the fullness of divine meaning. Thus, Cajetan argues the point that while the virtue of religion binds everyone both

---

sos intrinsecus per hanc Deo applicant."

[68] See *Summa theologiae* IIa-IIae q. 85, a. 3, ad 3. C. E. O'Neill, O.P., *Sacramental Realism* (Wilmington, DE, 1981), pp. 111–112 points out the significance of this precision for the doctrine of the Eucharist.

to offer general sacrifices and to direct his or her heart toward God, only the priests of the new law, who are specially configured to Christ by the sacrament of holy Order, can offer the perfect sacrifice that occurs in every Mass. [69] But the notion of sacrifice is analogical, for it can be used to describe the sacrifices that form part of the everyday life of the Christian as well as the eucharistic mystery of the new law. The Irish theologian Colman O'Neill makes the following comment concerning the place that sacrifice holds in the Christian life.

> Redemption is a work of divine love, calling up sacrifice in the person of Christ only in order that it might be created as well in the hearts of all who accept this mystery. When sacrifice, understood as human response to God's creative act of mercy, is made the central category of thinking about the Christian mystery, other, more restricted categories adopted by the Christian tradition can be given their due importance. [70]

St Augustine's *De civitate Dei* provides the patristic inspiration for incorporating the religious notion of sacrifice into a general theological conception of the Christian life. [71]

6.2. VOWS

Because a vow by definition promises some future good to God, vows are to be distinguished from the acts of religion that offer something here and now to God, such as sacrifice, oblations, the first fruits of the harvest, and tithes. A vow represents a deliberate and free promise made to God concerning a possible and better good. [72] As an act of the virtue of religion, the obligation of keeping a vow rests on the excellence of the divine majesty, and so vows can form an important element in the life of one set upon the pursuit of moral truth and goodness. Aquinas's understanding of the importance of the vows of religion reflects some of the concerns of the anti-mendicant controversy that bedeviled the development of religious life at Paris during the course of the 13th century. However, as acts of the virtue of religion, a person may vow an extensive range of promised goods other than "the evangelical counsels of chastity consecrated to God, poverty and obedience." [73] So even though the

---

[69] *In secundam secundae*, q. 84, a. 4: "In art. IVo, habes quod duo genera sacrificii sunt omnibus communia: scilicet interioris mentis oblatio per devotionem et orationem, et oblatio actuum aliarum virtutum. Tertia autem sacrificii genus est proprium sacerdotibus et ministris Ecclesiae ... "

[70] C. E. O'Neill, "The Fullness of Christ's Sacrifice," *Word & Spirit* 5 (1984): 44–60 makes this important qualification concerning the place of sacrifice in Christian practice.

[71] See Bk 10, chap. 6.

[72] See *Codex Iuris Canonici*, can. 1191.1.

[73] *Lumen gentium* chap. 6, no. 43.

vows of religion hold a central place in the life of the Church, every Christian can consecrate something to God by means of a vow. [74]

Because a vow implies a promise to do something or to omit doing something, it presupposes that one making a vow observe the ordinary prudence that guides any authentic moral action. Thus, according to the tradition, three things are required for a vow: "First, deliberation, second, a resolution of the will, and third, the promise, which completes its character." [75] Deliberation forms an important part of the resolve to promise something by vow; in fact, St Jerome chides the Old Testament saint Jephthah for lack of discretion when the latter vowed, if victorious, to sacrifice the first living thing he encountered upon return from his battle with the Ammonites. [76] In any event, the resolve and promise to accomplish a greater good constitute the distinctive notes of a vow. Because vows concern the promise of a greater good, neither the impossible nor the inevitable can properly fall under a vow.

While suitable detachment and reasonable poverty, the conduct of a chaste life, and a right sense of obedience belong to the very nature of Christian life, a person may still bind himself by vow to promise these goods in a determined way, viz, in a greater fashion. Aquinas especially grasps the special meaning and utility of a vow when he declares that one who makes a vow "immovably dedicates his will to good." [77] Thus, to renounce the radical possession or even the free use of material goods, to renounce the right to married love, and to choose to bind oneself to the lawful determinations of a religious superior form a specific way of promising the greater good. As a properly religious act, every vow serves the pursuit of a person's ultimate perfection and happiness; St Augustine clearly makes the theological point when he says that "what is given to God is added to the giver." [78]

The virtue of religion also regulates those circumstances in which a creature uses something that belongs properly to God – for instance, when a person invokes God's name, as happens when taking oaths, swearing, and in the use of invocations. An oath serves to confirm one's own statement or affirmation about a given matter of testimony. Swearing or adjuration employs the holy

---

[74] See *CIC*, can. 1191, no. 2 and chapter 6 of the Dogmatic Constitution on the Church, *Lumen gentium*, "On Religious."

[75] See *Summa theologiae* IIa-IIae q. 88, a. 1.

[76] The incident is recorded in Judges 11: 30. See Peter Comestor, *Historia Scholast*. 12 (*PL* 198: 1284): "In vowing he was foolish because he did not use discretion, and in keeping the vow he was impious." However in *Summa theologiae* IIa-IIae q. 88, a. 2, ad 2, Aquinas discovers a reason for the tradition of numbering him among the saints of the old dispensation, and maintains that even the evil act of killing his own daughter, for which Jephthah duly repented, holds a figurative meaning of something good.

[77] *Summa theologiae* IIa-IIae q. 88, a. 4.

[78] St Augustine, *Epistola* 127 (*PL* 33: 486).

name as an instrument to induce others to do something. Invocation denotes a prayer or hymn of praise that includes reference to the Godhead.

The possession and exercise of the infused virtue of religion specifically implies our involvement in the economy of salvation. Within the logic of the incarnation, God commits to the human person the use of created realities as instruments of divinity. Therefore, the Christian religion especially involves the sacramental system of the new law. In structuring the *Summa theologiae*, Aquinas places his treatment of the sacraments after that of the incarnation itself. Still, the relationship of infused religion to the cardinal virtue of justice implies that divine justification analogously includes some reference to a right ordering or balance of the *imago Dei*. By contrast, superstition, idolatry, and divination (the wrongful foretelling of future events) represent radical departures from the worship of the true God. Aquinas associates these practices largely with those who lived during the period of the old law, when knowledge of true religion was confined by the limits of images and foreshadowing. But the temptation to subvert the purposes of true religion by the use of artful simulations of religious practices remains even today a challenge to Christian believers. In addition, tempting God, perjury, and sacrilege represent vices against the virtue of religion, for in these cases a person wrongfully employs holy things. Endeavoring to traffic in the very gifts that the Holy Spirit gives to the Church after Christ's resurrection, simony represents a special affront to the divine majesty. Significantly, the New Testament marks this irreligious act out for special reprehension (see Acts 5: 1 – 11).

7. THE GIFT OF PIETY

Because the life of divine charity raises up the human person beyond the limitations of mere human ingenuity, each one of the moral virtues enjoys the special aid of the gifts of the Holy Spirit. These gifts are rightly referred to as *instinctus*, for they operate in us not after the manner of deductive reasoning, but after the fashion of an inborn touch or genius. Since the gifts work only in the believer, religion – outside of the realm of the Christian gospel – is a movement toward God that is entirely constrained within the limits of creaturely ways. But Jesus reveals that the God of Abraham, Isaac, and Jacob is his Father, so that all who share in the grace of Christ participate in his sonship as either sons or daughters.

The gift of Piety helps to make us effective children of the heavenly Father. Cajetan explains its special significance when he observes that this gift illumines the just believer to embrace every person, and indeed everything, as a child or possession of the heavenly Father – "ut filios et res Patris." This gift accordingly brings to an evangelical perfection whatever remains of the juridical and limited in the exercise of justice, thereby transforming in a mysterious way this heaven and this earth into the new heavens and the new earth (Rev 21: 1).

And because haughty people use other persons and things according to their selfish designs, the Christian tradition associates with the gift of Piety, the second Beatitude, "Blessed are the meek, for they will inherit the earth" (Mt 5: 5). Meekness marks the Christian character with strength, not servitude. Nietzsche's deranged prophecies about the modern era, unfortunately confirmed in much that the 20th century witnessed, illustrate the end to which a world of egoists tends. But the gift of Piety represents a strong spirit, and those who enjoy its grace and power are readied for creating a just order and measure in the world. In medieval art, justice is frequently represented with a balance and scroll; for example, at the cathedral of Hildesheim, the scroll bears the words from the book of Wisdom, "Omnia in mensura et pondere pono" (Wis 11: 21). Divine wisdom has arranged all things by measure and weight, and the virtue of justice makes it possible for the Christian believer to recognize and achieve the proper balance in everything that concerns the coming of God's reign.

CHAPTER 6
FORTITUDE AND THE COURAGE OF CHRIST

1. CHRISTIAN ANTHROPOLOGY AND HUMAN EMOTION

According to the constant teaching of the Church, human reason grounds free choice, and both capacities, intellect and will, together constitute the human person's specific humanity. The intellectual powers of the human soul (both reason and will) distinguish human persons from all lower forms of vegetative and sentient life. In order to recall this important truth, *Gaudium et spes* cites Psalm 8: 5–7: "Yet you have made them a little lower than God, and crowned them with glory and honor. You have given them dominion over the works of your hands; you have put all things under their feet, all sheep and oxen, and also the beasts of the field."[1] In his treatise on the creation of the human person, Aquinas distinguishes between the substance of the soul and its powers.[2] While the intellectual or rational powers identify the human being as such, the human soul also includes vegetative powers (nutrition, growth, and generation) and sensitive powers (the five external senses and the four internal senses: memory, imagination, the *sensus communis* and the *vis cogitativa*).[3] Although he denied the plurality of forms in the one substance of a human being, Aquinas does maintain a plurality of powers, really distinct from the soul and from each other. This conception of human psychology, which the Christian tradition has largely made its own, does not, however, force a metaphysical schizophrenia onto our conception of the human person. For in every action

---

[1] *Gaudium et spes*, no. 14.

[2] *Summa theologiae* Ia q. 77. Required background for Aquinas's discussion of the moral virtues includes a basic knowledge of his conception of the human person and the operative capacities that belong to the person. The following texts provide a helpful summary of this material: *Summa theologiae* Ia qq. 7583 (this tract on the nature and abilities of the soul is available in volume 11 [edited by Timothy Sutton] of the Blackfriars *Summa*); Etienne Gilson, *The Christian Philosophy of St. Thomas Aquinas*, trans. from the 5th ed. by L. K. Shook (New York, 1956) Part Two, chapters 4, 5, 6, & 8; W. A. Wallace, O.P., *The Elements of Philosophy* (New York, 1977), pp. 7184, offers a very concise treatment of the required material, but he does provide references to the pertinent articles in the *New Catholic Encyclopedia*.

[3] *Summa theologiae* Ia q. 78. Aquinas next considers the general features of the intellect in q. 79.

that an individual performs, the human being, as one substance or supposit, remains a single subject of operation, an undivided *agens* or acting person.

In a broad sense, each power or capacity of the human soul is characterized by love, a reaching out toward what perfects a particular power and, indeed, the very person who acts. Human intelligence loves truth; human willing loves the good. This, in the words of Dante, "is the Love that moves the sun and the other stars."[4] The dynamism of the appetitive powers in particular deserves to be called love. And in the human person, the rational animal, we distinguish sense appetite – the human passions or emotions – from intellectual or rational appetite. In order to delineate accurately the moral virtues that are *circa passiones*, namely, those that moderate human passions, the difference between the sense appetites and the intellectual or rational appetite remains central.

Sensitive love (*amor sensitivus*) is the complacency of the sensitive powers in their respective objects, such as happens in brute animals. In this context, "object" is anything considered as terminating and specifying an elicited act, cognitive or affective. Sense appetite is aroused by values sensibly perceived or imagined, whereas intellectual affectivity, or will, is the power to enjoy things that come within the focus of understanding.[5] Rational love differs from sensitive love in that its object is the good as known by the intellect. Moreover, in human choosing, the good intended is itself determined by choice. The medieval historian Étienne Gilson explains this major implication of the human ability to love rationally.

> In this life, confronted as it is with a multiplicity of partial goods, human intellectual love enjoys the kind of freedom proper to free choice. Man freely chooses the objects of his love following the judgments of his intellect on their comparative goodness and the consecutive movements of his will.[6]

Freedom, then, is possible for the human person because, and insofar as, no particular object necessitates the attention of his mind. Because the human will is an intellectual appetite, the choosing person approaches the good only under the appearance of a particular and concrete thing. A choice of will of course involves the whole human person, the origins of whose intellectual life lie in sense knowledge. Virtuous choice, imperated through intelligent command characteristic of prudence, effectively engages every necessary human resource within the person toward the accomplishment of a good end.

Even some classical philosophers recognized the difference between deliberate choice and sense desires. In his treatise *On the Soul* (the *De anima*) Aristotle, for instance, distinguishes the two powers of appetite; moreover, he

---

4   Dante, "Il Paradiso," 33, 145.
5   The phrase comes from the helpful appendices by Timothy Sutton, O.P., in volume 11 of the Blackfriars translation of the *Summa theologiae* (1a. 75–83), *Man*, p. 252.
6   Étienne Gilson, *Elements of Christian Philosophy* (New York, 1960), p. 257.

asserts that the lower appetites of sense can participate in the higher one of reason.[7] And Aquinas accepts as fully compatible with Christian revelation that the appetitive dynamism in the human being "is born to be moved as a result of apprehension."[8] Even if emotionality is sub-rational in its own right, still it is naturally ordered to be controlled and directed by reason. However human nature in itself possesses scant resources for bringing about this state of moral equilibrium, and although this common experience seems to have escaped the notice of even so prominent a moral philosopher as Immanuel Kant, many people experience the utter helplessness of their will power to manage sense urges.

In Aquinas's account of the emotional life, the sense passions fall into two main categories: the contentious emotions of the irascible power and the impulse emotions of the concupiscible power. In a brief text, Aquinas summarizes the main lines of what Christian anthropology teaches about the emotions:

> The object of the concupiscible power is straightforward sensible good or evil, namely, what is pleasurable and painful. But conflict and stress arise from time to time about obtaining the one or avoiding the other; the situation is not simple, and good and evil as invested with the qualities of hardness or difficulty are then the objects of the irascible appetite. Some emotions, such as love and hate, desire and aversion, pleasure and sorrow, answer to the former appetite, while others such as courage and fear, hope and despair and anger answer to the latter.[9]

The Christian theologian need make no apology for introducing an adequate account of the emotional life into a discussion that explains the dynamic unfolding of the divine image in the human person. Using his own language and categories such as Spirit and flesh (Rom 8: 5), St Paul recognizes the facility with which emotional and other disturbances can occur within the Christian, thereby corroborating that the spiritual life is never that of a pure or disembodied spirit. In fact, St Paul correctly points out that the sense and other powers within the human person can rebel against the norms of the eternal law. Recall his comments apropos of human existence without Christ: "For I know that nothing good dwells within me, that is, in my flesh. I can will what is right, but I cannot do it" (Rom 7: 18).

There are other terms that refer to the generically different appetites that govern emotional interactions. Since the concupiscible appetites constitute passions of attraction, they are sometimes referred to as the impulse emotions; for they account for the effortless responses that the person makes when con-

---

[7]   Aquinas actually quotes the *Politics* Bk. 1, c. 2 (1254b5) in the text of *Summa theologiae* Ia-IIae q. 56, a. 4, ad 3.

[8]   *Summa theologiae* Ia q. 80, a. 1.

[9]   See the discussion of this important matter in *Summa theologiae* Ia-IIae q. 23, a. 1.

fronted with a simple, *viz*, uncomplicated, good or evil object. [10] These impulse emotions, as I have said, are six in number: love and hate, desire and aversion, joy and sorrow. On the other hand, since the irascible appetites amount to passions of attack, they are sometimes referred to as the contentious emotions; for they account for the human response to an arduous good or an especially difficult evil. Again, the contending emotions are five in number: hope and despair, fear and courage, and anger. Anger represents the railing of the emotions when an evil has already befallen a person. Because appetite by definition seeks rest in the object with which it is engaged, there is no counterpart for anger with respect to the good. Indeed, when the good, especially the ultimate good, befalls the human person, all appetite ceases. In their respective orders, the proper attainment of sense good, moral good, and theological good comprise moments of rest for the human person. For God, infinitely perfect and blessed in himself, according to a plan of pure goodness, has freely created humankind so that men and women might share in God's blessed life, his perfect rest in the good. [11]

The Christian tradition considers the irascible and concupiscible powers in two ways: first, in themselves, as they form part of the sensitive appetites; second, as they share in the life of reason, which, as Aquinas observes, the emotions are meant to do in intelligent animals. Because of St Paul's theological observations in the Letter to the Romans on the contrasts between Spirit and flesh and sin and law – "To set the mind on the flesh is death, but to set the mind on the Spirit is life and peace" (Rom 8: 6) – Christian theology must give an adequate explanation of the way reason affects the emotional life. Aquinas's account of the interaction between reason and the emotional life does full justice to the psychosomatic unity of the human person, and at the same time describes the important role that the virtues play in a life of Christian excellence.

> The body is ruled by the soul, and the irascible and concupiscible powers by reason, but in different ways. The body blindly obeys without contradiction where it is born to be moved by the soul. Hence Aristotle says that "the soul rules the body with a despotic rule," as a master rules his slave: here the body's entire movement is attributed to the soul. For this reason virtue is not in the body but in the soul. The irascible and concupiscible powers, however, have no such blind response. Instead, they have their own proper movement, by which, at times, they go against reason; hence Aristotle says that reason rules the irascible and concupiscible powers with political control, as free men are ruled who have in some

---

[10] In *Summa theologiae* Ia-IIae q. 23, a. 4, Aquinas devotes a long article to the explanation of the grounds for distinguishing eleven passions of the soul.

[11] *The Catechism for the Catholic Church*, prol., no. 1.

matters a will of their own. This is why virtues are required in these powers, so that they may be well fitted for operation. [12]

Because of this sharing in the life of reason, "the irascible or the concupiscible power can be the seat of human virtue, for in so far as each participates in reason, it is a principle of a human act." [13] While the virtuous development of the sense appetites requires that they be "ruled" by right reason, this rule is not something extrinsic to the particular character of the sense appetites. Because they can be inwardly shaped by reason, these seats of human emotion possess the capacity for authentic virtuous formation. They constitute, then, true seats, as the scholastic theologians say, for virtue.

Sound moral theology must provide a psychological basis for its claim that virtue can radically transform human behavior of every sort. Consider the example of the virgin martyrs in the early centuries of the Church. Ordinarily, a life-threatening danger such as the sure promise of execution would so excite the sense appetites that a person would immediately act so as to avoid death. But an intelligence informed by faith can discover the particular moral truth that this threat should be withstood for the sake of the gospel. And in freedom, these youngsters effectively chose to withstand the emotional pressure to capitulate to the demands of the tyrant. We can also find examples from everyday life. For instance, many people experience themselves pulled toward indulgence in unvirtuous venereal pleasure because the sense appetites spontaneously react to objects of attraction, both real and imagined. But a well-formed moral conscience knows the moral truth that a rectified love of friendship excludes carnal communication outside of lawful marriage. [14] And so the tempted person, who, as St Augustine says, "loves God with an undivided heart that no evil can shake loose," can choose to withstand such an attraction and instead exercise the freedom to conform to moral truth. [15] "But you are not in the flesh," St Paul assures the Romans, "you are in the Spirit, if in fact the Spirit of God dwells in you" (Rom 8: 9). The grace of the Holy Spirit conforms the Christian to full moral truth.

Because sense desire in itself remains rationally indiscriminate, nothing in either the irascible or concupiscible appetites enables these sense powers to differentiate whether it is reasonable to seek a particular good or to avoid a particular evil. Only the intellectual virtue of prudence can discern the good-as-meant, or how this particular sense good or sense evil should be virtuously embraced or courageously avoided. Aquinas says that the "intellect penetrates

---

[12] *Summa theologiae* Ia-IIae q. 56, a. 4, ad 3.

[13] See *Summa theologiae* Ia-IIae q. 56, a. 4.

[14] In fact, as *Summa theologiae* Ia q. 82, a. 4 ad 1 points out, there is an essential difference ("per se") between what the intellectual appetite wants and what the sense appetites want.

[15] *De moribus ecclesiae catholicae*, Bk 1, chap. 25, no. 46 (*PL* 32: 1330–1331).

the will with its act and object the way it does any other particular objects of understanding, like stone or wood, which all fall within the field of being and truth." [16] Such penetration is possible because, as the Second Vatican Council teaches, the human being remains "a unity of body and soul." [17] And so there exists a similarity between the relationship of prudence to the behavioral virtues and how the intellect lays hold of any knowable object. Virtue, in other words, puts reason into emotion. The ordering of the lower powers to the higher betrays the divine design of creation; in the human person "the elements of the material world, which reach their peak in humankind, raise their voice in free praise of the Creator." [18] When the human person follows a life of courage and moderation, he or she contributes to this chorus of praise by withstanding the "rebelliousness of the body." And so the Second Vatican Council affirms that "human dignity itself requires us to glorify God in the body (see 1 Cor 6, 13–20) and not to permit the body to serve the evil inclinations of the heart." [19]

2. THE VIRTUES OF PERSONAL DISCIPLINE

The treatment of the cardinal virtue of fortitude introduces the complex of moral virtues that Christian usage designates as the virtues of personal discipline. Of course by definition, every virtuous *habitus* infuses the discipline of reason into some area of human conduct, but because the cardinal virtues of fortitude and temperance immediately moderate the human emotions, these virtues especially are said to shape one's personal comportment. By distinguishing between the virtues of operation (associated with justice) and the virtues of personal discipline, the Christian moral tradition emphasizes that cardinal fortitude and temperance indeed form genuine virtues of the sense appetites. And since they moderate the emotional life or the sense passions (in Latin, the *passiones animae*), the virtues of personal discipline are sometimes referred to as virtues *circa passiones*; whereas the virtues of cardinal justice, because they regulate human interactions, are called the virtues *circa operationes*.

As qualities of the Christian life, the moral virtues of personal discipline shape and conform the emotions to the measure that corresponds to how God knows the world to be. In the moral psychology of the Christian believer, the virtues of personal discipline accomplish two objectives. On the one hand, these virtues affect the rational appetite or the will. Unruly emotions pose the most serious threat to maintaining a watchful prudence. By connaturalizing the

---

[16]   *Summa theologiae* Ia q. 82, a. 4 ad 1.

[17]   *Gaudium et spes*, chap. 1, no. 14.

[18]   Ibid.

[19]   Ibid.

irascible and concupiscible appetites to reach out for the authentically good ends of human life, the virtues *circa passiones* steady a person for making the right prudential choice. The second objective affects the sense appetites or emotions themselves. As real operative *habitus* of the human soul, the virtues *circa passiones* provide the actual operational principles for achieving any good action. In moral circumstances that involve the emotional life, the temperate and courageous person, then, both acts through and realizes the virtues of personal discipline. While in a certain sense the virtues of personal discipline cause a person to make a right choice, these virtues do not strictly speaking elicit choice, since this specifically human activity belongs to will itself. Rather, the virtues of personal discipline both facilitate virtuous choice and, by the ordering of the passions, eliminate emotional dispositions that would otherwise obstruct the realization of the virtuous life. In order to account for this full picture of human subjectivity, the scholastics said that the virtues of personal discipline bring about, especially in the sense appetites, what they termed *choice by participation*. In other words, because the emotions are conformed to virtue's measure, they can be said to enjoy a certain voluntariness; and in this sense, even the sense appetites are sources for fully human activity.

The principles of Aquinas's moral psychology uphold the importance of the whole person as the fit subject for human activity; his Christian account of how one lives a moral life never supposes a crypto-spiritualism in which the will holds (explicitly or covertly) an exaggerated predominance in the moral life. Because Christian life does not simply embody a spiritual ideal, moral realism unequivocally rejects all forms of anthropological dualism. Furthermore, because it recognizes that human personal existence comprises a unity of body and soul, sound moral teaching holds that the concupiscible and irascible sense appetites possess the capacity for true virtuous formation ordered to the authentic finalities of both nature and grace. Amid the exuberance and the dejection, the foolhardiness and the fear of anyone's emotions, moderation, stability, and rectitude are quite possible. The rule of reason does not refuse to recognize the good within the object of the appetites, but it is aware that a particular good must be appreciated within the context of the whole human good. At the time, in the place, and in the way the limitations of the sense objects allow, the appetites may give themselves to their proper objects. [20] Even within the life of grace and infused virtue, the emotions figure in achieving the best that human life can promise. Because the several capacities or powers of the

---

[20]   For this account, I follow W. D. Hughes, "Virtue in Passion," in *Virtue*, vol. 23 of the Black-friars translation of the *Summa theologiae* (London/New York, 1969), pp. 245, 246. For further information on how the scholastics understood human emotion see Mark D. Jordan, "Aquinas's Construction of a Moral Account of the Passions," *Freiburger Zeitschrift für Philosophie und Theologie* 33 (1986), pp. 7297.

rational soul (*potentiae animae*) all belong to a single subject that we call the acting person, the Christian tradition includes the conviction that moral truth affects every aspect of a human personality. "Just as it is better for someone both to will the good and to do it by an external act," explains Aquinas, "so it also belongs to perfect moral good that we be moved toward the good not only through our will but also through our sense appetites, according to the saying of the Psalm 83: 3, 'My heart and my flesh have rejoiced in the living God.' "[21] Grace permeates nature, neither destroying it nor leaving it alone.

Today, rationalist moral theories maintain a highly skeptical outlook about the chances of achieving an authentic humanization of the emotional life. This represents a complete failure of nerve about what the French poet Charles Peguy calls the "climate of grace." But a full theological vision, such as one finds in the writings of von Balthasar, consistently places the order of grace firmly *within* the natural world.[22] For different reasons, the Christian Platonisms that developed in the 12th century and continued in the 13th reacted negatively to Aquinas's bold attempt to incorporate even the most unruly sense urges, *viz*, the sexual urge, into the universe of truly moral comportment shaped by grace. Moreover, the tendency to exclude the power of divine grace from the realm of the sense life enjoys some impressive "patron saints." St Bonaventure, for instance, could not bring himself to believe that something as divine as infused virtue could abide in the same powers or capacities as disordered sense urges and human concupiscence. For concupiscence, according to some theological views, especially marks the effects of original sin, the primary alienation of the human person from God. Accordingly, Bonaventure explains infused temperance and fortitude as dispositions of the will that only influence the emotions.[23] But for Aquinas, while the *passiones animae* remain neutral in themselves, they receive their true moral character from our personal determinations insofar as the virtuous man or woman authentically directs these sense urges toward the achievement of moral good. In sum, moral realism rejects the view that the rational part of the soul forms the only significant characteristic of the moral person. Virtue shapes the whole body-soul composite, the *per se unum* that is the human person, with the result that the practice of virtue need not always entail a conscious figuring out of what one ought to do; sometimes the *recta ratio agibilium* – the truth about what to do here and now – flows directly from well-ordered and fully developed sense passions.

---

[21] *Summa theologiae* Ia-IIae q. 24, a. 3.

[22] See his *Studies in Theological Style: Lay Styles*, ed. and trans. Joseph Fessio and John Riches (San Francisco, 1986), p. 404.

[23] For further information, see my *The Moral Virtues and Theological Ethics* (Notre Dame, IN, 1991).

3. VIRTUE AND VALUE-FREE THEORIES

Contemporary empiricist views about human psychology account for the human emotions in a way that differs considerably from that advanced by classical anthropology and theology. One significant difference lies in the way practitioners of each approach morally evaluate emotion. While classical theology recognizes the moral neutrality of the human emotions as such, any particular expression of emotion is good or bad depending on how it measures up to the rule of prudence; value-free empirical determinations, on the other hand, are those that are made without a fixed relationship to moral good. But views about what constitutes the true nature of the human person distinguish most sharply clinical views about human emotions from those of Christian theology. Because there is no agreement about what constitutes human fulfillment, secularist practitioners are free to establish their own hierarchy of values. And because there exists no consensus among secular thinkers as to what promotes human well-being, professional psychologists hold different opinions as to what kind of emotional life suits human moral maturity. Clinical psychologists are left to ascertain only whether a particular emotional bent is constructive or destructive for an individual person. Of course, Christian revelation, since it can communicate the truth about being human and acting well, requires that the believer judge the moral value of sense urgings according to the measure of right reason. Eternal law establishes the norm or pattern for right human conduct. As a result, the Christian moral theologian may not suspend a judgment of moral truth in order to accommodate value-free psychological theories about the emotional life.

Since the sense appetites remain true seats of virtue, prudence shapes these powerful sources of human activity toward the accomplishment of the end of human flourishing. In the human person, the conformity of sense appetite to reason transpires in freedom, and not in a vitalist or mechanistic way, as though the human person were a steam-driven engine that required occasional release in order to avoid exploding. Rather, by taking a reasonable and integrative approach to human emotions, the Christian tradition avoids the reductionism that identifies the human person with the sum total of his or her sense urgings.

The virtues of personal discipline concern two general areas of activity for the preservation of human life. The cardinal virtue of temperance along with its allied virtues principally concern various forms of proper restraint in the moral life, while the cardinal virtue of fortitude and its allied virtues mainly strengthen or bolster the emotional life. Of course, because the human person – the *per se unum* – grounds every emotional response in the unity of a created personhood, these general features or characteristics of the emotional life remain closely associated. However, the formal distinction between restraining and strengthening does serve the purposes of methodology and pedagogy. In particular, fortitude and temperance provide the Christian theologian with a way to explain the numerous texts in the Sacred Scriptures that encourage the Christian believer to control his or her passions. "For the grace of God has appeared, bringing salvation to all, training us to renounce impiety and worldly passions, and in the present age to live lives that are self-controlled, upright, and godly" (Tit 2: 11,12).

Because God sent his Son in the "likeness of sinful flesh" (Rom 8: 3), authentic Christian humanism must account for the full transformation of all human capacities. As a man, Christ himself enjoys a fully developed and entirely rectified emotional life. Furthermore, because everything that the Son of God assumed for our salvation enters into the mystery of our redemption, Christians believe that gospel truth and virtue impact on human emotional life. Nothing other than a transformation of this kind would do justice to the "new creation" (2 Cor 5: 17) that comes with the grace of baptism. On this basis, we can conclude that Christian theology does not configure well with certain prevailing philosophical spirits. Three philosophical schools in particular offer special resistance toward a virtue-centered moral theology that effectively touches the emotional life: Platonism, Stoicism, and Cartesianism.

First, Platonism. Although the early Church endeavored to make Platonic anthropologies fit Christian theology, since the 13th century there has been general agreement that, without significant modification, a full-scale Platonist anthropology does not serve well the central claims of the Christian message. For Platonism conceives the soul as a motor for the human body, instead of its substantial form. This outlook leaves little room for a doctrine about the humanization of human biological structures, especially the sense passions; indeed, Platonist-inspired spiritualities eschew the emotions as suitable for virtuous formation. Next, Stoicism. Because this popular world outlook considers the potential unruliness of the emotions as causes for special precautions and even for regret, the Stoic outlook, despite the best efforts on its behalf by certain Christian ascetics, offers little of substance to help develop authentic virtue in the emotional life. Aquinas especially points out the incompatibility of Christian moral realism with the Stoic ideal of *ataraxia* and of *apatheia* when he underscores the potential moral value of anger. "Sharp reaction to a vexatious situation," he writes, "is characteristic of anger, and so it works directly with fortitude in attacking." [24] Third, an authentic Christian teaching on the emotional life remains difficult to reconcile with the principal anthropological features of Cartesianism. The Cartesian spirit in philosophy strongly links human personhood with human consciousness, thereby emphasizing ra-

---

[24] *Summa theologiae* IIa-IIae q. 123, a. 10, ad 3.

tionality as the constitutive element of the *humanum*. As a result, Cartesian-influenced thinkers tend to identify the process of humanization with the person's ability to provide a rational expression for every experience. (An example of this is found in the trend that considers education to be the best remedy for moral disorder.) Because moral truth rectifies not only the reflections of reason but also the movements of the emotions, Christian moral realism offers a starkly different outlook on the emotions within the Christian life.

4. THE CARDINAL VIRTUE OF FORTITUDE

Like all of the virtues *circa passiones*, fortitude remains ordered to the humanization of the sense appetites, that is, toward bringing the appetites into conformity with the rational good. [25] In particular, courage stops us from being repelled unreasonably by difficulties. More than any other classical Christian author, Aquinas develops a profoundly systematic reflection on the virtue of fortitude. [26] Moreover, in discussing Christian fortitude, Aquinas especially shows that Aristotle's notion of courage fails to provide a paradigm that fits neatly into a complete vision of Christian humanism. Some persons, it is true, may enjoy a physical stature that well suits them for combat, but Aquinas insists that true Christian fortitude is a form of spiritual bravery. Building on Aquinas's views, Josef Pieper uses this conception of fortitude to challenge the often-repeated, but utterly erroneous, position of Nietzsche that Christianity amounts to a religion of slaves and that instruction in gospel truth only fosters an unhealthy psychological attitude of submission. [27]

Fortitude is a virtue of the irascible or contending appetite. The irascible appetites come into play when a person faces complex and difficult situations, such as those circumstances that require one to face up to special evils. In the discussion of theological hope, we pointed out that two alternatives face the person confronted with a difficult good. One is hope, a confident tendency toward an arduous, future possible good; the other is despair, the turning away from such a good as impossible of attainment. In their most basic forms, hope and despair are movements of the irascible appetite elicited by the presence of sense goods difficult to obtain. But in the face of a difficult evil, different

---

[25] Cajetan provides a fine commentary on the way this works. See his *In secundam secundae* q. 123, aa. 1, 2.

[26] Aquinas probably wrote the small treatise in the *Summa theologiae* IIa-IIae qq. 123–140 at the end of his life, *viz*, around 1272 in Italy. He had completed commentary and notes on Aristotle's *Nicomachean Ethics*, but the major influence in the treatise derives from his meditation on the passion of Christ and the witness of the Christian martyrs. See M.-J. Congar, O.P., "Le traité de la force dans la 'Somme théologique' de S. Thomas d'Aquin," *Angelicum* 51 (1974), pp. 331–348.

[27] See his *The Four Cardinal Virtues*, trans. Richard and Clara Winston (New York, 1965).

emotional reactions set in. In the Christian view the virtue of fortitude chiefly addresses "fears of difficulties likely to cause the will to retreat from following the lead of reason." [28] The Christian believer, says St Augustine, "loves God with an undivided heart that no evil can shake loose." [29]

As with every authentic practice of moral virtue, the person of fortitude must rely on true prudence in order to figure out the proper course of brave action. [30] Because Christian prudence is at work in every behavioral virtue, fortitude does not ape the bravery of Aristotle's soldier of fortune. [31] At least five different circumstances provide the opportunity for mock courage: when someone is ignorant of a danger involved, too optimistic about the nature of the danger, overly confident concerning his abilities, moved by untoward emotions of anger or depression, or is overly motivated by bounty-seeking. In these cases, people may in fact perform brave actions, but they do not possess the virtue of fortitude. Furthermore, because they lack the proper direction that prudence alone can impart, actions in these circumstances do not build character.

Because it restrains the urge to abandon activity in the face of obstacles to seeking the good, the virtue of fortitude restrains our fears – *cohibitiva timorum*. At the same time, fortitude moderates deeds of daring and audacity – *moderativa audaciarum*. So fortitude deals with fear and daring, restraining the first and imposing a balance on the second.

We define virtue by the maximum that it can achieve. "Fortitude," writes Aquinas, "is properly employed in sustaining all misfortunes. But a man is not unreservedly considered brave because he endures just any sort of trouble, but only because he endures even the greatest evils well." [32] Fear of the dangers involved with death particularly concern cardinal fortitude. Natural law inclines the human person to protect the substantial being of his or her individual human nature. However, when a person is confronted with the prospect of dying for some greater good cause, whether it be in defense of a fatherland or for the Christian faith, fortitude overcomes even love for one's own life. Since death spares no one, fortitude becomes every man and woman; moreover, the inevitable threat of death establishes the indispensable place that fortitude keeps in human life.

Warfare especially occasions the risk of death. Since the Christian tradition has never sanctioned pacifism as the only response to unjust aggression, a just

---

[28] *Summa theologiae* IIa-IIae q. 123, a. 3.

[29] *De moribus ecclesiae catholicae*, Bk 1, chap. 25, no. 46 (*PL* 32: 1330–1331).

[30] Aquinas recognizes that there are many possibilities for false bravery; see *Summa theologiae* IIa-IIae q. 123, a. 1, ad 2.

[31] See *Ethics* Bk 3, chap. 8 (1116a16).

[32] *Summa theologiae* IIa-IIae q. 123, a. 4, ad 1.

war – one that defends the common good – remains a theoretical possibility, although the destructive force of modern armaments makes prudent deliberation on a war's expediency urgently necessary. Still, sometimes men and women are called into perilous circumstances in order to maintain the good order of peace. On this account, the Church continues to recognize the moral value of military service: "Those who are dedicated to the service of their country and are members of the armed forces," *Gaudium et spes* affirms, "should regard themselves as ministering to the security and freedom of their peoples, and while they are performing this duty in the right manner they are genuinely contributing to the establishment of peace." [33] In order to fulfill this role, those who volunteer or are justly bound to military service especially need fortitude. Christian hagiographers like to remind us that the professional soldier constitutes the largest single profession of those listed in the Roman martyrology. And among the ancient depictions of the Savior, such as the mosaic in the vestibule of the archiepiscopal chapel in Ravenna, we find Christ depicted as a warrior.

Although fortitude primarily concerns the courageous response in the face of death, it extends as well to other occasions, especially those that a person may encounter in the service of virtue:

> But a brave person is rightly concerned with the dangers of any other death [besides in battle], particularly as such a one may undergo the peril of any kind of death in the service of virtue; for example, when a man does not shrink from attendance on a sick friend for fear of deadly infection, or when he does not shrink from a journey on some matter of duty because of fear of shipwreck or bandits. [34]

Since no Christian believer passes through life without confronting difficulties of this kind, the virtues of fortitude serve a vital function throughout the Christian life. In medieval iconography, such as in the painting in the Chapel of All Saints at Ratisbon, the figure that represents fortitude wrestles with a lion. This image of true Christian strength reminds us that the believer must be ready to confront even the most ferocious challenges that the world sets up against the truth of life – the *veritas vitae*. And because he knew that adverse circumstances would inevitably confront those who believed in his name, Jesus himself encouraged his disciples to maintain a courageous spirit: "In the world you face persecution. But take courage; I have conquered the world" (Jn 16: 33).

Because great evil causes great fears, the principal act of fortitude involves endurance; to be brave is to endure (*sustinere*) hardships. Bearing up characterizes the work of fortitude more than attacking. Because an actually present evil

---

[33] *Gaudium et spes*, no. 79.
[34] See *Summa theologiae* IIa-IIae q. 123, a. 5.

brings its own seriousness and challenges, the emotions of daring or courage enjoy their own inbuilt moderation. So the virtue of fortitude concerns attack (*aggredi*) only in a secondary way. However, the endurance that comes from fortitude does not cultivate a passive quality of the soul; rather it represents an active and positive quality of character that allows one to cling to some good in the face of evil. Being a distinctively Christian endowment, "the virtue of fortitude," observes Josef Pieper, "keeps man from so loving his life that he loses it." [35]

Like each virtuous *habitus*, fortitude makes its special object, namely the endurance of evil, prompt, joyful, and easy. But the emotion of joy or delight seems incompatible with the experience of evil. In what does the brave person delight? The brave person delights in the exercise of virtue and its end. "Acts of the virtues cause delight chiefly because of their ultimate end," says Aquinas, "but in themselves they can be painful." [36] And he goes on to cite Aristotle: "The exercise of every virtue is not pleasant except insofar as it attains its end." [37] But in another sense the brave person has cause for sorrow. For such a one must ponder the loss of life or experience the pain of body. Therefore the virtue of fortitude does not necessarily entail conscious delight; it is enough that the brave person is not depressed by the evil circumstances that he or she faces. [38] And so the Church sees no contradiction between Christ's agony on the cross, even his experience of abandonment by the Father, and the joyful embrace of God's holy will that gives his physical sufferings their salvific value for the human race.

5. FORTITUDE AND MARTYRDOM

The Christian theologian recognizes that fortitude belongs in an eminent way to the martyrs of the Church. As the original Greek term implies, the martyr witnesses to someone and something. In the witness of martyrdom, we can discern three specific virtues that are at work: charity, faith, and the moral virtue of fortitude. Aquinas describes this as follows:

> Charity does prompt the act of martyrdom as its first and most important moving force by being the virtue that commands it [*per modum virtutis imperantis*], but fortitude does so as the directly engaged moving force, being the virtue that brings out [*per modum virtutis elicientis*] the act. Charity therefore is the directing virtue, and courage the eliciting virtue in the act of martyrdom; and so it

---

[35] Pieper, *The Four Cardinal Virtues*, p. 134.

[36] *Summa theologiae* IIa-IIae q. 123, a. 8, ad 2.

[37] *Nicomachean Ethics* Bk 3, chap. 9 (1117b15).

[38] *Summa theologiae* IIa-IIae q. 123, a. 8.

manifests both virtues. But like any act of virtue, it gets its meritorious nature from charity; so without charity it is of no value." [39]

In the language of the scholastics, martyrdom remains an elicited act of fortitude and a commanded act of theological faith and charity. In other words, the goodness of God becomes the source and ultimate motive for the martyr's act, for charity unites the person who suffers for the truth of the Gospel or for some Christian virtue to the very power of God himself. Theological faith provides the specific adherence that distinguishes Christian martyrdom from political assassination or dying for an ideological cause. But the courage to face death flows from the virtue of infused fortitude, for it belongs to the brave person to face death without flinching. Consider the composure of the English Renaissance martyr St Thomas More when he mounted the scaffold.

The French spiritual author Louis Bouyer explains that the early Church interpreted martyrdom as something more than an exercise of the moral or even theological virtues. "The Christian martyr," he writes, "is distinguished not only by faith in Christ, but by the explicit connection of his death with Christ's." [40] In the acceptance of martyrdom, the Christian believer achieves the perfect imitation of Christ. Indeed, during the period of persecution against the Church, some believers wanted even to surrender themselves to hostile civil authorities as volunteers for martyrdom. Though the practice was discouraged by the legitimate Pastors of the Christian Church, it discloses how much Christ's courage inspired the earliest Christian believers. So much did martyrdom shape the piety of the early Church that the 4th-century bishop and historian Eusebius of Caesarea says of the early Christians that they "loved to reserve the title of martyr to Christ, the 'faithful and true witness' (Rev 3, 14), the first-born from among the dead, the prince of the life of God." [41]

6. THE VICES AND SINS AGAINST FORTITUDE

The vices against fortitude include timidity or cowardice as its defective form and fearlessness and reckless daring as its excessive forms. The coward refuses to endure the hardships that doing the good entails; he recoils from the discomfort that accompanies the completion of any arduous effort. This vice is especially unwelcome in the person who is charged with the preaching of the gospel or the care of souls, for timidity of spirit often leads to compromise of the truth. Reckless daring also jeopardizes the successful achievement of important projects, especially when it masquerades as a sophisticated bravado

---

[39] See *Summa theologiae* IIa-IIae q. 124, a. 2, ad 2.

[40] See his *History of Christian Spirituality* I, *The Spirituality of the New Testament and the Fathers*, trans. Mary P. Ryan (London, 1963), p. 193.

[41] Eusebius, *Ecclesiastical History* 5, 2, no. 5.

or appears in the guise of a naive spirit. Fortitude and prudence work together, for the Christian believer requires a perceptive spirit when it comes to making an accurate assessment of the difficulties that confront the preaching of the gospel. Fortitude strengthens the Christian's resolve to resist temptations and to overcome the difficulties that one encounters in leading a moral life.

The capital vice that erodes fortitude is sloth, a state of dejection that gives rise to torpor of mind and felling of spirit. Following the language of W. H. Auden, the modern period is sometimes called the "age of anxiety," referring to the prevalence of a sluggishness that can so sap a person's strength that he or she loses a real desire for anything, even for the most simple forms of good. This oppressive sorrow can so weigh on a person's mind that all thought of exercising virtue causes dread and immobility. The slothful person grows increasingly suspicious of everything, exaggerating difficulties and discerning evil where it does not exist. The only antidote for this debilitating condition that today afflicts so many persons, even those of good will, is fortitude.

Our blessed Lady, whom Christian piety invokes as Comforter of the Afflicted and Cause of our Joy, serves as a special intercessor against the depressed and depressing disposition of sloth. At the foot of the cross, Mary shares the passion of her Son in a preeminent way, and so her maternal mediation takes on a new and definitive significance. "The words uttered by Christ from the cross," Pope John Paul II says, "signify that the motherhood of her who bore Christ finds a 'new' continuation in the Church and through the Church, symbolized and represented by John." [42] During the course of the late Medieval period, the custom of portraying Mary in a dead faint at the moment of Christ's death replaced the long-standing practice of depicting her in a serene and composed manner. In his commentary on Aquinas's treatment of fortitude, Cajetan takes exception to this artistic license. He explains that since our blessed Lady shares in the fortitude of her Son, an upright stance instead of a swooning faint better represents the patient composure that she maintained while standing at the foot of the cross. [43] As the Mother of Sorrows, Mary enables all those who invoke her maternal intercession to practice patient endurance in times of trouble, even of the most painful and aggravating variety.

---

[42] *Redemptoris Mater*, no. 24.
[43] *In secundam secundae*, q. 123, a. 8, no. II.

7. THE COMPONENTS OF FORTITUDE, AND THE GIFT OF THE HOLY SPIRIT

Because death constitutes the formal object of fortitude, there are no subdivisions of this virtue to compare with the subjective parts of prudence – individual, political, and military. There is no way to subdivide death, which is sometimes called the great equalizer. However, fortitude does possess what we have earlier described as integral and potential parts. These can be conveniently organized under two headings: (1) the virtues of enterprise or attack, and (2) the virtues of support. Both the integral and potential or allied parts of the cardinal virtue of fortitude bear the same names. As integral parts, these dispositions refer to the psychological traits that distinguish a brave stance toward death. As potential parts, however, they constitute distinct *habitus* that regulate the proper restraint of fear and due moderation of daring in those situations that do not entail the full power of death's threat. [44]

The virtues allied to fortitude represent strong virtues, and they serve important roles in the life of the Christian. The principal potential parts of fortitude include magnanimity, which upholds us in the pursuit of great honor, and magnificence, which strengthens us at times of great outlays of money. These comprise the virtues of enterprise. But the potential parts of fortitude also include patience, which steels us against various kinds of affliction, and perseverance, which helps us persist in this effort over a long period of time. These comprise the virtues of support. In the Church of Saint Germain-en-Laye on the outskirts of Paris, the cenotaph of the exiled English King James II displays an epithet that captures the work of fortitude's potential parts: "Magnus in prosperis, in adversis maior." The courageous person shows greatness of spirit in good times and even greater resolve in trying ones. And because difficult circumstances can extend even over a long period of time, endurance in the face of evil provides one of the most challenging fields for maintaining virtue. Thus, perseverance further includes the virtue of longanimity, which reinforces one to accept postponement of expected relief from suffering, and the virtue of constancy, which braces a person against the threat of further obstacles that would delay finding relief from difficulty. Though each of these virtues represent distinct *habitus* within the family of the virtues of support, they all manifest a relationship to Christian patience.

Because of the example that Christ himself offers us in the gospels, spiritual authors single out patience as a virtue that particularly characterizes the Christian life. "Everything written before our time was written for our instruc-

---

[44] Aquinas discusses the virtues of enterprise (magnanimity and magnificence) and the vices that obstruct their exercise in *Summa theologiae* IIa-IIae qq. 129–135 and the virtues of support (patience and perseverance) in qq. 136–138.

tion," St Paul tells us, "that we might derive hope from the lessons of patience and the words of encouragement in the Scriptures" (Rom 15: 4). Just as Christ himself manifests solid patience in the face of evil, and thus illustrates the divine compassion, so too must the Christian believer maintain a patient stance toward the world. "The virtue of the spirit which is called patience," writes St Augustine, "is so great a gift of God that it is proclaimed as a mark even of him who bestows it on us." [45] The Christian believer, then, bears temporal hardships as a way of reflecting God's merciful forbearance with a fragile and sinful human race. In this way, the patient person becomes holy by interceding for those many persons who rebuff God's loving call for union with him through suffering. "Charity," St Paul insists, "is patient" (1 Cor 13: 4).

The Christian community must never abide pettiness or lavishness, discouragement or lack of interest, soft living or obstinacy; these represent the sins against fortitude's allied virtues. Rather, those who embrace the Christian life should know how to exhibit greatness in accomplishing the good and how to hold fast with the good, even if this activity entails patient waiting, persistence in an effort, or continuing in a strenuous way already undertaken. "In your struggle against sin," warns the Letter to the Hebrews, "you have not yet resisted to the point of shedding your blood" (Heb 12: 4).

Above all, waiting for the coming of the Kingdom requires a discerning patience and forbearance that eludes ordinary human calculation. In the "Admonitions" that St Francis of Assisi addressed to his first followers, the holy man of God lays great stress on the value of patience and humility for the *sequela Christi*. "We can never tell how patient or humble a person is," he says, "when everything is going well with him, but when those who should cooperate do the exact opposite, then we can tell. A man has as much patience and humility as he has then, and no more." [46] Though this degree of virtue may develop as a result of human strivings, we can expect to encounter patience and humility of this kind only in those who receive the virtue from Christ himself.

The gift of the Holy Spirit that we call Fortitude supplies the *instinctus* or special grace that directs believers to the right course of action toward building up the Church. Moreover, the Church's tradition appropriately associates a gift of the Holy Spirit with the virtue of fortitude, "for sometimes it does not lie within human power to attain the end of one's work, or to escape evils or dangers, since these sometimes press in upon us to the point of death." [47] But the Holy Spirit, Aquinas assures us, pours into our minds a certain confidence that we will reach eternal life and escape from all dangers. Because the moment of

---

[45] St Augustine, *De patientia* 1 (*PL* 40: 611).
[46] "The Admonitions," no. 13 in St Francis of Assisi, *Omnibus of Sources* (Chicago, 1973), p. 83.
[47] *Summa theologiae* IIa-IIae q. 139, a. 2.

death remains a crucial one in the salvation history of each person, the believer at that time especially requires this sort of divine help.

The tradition associates with fortitude the fourth Beatitude, "Blessed are those who hunger and thirst for righteousness, for they will be filled" (Mt 5: 6). In making this connection, we are reminded that the gift of Fortitude especially points to the realization of evangelical justice in the world. Fortitude concerns what is strenuous. "Now it is very laborious not merely to perform the virtuous actions which are generally called works of justice," says Aquinas, "but to perform them with an insatiable longing which represents a 'hunger and thirst for righteousness.' "[48] Because the Holy Spirit aids those who face special adversity in the pursuit of good objectives, this eschatological gift aids those who labor in the vineyard of the Church.

---

[48]   Ibid.

CHAPTER 7
CHRISTIAN MODERATION AND TEMPERANCE

1. HUMAN ACTION AND HUMAN BIOLOGY

Temperance first of all concerns the basic requirements for biological life, to which human beings find themselves specially and, at times, exceptionally attracted. While the virtues attached to cardinal fortitude remain distinct from those of temperance, the inclinations of the irascible or contending appetites – always and necessarily suppose the movements of the concupiscible appetites the simple and direct inclination or tendencies toward goodness and away from evil. In other words, the irascible appetites (hope and despair, fear and courage, and anger) come into play only when a set of circumstances makes the good to be achieved or evil to be avoided especially difficult or complex. However, the fundamental, ordinary response of the human emotions in front of a good or evil object always involves the dynamism of the concupiscible appetites.

As I have said, the concupiscible appetites include three pairs of *passiones animae*, namely, the emotions of love and hatred, desire and aversion, pleasure and sadness.[1] The virtues of temperance include a number of good *habitus* or qualities of character that enable the human person to restrain or moderate the movements of the concupiscible appetites. As elementary human capacities, the emotions of the concupiscible appetites principally secure goods indispensable for human flourishing. So, for example, the Church teaches that "the conjugal communion sinks its roots in the natural complementarity that exists between man and woman and is nurtured through the personal willingness of the spouses to share their entire life project, what they have and what they are. For this reason such communion is the fruit and the sign of a profoundly human need."[2] Furthermore, as the concupiscible appetites embody the human capacity to reach out toward good sensible objects such as food, drink, and sexual pleasure, these passions of the soul are also known as the

---

[1] For a fuller treatment of the passions in Aquinas's doctrine, see *Summa theologiae* Ia-IIae q. 23, a. 4.

[2] *Familiaris consortio*, 3, no. 19.

impulse emotions.[3] These impulse emotions concern goods that fall under two main headings: the good of nutrition, essential for the preservation of the individual, and the good of reproduction, essential for the preservation of the human species. Understanding the importance of virtuous temperance for sound moral theology requires a correct view of the place that biological needs have in a general description of human well-being.

Because these needs are rooted in human biology, the satisfaction of the basic human needs remains indispensable for human life. While biological needs figure importantly in virtuous prudence, at the same time, not every thirst, hunger, or sexual urge arises from and therefore represents true need.[4] Consider the example of a fine dinner. Of course, the need for food is one thing; lust for the pleasure of the palate is another. As a subjective part of the virtue of temperance, the virtue of abstinence concerns the lust for pleasure with comestibles, and through the right regulation of such desire properly fulfills the biological requirements of healthy nutrition. At the same time, true abstinence shuns the defect of boorishness, or the complete inability to appreciate the pleasures of the table, especially the refined ones.

In order to discuss the virtues that moderate the sense impulses of human nature, the moral theologian must consider the relationship between biological need and inclination or tendency. What is a tendency or inclination? In its most primitive form, tendency designates what the scholastics call appetite (*appetitus*), *viz*, the simple inclination or movement found in any living subject toward a convenient object. When used to describe what satisfies an appetite, the term "convenient (*conveniens*) object" implies that a specific reality is able to perfect a given subject endowed with appetite. For example, only potable liquids serve as fitting objects for the human tendency to thirst. Aquinas expresses this anthropological axiom as follows:

> By its nature each thing is bent on what fits it. And so human beings naturally crave an enjoyment that matches them. As such they are intelligent beings; consequently the pleasures they are equal to correspond to intelligence. On these temperance puts no restraint, though it does on those that are against intelli-

---

[3]   Those who prefer a more literal translation of Aristotle's Greek speak about the affective orexis for the concupiscible or impulse appetites and the spirited orexis for the irascible or contentious.

[4]   Psychologists usually distinguish general biological needs from instincts. Instincts ensure that the necessary actions for a body's well-being, such as the coupling of male and female and the nursing of young offspring, transpire in the proper way, even without the benefit of previous learned experience. Instinctual behavior represents a kind of innate *savior-faire*, that is, the ability to operate according to a particular pattern that benefits the organism. Because instinctual behavior usually remains ordered to only one realization, and therefore does not form a suitable action for *habitus* formation, the moral theologian remains especially interested with instincts and needs.

gence. Clearly this is to agree and not to clash with the burden of human nature. Which is not to deny that temperance is against the grain for merely animal nature uncomplying with reason. [5]

This text explains that in order for appetite to operate properly in the human person, there must exist the potential for conformity between the human person and the good that satisfies his or her yearning. In the example of thirsting, for instance, saltwater never satisfies the human appetite for liquid intake.

In human conduct, ends are said to draw. By definition, then, the objects of human appetite exercise a specific kind of causal influence on the human person. If the object embodies some good that, when embraced in reasonable measure, perfects human nature, then the drawing attraction of such a good serves to promote the overall well-being of the human person. In other words, human drives serve, and in themselves do not threaten, the good of the human person. When, however, the sense appetites settle on objects the embrace of which causes harm to the person, then no virtuous measure can be determined for any inclination toward such objects. The unsuitable object of desire alone constitutes a moral disorder, as happens in those who fancy sexual activity with a person of the same sex. There are two ways, then, that the sense appetites can lead a person to act against the reasonable order of virtue: first by wanting more or less of a good thing than what right reason dictates serves the person's good, and second by wanting something that frustrates the Creator's design for human well-being. [6]

The scholastics further distinguish between natural appetites and elicited appetites. Natural appetite represents a particular organism's bent toward any good that authentically perfects its being. We see, for example, the sunflower's turning to the sun, the deer's panting after running streams, or the human person's seeking intelligent explanations for the physical world. In the case of natural appetites, the cause of the body's movement toward an object lies in the actual nature (*forma*) of what moves. Because the human person enjoys vegetative, sensitive, and intellectual powers, each one of these "forms" spawns its own kind of natural appetites; however, the one substantial form that constitutes the human soul ensures the unity of the human person in acting.

Elicited appetite exists only in those beings that are capable of sense knowledge or that possess some form of voluntariness that develops from cognition. For example, when most children learn to savor spinach and relish artichokes or when any student masters a particularly difficult academic discipline, they are said to have developed an elicited appetite for these things. Accordingly, elicited appetites appear as expressions of either sensuous appe-

---

[5]   *Summa theologiae* IIa-IIae q. 141, a. 1, ad 1.

[6]   See Congregation for the Doctrine of the Faith, "Letter to the Bishops of the Catholic Church on the Pastoral Care of Homosexual Persons" (Vatican City, 1986), no. 7.

tition, which spring from sense knowledge, or rational appetition or willing, which arise from a person's understanding or comprehension of what the desired object means in terms of human fulfillment. Since the human person is a knowing subject capable of development through learning, many elicited appetites, then, actually exemplify learned patterns of behavior. The human person learns – through instruction and experience – the pleasurableness, usefulness, and goodness of many things.

2. THE DIGNITY OF THE HUMAN PERSON

Today, the moral issues that arise in connection with the concupiscible appetites are often articulated and evaluated according to criteria established by the life sciences. Because the sense appetites lie so deeply embedded in the biological structures of the human person, the life sciences can provide useful data that aids our comprehension of the virtues of temperance. Still, the Christian believer recognizes that the gospel imparts a wisdom about human life that surpasses what scientific research, however technologically advanced it may be, can achieve. *Gaudium et spes* explicitly affirms the importance of evangelical truth when it comes to making final determinations about what best serves both human progress and dignity.

> As sharers in the light of the divine mind, human beings are correct in judging that by their intellect they are superior to the totality of things... The intellectual nature of the human person reaches its final perfection, and needs to do so, through the wisdom that gently draws the human mind to seek and love what is true and good, and which leads it through visible realities to those which are invisible.[7]

On this account, it is entirely wrongheaded for the Christian believer to agree to a radical separation between the spiritual and psychological orders, a separation that would render the gospel irrelevant to human psychological well-being. It is true that some Christian authors in spiritual theology write as if the natural and life sciences can provide the only real truths about human nature and psychology, whereas religious instruction and moral truth pertain to a realm of "spirituality" that never really touches the concrete life of the person. This approach can lead to a kind of dualism in the human soul, dividing it into a transcendental "spirit" that adheres to God mysteriously, and a more mundane psychological dynamism that can be completely explained by human science. But to divide the intellectual nature of the human person contravenes the clear teaching of the Church; in fact, as early as the ninth century, the Church in ec-

---

[7] *Gaudium et spes*, no. 15.

umenical council authoritatively affirmed that no such spiritual duality exists within the human person. [8]

Just as the gospel itself repudiates all insinuations of cosmological and psychological dualisms, Christian morality rejects all forms of material determinism in the human person. *Gaudium et spes* points to the excellence of the human soul as the grounds for recognizing the true dignity and vocation of the human person.

> Humankind is not mistaken in recognizing its superiority over bodily things and in considering itself not just as a particle of nature or an impersonal element of human society. By its interior life it far exceeds the totality of things, and it experiences this deep interiority when it enters into the heart where God, the searcher of hearts, is waiting and where it decides its own destiny in the sight of God. [9]

Christian believers possess the consolation of knowing that deliberate actions originate from "within them" (Jer 31: 33), that is, from what the Church's spiritual tradition calls the human heart. The virtues of temperance in particular indicate both the psychosomatic unity of the human person and the subordination of matter (including the matter of the human body) to the human vocation that realizes itself in intelligence and freedom.

Theological ethics must take full account of human needs and tendencies insofar as they form an integral part of human life. Nevertheless, because of the excellence of human interiority, no moral judgment can be made about human actions simply by reason of the fact that they allegedly fulfill needs or tendencies. To hold such a view implies an extraordinarily superficial assessment of human nature and conduct. The Church rather instructs the faithful to acknowledge the spiritual immortal soul along with the biologically rooted needs and tendencies, so as to "attain that profound truth about reality" and to avoid deceptive and misleading explanations of what it means to be fully human. [10] What *Gaudium et spes* calls the "profound truth of reality" (*profundam rei veritatem*) means the truth about the human person, but it also points to the truth about human conduct. The goal of virtue is to achieve the truth of life, the *veritas vitae*, and this happens only when the person brings his or her activity into a right conformity with the supreme norm for all human conduct, which, as St Augustine has instructed the Christian theological tradition, remains the eternal law.

---

[8] See IV Constantinople (*DS* 657).
[9] *Gaudium et spes*, no. 14.
[10] Ibid.

3. THE VIRTUE OF TEMPERANCE

Temperance particularly concerns pleasure. As a virtue, temperance embodies a measured temper communicated by intelligence that restrains our desire for what exerts strong attraction on the human person. Temperance, then, helps the human person deal with the lower goods that perfect the human person, those, moreover, that so easily engage human attachments. Within the classical distinction of the five senses, cardinal temperance primarily concerns the sense of touch, for one cannot accomplish the activities that it directs without some form of bodily contact. The Christian tradition usually places food and sexual gratification among the principal objects that provide the strongest pull, whereas moral theologians prefer to discuss the material objects of temperance in a strictly formal sense: whatever produces pleasurable sensation as a concomitant of appropriate activity with food or a sexual partner. So while well-tempered passion forms an essential characteristic of all virtue, temperance, nonetheless constitutes a special virtue, since we can identify its specific formal object. Aquinas introduces a further precision into the scope of temperance. "The virtue of temperance," he says, "is engaged first with emotions of desire and pleasure about goods of sense, and then as well with emotions of grief arising from their absence." [11]

Since it forms the *raison d'être* of temperance, we need to consider the phenomenon of pleasure. In the *Summa theologiae*, Aquinas adopts a philosophical definition that describes pleasure "as a movement of the soul, perceptibly establishing a person in a condition which is in harmony with human nature, and which is an instantaneous whole." [12] In order to clarify this definition, the scholastic commentatorial tradition proposes five conditions that must be fulfilled in order to verify the experience of pleasure. [13] First, in order for pleasure to occur, a subject must be conjoined to an object through a certain and definite operation. Second, the human person experiencing the pleasure must actually know that the object is present and that the connection exists. [14] Next, pleasure requires a movement of the appetite, *viz*, an active and present delight that results from the happy accomplishment of the operation. Then, because there exists a connaturality between the person experiencing the pleasure and the object, a certain ecstatic quality marks the achievement of fulfillment. Finally, the climax or term of the operation cannot leave some essential element of the pleasurable movement yet to be attained, for in that case, the person ex-

---

[11]   *Summa theologiae* IIa-IIae q. 141, a. 3.

[12]   See *Summa theologiae* IIa-IIae q. 31, a. 1. Aristotle's text comes from his *Rhetoric*.

[13]   See Cajetan's commentary *In primam secundae* q. 31, a. 1.

[14]   For further information on this point, see G. E. M. Anscombe, "Modern Moral Philosophy" in *Ethics, Religion, and Politics* (Minneapolis, MN, 1981), p. 27.

periences the emotion of hope instead of pleasure. When put into the context
of virtue, there is a relationship between the right ordering of one's life and the
experience of pleasure. In order to illustrate convincingly this thesis, Aquinas
maintains that in the state of original justice, men and women would have experienced greater sexual pleasure in coitus, for the restraint of sinful disorder
would not have been active. [15]

This phenomenological description of pleasure provides helpful information for developing consensus on important issues in moral theology that concern the human person's craving for pleasure. First, pleasure never occurs without a person engaging in some operation; this operation can be actually exercised or imagined, that is, represented by the internal senses. The operation,
then, serves as the principal basis for making a moral judgment about pleasure.
In itself, pleasure remains morally neutral and, as a physical experience, always good. However, the right relationship of object and operation is required
in order to establish the basic moral character of a given pleasure. Moreover,
since pleasure remains a delightful good, a *bonum delectabile*, Christian ethics
must ensure that this accompanies the embrace of an authentic good, a *bonum
honestum*. Because objects specify their actions, we determine both the physical feature and the moral meaning of pleasure by reference to some object that
justifies both the coming-to-be and the enjoyment of a given pleasure. [16] For
example, if a person claims pleasure from putting food into his ears, we have
grounds for questioning the good sense, and also the morality, of such "pleasurable" activity. And this same rule of measure holds true when it comes to
improper sexual conduct, of the kind that contravenes both the purpose and the
design of the Creator.

In the virtue of temperance, the natural finalities of the human operations
that serve nutrition and procreation establish the basic parameters for virtuous
living. Aquinas asks whether the needs of the present life set the standard for
temperance. [17] The formal measure for temperance lies in the ends of the operations that promote the preservation of both the individual human person and
the human species. In this sense, temperance does not differ from the other
virtues, though the physical ends whose attainment temperance regulates stim-
ulate reactions more immediate and felt than those controlled by the virtues

---

[15] See *Summa theologiae* Ia q. 98, a. 2, ad 3.

[16] See Thomas Gilby's important remark in *Temperance* (2a2ae. 141 – 154), vol. 43, p. 27: "To
be *delectabile* is the quality of an end, nevertheless the 'pleasure-extract' there is not the
end-cause as such; cf. the classical criticism of hedonism, Ia-IIae 4,2. It is a consequence of
that, namely the real value there, *honestum*. And this itself, while not a *utile*, may be an end
subordinate to a higher end, and so the pleasure it gives may in this sense be for a purpose,
cf. *Summa contra Gentiles* III, 27."

[17] *Summa theologiae* IIa-IIae q. 141, a. 6.

of justice and fortitude. Because of the importance that preservation of the human race holds as an end, a provident God left little to the personal taste and discrimination of individual men and women. Moreover, "sexuality," explains Pope John Paul II in *Familiaris consortio*, "by means of which man and woman give themselves to one another through the acts which are proper and exclusive to spouses, is by no means something purely biological, but concerns the innermost being of the human person as such." [18] And the moral theologian could easily adapt this principle in order to show that, for the human person, eating and drinking should also constitute distinctively human activities.

Christian moral theology identifies the pleasures of and desires for satisfying the senses of touch and taste as the principal matters of temperance. Temperance moderates the desires and pleasures of touch and, derivatively, the aversions and sorrows that arise when any sense is suitably deprived of its object. While the theologian ought not to ignore the sense pleasure that derives from the other senses, *viz*, from admiring looks, pleasant words, sweet smells, and other sensations, nevertheless, on account of its connection to nutrition, temperance especially (though secondarily) concerns the sense of taste. Unlike those theologies overly influenced by Stoic outlooks on life, Christian theology does not deem the necessary operations of life as regrettable. The theologian warns only against unreasonable indulgence. At the same time, as the workings of internal senses such as the imagination or fantasy demonstrate, the human person can attempt to infinitize sense pleasure that in itself is limited.

Some sinners strive to make an idol out of pleasure. These are the people who come to live only by their senses, so that carnal desires predominate in their lives to the exclusion of everything else. In other words, the shape of a person's emotional life actually dictates how he or she will discriminate among a range of options. Disordered desires obviously affect the practical judgment an individual makes about the use of certain goods, about how he or she approaches a desired end. Accordingly, the drunkard wants only more intoxicating liquid; the profligate seeks more sexual gratification; the glutton more food, and so forth. These are the carnal sinners, as Dante calls them in the *Inferno*, "who subject reason to desire." [19] But this exertion always concludes in personal disorder; for by definition, created goods remain limited, and so they never lead humankind to the "wisdom which gently draws the human mind to seek and love what is true and good, and which leads men and women through visible realities to those which are invisible." [20]

---

[18]   *Familiaris consortio*, no. 11.

[19]   *Inferno*, Canto V, 37–39: "Intesi ch'a così fatto tormento enno dannati i peccator carnali, che la ragion sommettono al talento."

[20]   *Gaudium et spes*, no. 15.

For reasons that largely derive from theological considerations of eschato-logical fulfillment or final beatitude, Christian ethics customarily distinguishes between the sense experiences of joy and pleasure. [21] In order to understand this distinction, we must recall that in the human person there are both external senses such as touch and taste and internal senses such as memory and imag-ination; furthermore, the concupiscible appetite can react to sensations from both of these sense powers. When the internal senses experience something good, the Christian spiritual tradition speaks about joy, but when the external senses are at work, it speaks about pleasure. Even though both internal and ex-ternal senses are presented with objects and receive their stimulation in differ-ent ways, they represent movements of the sense appetites in response to sense experienced objects. This distinction, of course, points up the importance of the imagination in the moral life. Self-indulgence by means of the interior senses, while less directly perceptible to an external observer, nonetheless causes the same moral harm as disordered self-indulgence through the external senses. From a different perspective, the distinction between pleasure and joy explains why the Christian martyrs claim to experience a profound joy even in the midst of their painful physical sufferings.

Because their objects concern the goods that least distinguish the human person from other living organisms, the virtues of temperance rank last on the hierarchy of objective worth. As a virtue of personal discipline, temperance concerns the use that the human person makes of some *thing* or object. Moder-ation's rule for using pleasurable things derives from how much we need them to live. Still, the virtues of personal discipline possess a social dimension. Un-limited self-gratification, whether it concerns comestibles or erotic gratifica-tion, bears directly on the way that a person is able to participate in the life of the community. The wisdom literature of the Old Testament greatly esteems moderation: "Do not follow your base desires," counsels Sirach, "but restrain your appetites. If you allow your soul to take pleasure in base desire, it will make you the laughingstock of your enemies" (Sir 18: 30–31). Among all of the vices, intemperance particularly affects the person's capacity for engaging effectively in social communication.

---

[21]   The scholastics considered that simple joy represents the fruit of the rational appetite (cf. *Summa theologiae* Ia-IIae q. 31, aa. 3, 4), whereas felt joy involves the sense appetites (*delectatio cum reduntia in appetitu inferiori*). Pleasure or *voluptas* means sense pleasure, and can unfold as a result of cognition (*delectatio secundum cognitionem*) which is called aesthesis (cf. *Summa theologiae* IIa-IIae q. 141, a. 4, ad 3 um), or from touch (*delectatio in ordine ad sensibilia tactus*), which is called carnal pleasure (cf. *Summa theologiae* Ia-IIae q. 31, a. 6; q. 32).

4. THE MAKEUP AND KINDS OF TEMPERANCE

When he talks about *verecundia* and *honestas* as related to cardinal temperance, Aquinas takes his cue, but not his entire teaching, from classical moral philosophy. As integral parts of a cardinal virtue, these qualities represent special sensitivities in the temperate person. The first of these, shame or *verecundia*, causes the temperate person to recoil from what is dishonorable and disgraceful. Sensitivity to shame (*verecundia*) does not form a distinctive *habitus*; rather, it denotes a certain psychological trait that promotes temperance in general. We can further describe this trait as a reserve and good sense that amounts to a right fear of being shamed by the commission of moral ugliness or disgrace. The trait promotes a repulsion against what does not conform to a proper moral comportment. Unfortunately, since people easily develop a preference for the morally ugly instead of what comprises the morally beautiful, these component elements of temperance easily fall dormant in human consciousness, resulting in a deformed moral conscience. Those who are brazen about vice no longer recognize the difference between the morally aesthetic and the ugly; and such people are said in fact to lack all shame. It can also happen that those advanced in age or true saints may lack feelings of shame, but this occurs only on account of the unlikelihood that persons of such qualities will commit intemperate acts. In any case, shamelessness, except among the saints, leaves a person liable to making gross misjudgments concerning what is proper and fitting in matters dealing with temperance.

The other integral part of temperance is a sense of honor or *honestas*. Like truthfulness, honor – because it signifies a certain gracefulness and beauty of spirit – represents a quality that marks the whole of the virtuous life. Some authors teach that it actually corresponds with spiritual beauty itself. "By the honorable,"says St Augustine, "I mean what is beautiful to the mind, and this we properly designate as spiritual." [22] It may strike one as odd, then, that Aquinas considers such an important quality of the moral life as only an integral part of the lowest moral virtue. But since *honestas* represents the realization of a true moral aesthetic, the person who possesses this trait instinctually rejects anything that smacks of the indecent and the morally ugly. In other terms, the honorable person always chooses the beauty and grace that, according to God's providential design, characterizes the moral life.

When it comes to drawing up a complete list of the potential parts of temperance, the moral theologian faces some perplexing questions. Since every virtue implies moderation of one kind or another – the so-called virtuous mean – it is difficult to identify the particular virtues that share directly in the power of cardinal temperance. Aquinas, for example, divides the potential

---

[22]   *83 Quaestiones* 30 (*PL* 40: 19).

parts of temperance among those that moderate our inner feelings and those that moderate bodily poise and other external things. The first category includes virtues such as humility, an important Christian virtue that moderates our self-appreciation, clemency and gentleness that moderate anger and the desire for revenge. Aquinas also includes in this list the act of continence – not, properly speaking, a virtue – for it does effect the moderation of particular movements of concupiscence at particular times. The second category of virtues includes modesty, which particularly concerns external deportment, decency in dress, which concerns moderation of style and fashion, and, of special note, the virtue of study, which, says Aquinas, moderates an excessive curiosity about learning. The supposition behind Aquinas's view comes from Aristotle, who affirmed that there exists among human beings a natural urge to find out. The sins against the potential parts of the virtue of temperance include: incontinence, wrath and cruelty, and inquisitiveness or useless curiosity.

5. CHASTITY, ABSTINENCE, AND SOBRIETY

The subjective parts of temperance are easy to identify. The specific types of virtues of temperance fall under two main headings, *viz*, those about the pleasures of the table and those about sexual gratification. [23] Abstinence is the virtue that moderates the desire for the pleasure of food and sobriety the virtue that does the same for drink, especially inebriating drink and other mind-altering substances. Both abstinence and chastity moderate pleasures associated with touch, but they remain distinct virtues because of the two operations, *viz*, ingestion and coitus, that generate their distinctive pleasures. [24] Chastity strictly speaking pertains to moderating sexual climax; whereas purity pertains to the desires, thoughts, words and actions that promote, foster, and initiate sexual union. [25] While chastity obviously constitutes a special virtue, there is a sense in which every virtuous act exhibits a certain chasteness of spirit. In a particularly beautiful phrase, Aquinas expresses the fundamental note that chastity ensures in the moral life. There is a metaphorical meaning to chastity, he says, "for if God is our heart's delight, our attachment is where it should

---

[23] Aquinas treats the virtues and vices concerned with nutrition in *Summa theologiae* IIa-IIae qq. 146 – 148 (abstinence about food) and qq. 149 – 150 (sobriety about food) and with procreation in q. 151, aa. 1 – 3 (chastity and orgasm) and purity in general (qq. 151, a. 4 – 154).

[24] See *Summa theologiae* IIa-IIae q. 151, a. 3, ad 2 where Aquinas reflects on St Augustine's estimate of conjugal pleasures.

[25] See *Summa theologiae* IIa-IIae q. 151, aa. 1, 2. The *ea quae sunt ad finem* that chastity promotes concern nothing less than the survival of the human race itself. False teachings about sexuality always ignore the fundamental reason for chastity.

be, and we shall refrain from enjoying things against his design." [26] Particular norms for human conduct in matters of conjugal and personal chastity always reflect the divine design, and so the freedom of spirit that those who are conformed to God's law enjoy eliminates all suggestion of undue restraint or repression.

Because the sense of touch plays such an important role in the preservation of human life, moral theology traditionally concerns itself with human sexuality. [27] The Augustinian doctrine on original sin contributed to some misunderstandings about the role that disordered concupiscence plays in the Christian life. While Aquinas modifies considerably the standard teaching of his day, he still recognizes that sexuality suffers more than other human capacities from the disorientation of original sin. [28] In other terms, he accepts the view that the capacities more closely linked to human biology are less able to withstand the disordering effects of sin than are the higher capacities. While this view has led some theologians to prejudice sexual pleasure in itself, Aquinas applies his principle so that even sexual ecstasy remains an authentic human good whose moral character depends on the "setting" in which the pleasure occurs. [29]

Given the vehemence that characterizes sexual pleasure, the fact that sense-pleasures in themselves provide no standard of moral good and evil remains an important truth for Christian ethics. [30] Human appetites decide only what is pleasurable, and in the state of fallen nature they sometimes run at odds with the reasonable good. Aquinas explains this important point of Christian anthropology in the following way:

> The gift bestowed upon man in his first state, as a result of which reason kept the lower parts entirely in check, and the soul kept in check the body, was not from the efficacy of any natural principles but from the efficacy of original justice, which was given by divine liberality over and above them. When this justice was removed by sin, man returned to a state which befitted him according to his own natural principles... Just as man naturally dies and cannot be restored to immortality except miraculously, in the same way the concupiscible power naturally tends to what is pleasurable... even outside the order of reason. [31]

Because of original sin, erotic pleasure requires the attention of a special moderating virtue. But the Christian tradition encourages a balanced interest in sexual morality. Moreover, the Christian faith assures the believer that Christ

---

[26] *Summa theologiae* IIa-IIae q. 151, a. 2.

[27] For background, see *Summa theologiae* Ia-IIae q. 31, a. 6.

[28] See *Summa theologiae* Ia-IIae q. 83, a. 4.

[29] For more information, see *Summa theologiae* IIa-IIae q. 141, aa. 4,5.

[30] See *Summa theologiae* IIa-IIae q. 153, a. 2. Also, since "our genital motions are less subject than our other bodily members to reason," temperance must regulate everything that relates to promoting sexual climax, e.g. looks, kisses, embraces.

[31] *De veritate* q. 25, a. 7.

himself provides the balance; or as Origen insists, Christ is the substance of the virtues. Because the experience of pleasure forms part of the original integrity of man and woman, "conjugal love," says Pope John Paul II, "reaches that fullness to which it is interiorly ordained [in] conjugal chastity." [32] As a specific part of temperance, conjugal chastity, the Pope continues, "is the proper and specific way in which the spouses participate in and are called to live the very charity of Christ, who gave himself on the cross." [33]

Even the classical philosophers remarked on the unruly character of sexual urges in the human person, judging that they possess, as it were, a life of their own. And St Paul registers a similar view concerning the power which the "law of the members" exercises in our lives (see Rom 7: 23, 24), by which he of course means the movement of all the human appetites after the loss of original justice. In the Christian life of faith and sacraments, infused virtue actually and directly affects the sense appetites. Aquinas supports this claim by appealing to the Pauline teaching on Spirit and law:

> Infused virtue is of value in that, even though the passions be felt, still they in no way gain control. For infused virtue effects that a man in no way obey the concupiscences of sin; and while this virtue remains, it does this infallibly. Acquired virtue falls short in this respect, although in only a few instances, as other natural inclinations fail in only a minor part. Hence the Apostle declares in Romans 7: 5,6: "While we were living in the flesh, our sinful passions, aroused by the law, were at work in our members to bear fruit for death. But now we are discharged from the law, dead to that which held us captive, so that we are slaves not under the old written code but in the new life of the Spirit." [34]

In other terms, the infused virtues conform unruly sense appetites to the law of reason as Christ perfects it in the evangelical law. This ordering of the emotions or passions happens through what Aquinas calls the "impression of reason" on the appetites, so that by reason of his or her conformity to Christ, the Christian believer enjoys the power to achieve a rectified emotional life. [35]

But must the Christian theologian insist on reasonableness even in the context of sexual effervescence? Cajetan observes that one has to distinguish between an intermission of reason that leaves intelligence in a state of suspension and one which leads to a disordering of reason. Virtuous sex falls into the first category; intoxication provides an example of the second. In this regard, it is important to recall that Aquinas felt that, on the basis of the more profound harmony between the human powers which existed in pre-lapsarian man and woman, coitus would have been more pleasurable in the state of original jus-

---

[32] *Familiaris consortio*, no. 13.

[33] Ibid.

[34] *De virtutibus in communi* a. 10, ad 14.

[35] *Summa theologiae* Ia-IIae q. 60, a. 1.

tice than it is now, "for the pleasure of sense would have been all the greater, given the greater purity of man's nature and sensibility of soul." [36] Moreover, Aquinas held this view in opposition to the Franciscan school represented in the 13th century by Alexander of Hales and St Bonaventure. Even today, the Church recognizes that communication in charity between spouses enhances the warmth of spousal love. So there is nothing in Christian teaching that would allow one to conclude that Christianity covertly promotes the fear that sex makes people behave more like animals. Rather Christian truth invites men and women to embrace the honest realization that disordered sex does mar the beauty of the creature in a way that other capital sins do not, "for a person sunk in carnal delights," Aquinas warns, "has no taste for spiritual joys." [37]

The rectification of the sense appetites exists preeminently in the case of Christ, who had full and strong human passions or emotions that remained rightly ordered from within because his virtues of moderation and strengthening were so perfect in their formation. [38] What the grace of union accomplishes in Christ, chastity infused with charity effects in the one united with Christ. The French poet Charles Péguy gives this mystery poetic expression.

Car le surnaturel est lui-même charnel,

Et l'arbre de la grâce est raciné profond

Et plonge dans le sol et cherche jusqu'au fond

Et l'arbre de la race est lui-même éternel. [39]

Grace perfects nature, *gratia perficit naturam*. "The virtue of chastity," says one author, "is a perfect virtue because it consists in making sexual desires and joys participate in the reasonable order of the love of moral beauty, but it comes up against a great resistance of the passions become anarchic since original sin." [40] But through the healing power of divine grace – *gratia sanans* – Christ conquers sin in each one of his disciples. Chastity, as Pope John Paul explains in *Familiaris consortio*, touches directly on divine charity and, thereby, aids the principal commandment of the law that forbids placing any creature or created thing before God. As with every virtue, grace conforms human nature – in this instance, the emotional life – to the good of divine truth. And because of this union of hearts between the believer and Christ, divine grace frees the human person to join in the perfect worship of Christ the high priest. Pope John Paul

---

[36] See *Summa theologiae* Ia-IIae q. 98, a. 2, ad 2.

[37] *Summa theologiae* IIa-IIae q. 153, a. 5.

[38] See *Summa theologiae* IIIa q. 15, a. 2.

[39] Charles Péguy, *Eve* in *Oeuvres poétiques complètes* (Paris, 1941), p. 813: "For the supernatural itself is carnal, / And the tree of grace is rooted so deeply / And seeks the depths and sinks in soil so steeply / And the tree of the race itself is eternal" (translated by Fr Kevin McCaffrey, O.P.).

[40] Albert Ple, O.P., *Chastity and the Affective Life*, trans. Marie Claude Thompson (New York, 1966).

II recalls the New Testament parallel between unchastity and idolatry: "The same sin which can harm the conjugal covenant becomes an image of the infidelity of the people to their God." [41] Because unregulated emotion of any kind thwarts the realization of divine truth, every offense against chastity represents a miniature idolatry. The special gravity of lechery lies in its capacity to wean a person away from a full-hearted love of God.

Because the most important vocation for the Christian believer is to become a saint, the New Testament teaches that the contemplation of divine truth is more important than the pursuits of marriage. For this reason, both married persons and those who remain celibate are bound to give themselves as fully as possible to a life of prayer and worship. "Marriage and virginity or celibacy," says Pope John Paul II, "are two ways of expressing and living the one mystery of the covenant of God with his people." [42] Just as Christian martyrdom illustrates fortitude in an exemplary way, so the consecrated virgin or celibate must maintain a chaste love for those whom they serve. In this exercise of celibate chastity, moreover, they become spiritually fruitful, the fathers and mothers of many whom they bring to life in the Christian faith. And so the Church considers virginity and celibacy as a sign of the eschatological marriage of Christ with the Church; for those who dedicate themselves to this way of life liberate the heart "so as to make it burn with greater love for God and all humankind." [43] Because he considers this greater love as objectively associated with virgins and celibates, who dedicate themselves more completely to the contemplation of divine truth, Aquinas argues that these states of life retain their special eminence in the Church. [44]

Some theological opinion maintains that virginity in itself constitutes a better way of life. Whether this is true or not, the position provides a starting point for discussion with those who appraise virginity and celibacy as having only pragmatic value. Still, even Christian virginity remains a means to God; it is not an end in itself. Aquinas approvingly quotes St Augustine on the relative perfection of the celibate vocation: "Virgins follow the Lamb wherever he goes because, as Augustine puts it, theirs is the imitation of Christ by integrity

---

[41]   *Familiaris consortio*, no. 12.

[42]   *Familiaris consortio*, no. 16.

[43]   *Perfectae caritatis*, no. 12. In *Summa theologiae* IIa-IIae q. 152, a. 1, Aquinas explains what he considers essential to virginity: "Since virginity is defined in terms of moral integrity, the unbroken hymen is incidental to it, the immunity from the pleasures of orgasm is like its material, whereas the purpose of perpetually abstaining from this pleasure gives it completion and meaning." See also, a. 3, ad 2 & ad 3 for Aquinas's teaching on virginity *in præparatione mentis*, and his view on regaining the virtue of virginity through repentance. In the male, the waste of semen (outside of what occurs in the course of nature – the nocturnal emission) marks the end of physical virginity.

[44]   See *Summa theologiae* IIa-IIae q. 152, a. 2.

of flesh as well as of soul. So virgins follow in more ways, but not necessarily more closely, for other virtues cleave to God more closely by conformity of mind." [45] In this text, both Aquinas and Augustine make reference to the theological virtues of faith, hope, and charity. These virtues, that are given to every believer in grace, constitute the one true state of perfection for the human person. To fulfill perfectly this vocation, moreover, is the call directed to every member of the Church.

6. THE VICES OPPOSED TO TEMPERANCE

The vice opposed to temperance is intemperance. Intemperance results from the pursuit of sense pleasures outside the order of right reason. Even Aristotle recognizes that intemperance especially corrupts practical reasonableness; *intemperantia maxime corrumpit prudentiam.* [46] Since sins of intemperance impair one's ability to recognize the standards of graceful beauty, disordered lust handicaps intelligent behavior in a particular way. [47] Common experience shows that intemperance strikes at probity, decorum, and the like; indeed, people customarily hesitate to speak about sins of intemperance, more than they do about objectively graver sins. But as with every moral virtue, temperance has a defective form that appears to resemble more closely the practice of the cardinal virtue than its exaggerated form does. Temperance moderates passion; it does not destroy it. And, because the vice of unfeelingness or insensitivity restricts a person's capacity to enjoy pleasure, it represents a vicious deformation of true temperance. [48] But the Christian enjoyment of pleasure does not serve as the only principle in the moral life. The Christian life still requires the practice of asceticism, especially in those who devote themselves to contemplation and the study of divine matters and who, for that reason, should withdraw more from the allurement of carnal affairs. [49]

Intemperance particularly identifies the morally immature person; and such a one typically manifests unreasonableness and resistance to correction. And on account of this intransigence, intemperance usually warrants strong and immediate correction. So, while intemperance ranks far from being the worst of sins, it nonetheless is associated with a kind of shame that brings reproach (*ex-*

---

[45] *Summa theologiae* IIa-IIae q. 152, a. 5.

[46] For Aquinas's commentary on this important principle, see *De malo* q. 15, a. 4.

[47] Aquinas holds, however, that rightly ordered lust figures into the divine plan for virtue: "The fact that the reason's free attention to spiritual things cannot be simultaneous with [venereal] pleasure does not show that there is something contrary to virtue here, any more than when the reason suspends its activity according to right reason. Otherwise it would be against virtue to go to sleep." See *Summa theologiae* IIa-IIae q. 153, a. 2, ad 2.

[48] See *Summa theologiae* IIa-IIae q. 153, a. 3, ad 3.

[49] *Summa theologiae* IIa-IIae q. 142, a. 1.

probrabilis) upon those who indulge themselves without moderation. "Intemperance," says Aquinas, "is grouped among the carnal vices, which, according to Gregory the Great, 'although less culpable are more infamous.' " [50] To put it differently, because it skirts the proper measure that human actions should possess as regards rectitude, probity, decorum, and the like, intemperance especially erodes the moral beauty that distinguishes a person of upright life.

While he squarely rejects the view that the pleasure of sexual intercourse inevitably begets some sin, Aquinas devotes considerable attention to the capital vice of *luxuria*, which is the generic name for all sins against chastity and purity. [51] Right reason establishes both an order and a measure for venereal pleasure; lechery violates this order and measure, with the result that a person oversteps the proper norms for conduct in matters pertaining to sexual pleasure (*ut ordinem et modum rationis excedat circa venera*). Order refers to the proper setting for sexual activity; measure applies to the proper amount of pleasure that the right setting calls for. These norms are invariable and precise: the only order for sexual activity exists between lawfully married man and woman; the measure for sexual gratification is that which respects both the unitive and procreative purposes of marriage.

Christian discussion of the specific kinds of debauchery includes an analysis of simple fornication, seduction, rape, adultery, incest, and sacrilege, which are treated as serious expressions of the vice of venery, as well as the "sins against nature." [52] The sins against nature include masturbation, [53] bestiality, homosexual acts (sodomy), and violations of the natural style of heterosexual intercourse. Aquinas judges these as more serious expressions of vice than the other forms of *luxuria* because such activities more clearly depart from embodying the purposes and designs of sexual communication. At the same time, Aquinas would maintain that, because of the harm rape causes to the bond of charity, the seriousness of rape – to cite one example – ordinarily surpasses that of solitary masturbation. For the Christian life, charity remains the principal good that chastity or any virtue embodies. [54] Thus in his *Moralia*, St Gre-

---

[50] *Summa theologiae* IIa-IIae q. 142, a. 4.

[51] See *Summa theologiae* IIa-IIae q. 153, a. 2, ad 2: "The virtuous mean lies in agreement with right reason, not in the amount of material. Consequently the abundance of pleasure in a well-ordered sex-act is not inimical to right reason."

[52] For further information, see *Summa theologiae* IIa-IIae qq. 153 – 154.

[53] See *Summa theologiae* IIa-IIae q. 153, a. 3, ad 1 on the reason for the malice of masturbation and other auto-erotic acts that lead to sexual climax. The wrong does not consist in the wastefulness of the male semen, but in the dislocation of gratification from its condition, of being shared between persons.

[54] *Summa theologiae* IIa-IIae q. 151, a. 2.

gory the Great takes pains to illustrate how the vices associated with lechery especially work disorder in the pursuit of the entire moral life. [55]

The sins against the other principal virtues of temperance, *viz*, abstinence and sobriety, are gluttony and drunkenness respectively. *Gula*, says Henry Fairlie, is more concerned about eating than about food. As with all sins, gluttony makes us solitary, even at a table of sharing. [56] All the more does this sad commentary apply to those who fail in reaching the proper mean when using inebriating liquors or other mind-altering substances.

7. INFUSED TEMPERANCE AND CHRISTIAN HUMILITY

Like the virtue of fortitude, Christian temperance serves the needs of the Church. As a gift that observes the norm of grace, infused temperance may observe a different rule or measure with respect to food; this happens in fasting and abstinence or even with regard to sexual abstinence, as is the case with consecrated chastity and celibacy. Although in his mature schema, Aquinas assigns no gift of the Holy Spirit exclusively to cardinal temperance, he does indicate that the most appropriate gift is Fear of the Lord. [57] And he gives the following explanation. Although they embody in a certain sense only peripheral and surface gratifications, temperance's objects exercise such an attractive power on the human person that they risk throwing off the sway of reason and God's law in order to attain them. In his *Spiritual Exercises*, St Ignatius lays down the principle and foundation for the Christian life: we exist to praise, reverence, and serve God. A loving and chaste fear helps us to keep a proper poise and to live out this principle. The gift of Fear of the Lord aids all the virtues of cardinal temperance, that is, all the virtues of the general type of moderation, so that they keep the Christian properly focused on the important matters of life, but especially interested in the pursuit of divine goods.

In speaking about the first Beatitude, "Blessed are the poor in spirit, for theirs is the kingdom of heaven" (Mt 5: 3), which the spiritual tradition associates with Fear, Aquinas summarizes his Christian theology of temperance and humility:

> In a proper sense, poverty of spirit does correspond to fear, the reason being that filial fear is connected with showing reverence to God and being subject to him, and so the consequences of such subjection are likewise attributed to the gift of Fear. Resulting from such submission of self to God is a disinclination to seek glorification in oneself or in any other except God. For this would be irreconcilable with perfect subjection to God; and, in effect, this is what is meant

---

[55] See *Moralia* 31, 45 (*PL* 41: 436). Also, Aquinas in *Summa theologiae* IIa-IIae q. 153, a. 5.

[56] Henry Fairlie, *The Seven Deadly Sins Today* (Notre Dame, IN, 1979), pp. 155ff.

[57] See *Summa theologiae* IIa-IIae q. 141, a. 1, ad 3.

in the Psalm, "Some put their trust in chariots and some in horses, but we invoke the name of our God."

Perfect fear of God, then, accounts for the fact that one seeks neither self-exaltation in a spirit of pride nor the eminence that can be gained through exterior goods, such as honors and wealth. These attitudes characterize poverty of spirit. [58]

The fulfillment of the Christian life remains conformity to Christ that is progressively achieved through a life of self-emptying love. Because of the dynamics of divine grace, the beatitude of poverty of spirit epitomizes the disposition required in order to fulfill the evangelical law. As the humble handmaid of the Lord, the blessed Virgin Mary embodies the "obedience of faith" (Rom 1: 5) that, on St Paul's authority, must characterize every Christian believer on pilgrimage to God.

From this meditation we learn that, in a certain sense, humility crowns the life of Christian love, even as it provides the first steps for beginning the life of charity. However, this virtue that ranks so importantly in the Christian view of life falls only among the potential parts of temperance. Humility belongs to the virtues of moderation because it restrains the craving that people experience for the esteem of others. Recall that Aquinas orders the virtues according to their formal type, not necessarily by their position in the hierarchy of gospel values. In any event, Aquinas discovers nothing in the writings of Aristotle to aid his presentation of Christian humility. Indeed, because humility moderates reaching for the stars, this virtue actually seems to oppose the super-virtue of philosophical ethics which is magnanimity. Magnanimity affirms and sustains the hope for some great good; humility restrains the soul lest it push forward immoderately toward the achievement of great things. In the paradox of Christian grace, both objectives remain realizable for the humble person who puts his trust in the Lord.

In his treatment of the virtue of humility, Aquinas acknowledges the influence of St Benedict and the recognized twelve steps of humility found in the *Rule* that bears his name. In the Church, the monastic program illustrates that the moral virtues associated with the practice of religion, namely humility, hope, and love, represent the basic configuration of the Christian life:

Now, therefore, after ascending all these [twelve] steps of humility, the monk will quickly arrive at that "perfect love" of God which "casts out fear" (1 Jn 4: 18). Through this love, all that he once performed with dread, he will now begin to observe without effort, as though naturally, from habit, no longer out of fear of hell, but out of love for Christ, good habit and delight in virtue. All this the

---

[58] See *Summa theologiae* IIa-IIae q. 19, a. 12.

Lord will by the Holy Spirit graciously manifest in his workman now cleansed of vices and sins. [59]

Because humility and theological hope are connected, the gift of Fear of the Lord aids the humble person to find true and lasting peace within the *communio* of divine charity. For when a person recognizes his inadequacy before God, such a one turns to the merciful omnipotence of the heavenly Father in order to attain the help that he or she needs.

Humility moderates our emotions. While acquired humility is possible, especially in the religious person who exhibits the characteristic acts of submission, prayer, and obedience, because of its relationship to divine grace and the example of Christ, infused humility is of great interest in theological ethics. Christian art and literature bear witness to the emphasis that spiritual authors have put on the virtue of humility. In the 12th-century *Liber floridus Lamberti*, an illustrated encyclopedia that shows the reader the "Good Tree" of virtues as a symbol of the Church, humility is accompanied by two angels of peace ("*Angeli pacis*"), harbingers of the blessed happiness to which the virtuous man or woman may attain.

As a positive quality of character, humility represents "the reverence a person bears toward God, which prevents one from claiming more than is due to a person according to a divinely appointed lot." [60] Cajetan says that the humble person considers himself or herself *ut indignus* as unworthy, but the humble person is also abidingly conscious that everything he or she has received comes from God. The saints who show us the way of spiritual childhood help us to recognize this ideal, for they are the ones who have done God's will throughout the ages. True prudence ensures that Christian humility never becomes identified with forms of subservience; our blessed Lady, the handmaid of the Lord, remains the exemplar of this particularly Christian posture. For among the saints, the Church recognizes as the spiritual mother of all sanctity and virtue, the blessed Virgin Mary. St Ambrose of Milan compares our blessed Lady to a mirror which reflects all the virtues: "Therefore, let the life of virginity of Mary which has been described be for you just like an image, from which the appearance of chastity and the form of virtue shine forth as from a mirror." [61] Virginity is the source of motherhood in the Holy Spirit. The blessed Virgin Mary is a mother in the spiritual order for all those who are united with her Son in the one Church. And so believers confidently turn to her as one who molds them into the perfect image of the Father's glory. And this filial invoca-

---

[59]   *The Rule of St Benedict*, chap. 7.

[60]   *Summa theologiae* IIa-IIae q. 161, a. 2, ad 3.

[61]   "Sit igitur vobis tamquam in imagine descripta virginitatis vita Mariae, de qua velut speculo refulgeat species castitatis et forma virtutis" (*De virginibus*, Bk 2, chap. 2 [*PL* 16: 208]).

tion of the blessed Mother of Christ does not disappoint: "Ipsam rogans non desperas, ipsam cogitans non erras." [62]

---

[62] St Bernard, *Homilia* 2, super "Missus est."

Bibliography

The following bibliography includes specific studies on virtue and the moral life. For a general introduction to Thomist perspectives and doctrines, see Brian Davies, *The Thought of Thomas Aquinas* (Oxford: Clarendon Press, 1992) and Jean-Pierre Torrell, *Initiation à saint Thomas d'Aquin. Sa personne et son oeuvre* (Paris-Fribourg: Cerf-Editions universitaires, 1993) ET: *Saint Thomas Aquinas. The Person and his Work* (Washington, D.C.: The Catholic University of America Press, 1996). And for more general questions of Thomist virtue theory, see Romanus Cessario, *The Moral Virtues and Theological Ethics.* (Notre Dame, IN: University of Notre Dame Press, 1991) and Benedict M. Ashley, O.P., *Living the Truth in Love* (New York: Alba House, 1996). For a general introduction to Thomist moral theology, see Servais Pinckaers, O.P., *The Sources of Christian Ethics*, trans. Sr Mary Thomas Noble, O.P. (Washington, D.C.: The Catholic University of America Press, 1995) and Romanus Cessario, O.P., *Introduction to Moral Theology* (Washington, D.C.: The Catholic University of America, 2001).

Part I: The Theological Virtues

Chapter 1: Faith and the Life of Christian Virtue

1. Cessario, Romanus, O.P., *Christian Faith and the Theological Life* (Washington, D.C.: The Catholic Univesity of America Press, 1996).
2. Aubert, Jean-Marie. "La spécificité de la morale chrétienne selon saint Thomas." *Le Supplément* 92 (1970): 55–73.
3. Aumann, Jordan. "Mystical Experience, the Infused Virtues and the Gifts." *Angelicum* 58 (1981): 33–54.
4. Bourgeois, Daniel. "*Inchoatio vitae aeternae.* La dimension eschatologique de la vertu théologique de foi chez S. Thomas d'Aquin." *Sapienzia* 27 (1974): 272–314.
5. McInerny, Ralph. *Aquinas on Human Action. A Theory of Practice.* Washington, D.C.: The Catholic University Press of America, 1992.
6. Pieper, Josef. *Belief and Faith.* New York: Pantheon, 1963.
7. Spicq, Ceslaus. *Connaissance et Morale dans la Bible.* Fribourg, Presses universitaires, 1985.

Chapter 2: Theological Hope and Christian Expectation

1. Bernard, Charles A. *Théologie de l'espérance selon s. Thomas d'Aquin.* Paris: Vrin, 1961.
2. De Letter, P. "Hope and Charity in St. Thomas." *The Thomist* 13 (1950): 204–248; 325–352.

3. Gillon, Louis B. *Cristo e la teologia morale*. Rome, 1961.
4. Hill, William J. *Hope*, Volume 33 of the Blackfriars edition of the *Summa theologiae* 2a2ae. 17–22. London, 1966.
5. Knox, Ronald A. *Enthusiasm*. Westminister, MD: Christian Classics, 1983.
6. Pieper, Josef. *Hope*. San Francisco: Ignatius Press, 1986.
7. Ratzinger, Josef. *Guardare Cristo. Esercizi di fede, speanza et carità* (Milano, 1989).

CHAPTER 3: THEOLOGICAL CHARITY AND *Communio*

1. Abel, J. "L'influence de la charité dans la vie morale. Une controverse entre commentateurs de saint Thomas." *Recherches de théologie ancienne et médiévale* 37 (1970): 56–74.
2. Bobik, Joseph. "Aquinas on *Communicatio*. The Foundation of Friendship and *Caritas*." *The Modern Schoolmen* 64 (1986): 1–18.
3. Gilleman, G. *The Primacy of Charity in Moral Theology*. Trans. W.F. Ryan and A. Vachon. Westminster, MD: Newman, 1959.
4. Gilson, Etienne. "Wisdom and Love in St. Thomas Aquinas." *Aquinas Lectures*. Milwaukee, WI: Marquette University Press, 1951.
5. Meilaender, Gilbert C. *The Theory and Practice of Virtue*. Notre Dame, IN: University of Notre Dame Press, 1984.
6. Schockenhoff, Eberhard. *Bonum hominis. Die anthropologischen und theologischen Grundlagen der Tugendethik des Thomas von Aquin*. Mainz: Matthias-Grünewald-Verlag, 1987.
7. Wadell, Paul J. *The Primacy of Love. An Introduction to the Ethics of Thomas Aquinas*. New York: Paulist Press, 1992.

PART II: THE MORAL VIRTUES

CHAPTER 4: CHRISTIAN PRUDENCE AND PRACTICAL WISDOM

1. Gillon, L.B. "La hiérarchie axiologique des vertus morales selon saint Thomas." *Angelicum* 40 (1963): 3–24.
2. Inagaki, Bernard Ryosuke. "Habitus and Natura in Aquinas," in *Studies in Medieval Philosophy*. Edited by John F. Wippel. Washington, D.C.: Catholic University of America Press, 1987: 159–175.
3. Labourdette, Michel. M. "Conscience practique et savoir moral." *Revue Thomiste* 48 (1948): 142–179.
4. Langan, John P. "Augustine on the Unity and the Interconnection of the Virtues." *Harvard Theological Review* 72 (1979): 81–95.
5. Nelson, Daniel Mark. *The Priority of Prudence*. University Park, PA: The Pennsylvania State University Press, 1992.

6. Pieper, Josef. *Über die Klugheit*. Olten: Summa-Verlag, 1947.
7. Pinckaers, Servais. *Morality. The Catholic View.* South Bend, IN: St. Augustine's Press, 2001.

CHAPTER 5: CHRISTIAN JUSTICE AND HUMAN SOCIETY

1. Geach, Peter. *The Virtues*. Cambridge: Cambridge University Press, 1977.
2. Hugon, E. "La piété dans S. Thomas d'Aquin." *Vie Spirituelle* 15 (1927): 693–703.
3. De Koninck, Charles. "In Defense of St. Thomas: A Reply to Father Eschmann's Attack on the Primacy of the Common Good." *Laval Théologique et Philosophique* 1, No. 2 (1945): 9–109.
4. MacIntyre, Alasdair. *Whose Justice? Which Rationality?* London: Duckworth, 1988.
5. Mongillo, Dalmatius. "La struttura del 'De justitia'. *Summa Theologiae* II–II qq. 57–122." *Angelicum* 48 (1971): 355–377.
6. Pieper, Josef. *The Four Cardinal Virtues*. Notre Dame, IN: University of Notre Dame Press, 1965.
7. Wadell, Paul J. *Friendship and the Moral Life*. Notre Dame, IN: University of Notre Dame Press, 1989.

CHAPTER 6: FORTITUDE AND THE COURAGE OF CHRIST

1. Congar, Yves Marie. "Le traité de la force dans la *Somme théologique* de S. Thomas d'Aquin." *Angelicum* 51 (1974): 331–348.
2. Dent, N.J.H. *The Moral Psychology of the Virtues*. Cambridge: Cambridge University Press, 1984.
3. Ray, A. Chadwick. "A Fact About The Virtues." *The Thomist* 54 (1990): 429–451.
4. Roberts, Robert C. "Emotions Among the Virtues of the Christian Life." *The Journal of Religious Ethics* 20 (1992): 37–68.
5. Simon, Yves R. *The Definition of Moral Virtue*. New York: Fordham Univeristy Press, 1986.
6. Smith, Ignatius. "The Militant Christian Virtues." *The Thomist* 4 (1942): 193–220.
7. Yearley, Lee H. "The Nature-Grace Question in the Context of Fortitude." *The Thomist* 35 (1971): 557–580.

CHAPTER 7: CHRISTIAN TEMPERANCE AND HUMAN NEEDS

1. Carlson, Sebastian. "The Virtue of Humility." *The Thomist* 7 (1944) 135–78; 8 (1944) 363–414.

2. Cessario, Romanus. "The Meaning of Virtue in Catholic Moral Life: Its Significance for Human Life Issues." *The Thomist* 53 (1989): 173–96.

3. Fairlie, Henry. *The Seven Deadly Sins Today*. Notre Dame: University of Notre Dame Press, 1978.

4. Jordan, Mark D. "Aquinas' Construction of a Moral Account of the Passions." *Freiburger Zeitschrift für Philosophie und Theologie* 33 (1986): 71–97.

5. May, William E. *An Introduction to Moral Theology*. Huntington, IN: Our Sunday Visitor Publishing Division, 1994.

6. Plé, Albert. *Vie Affective et Chasteté*. Paris: Editions du Cerf, 1964.

7. Shivanandan, Mary. *Natural Sex*. New York: Rawson, Wade Publishers, Inc., 1979.